WITHDRAWN

THE PROGRESS OF THIS STORM

THE PROGRESS OF THIS STORM

Nature and Society in a Warming World

Andreas Malm

VERSO

First published by Verso 2018
© Andreas Malm 2018

The illustration titled 'View of a Coal Seam on the Island of Labuan', drawn by L. C. Heath, appeared in James Augustus St John, *Views in the Eastern Archipelago: Borneo, Sarawak, Labuan* (London: Thos. Maclean, 1847)

1 3 5 7 9 10 8 6 4 2

Verso
UK: 6 Meard Street, London W1F 0EG
US: 20 Jay Street, Suite 1010, Brooklyn, NY 11201
versobooks.com

Verso is the imprint of New Left Books

ISBN-13: 978-1-78663-415-3
ISBN-13: 978-1-78663-416-0 (US EBK)
ISBN-13: 978-1-78663-414-6 (UK EBK)

British Library Cataloguing in Publication Data
A catalogue record for this book is available from the British Library

Library of Congress Cataloging-in-Publication Data

Names: Malm, Andreas, 1977– author.
Title: The progress of this storm : on society and nature in a warming world / Andreas Malm.
Description: London ; New York : Verso, 2018. |
Identifiers: LCCN 2017036839 (print) | LCCN 2017045085 (ebook) | ISBN 9781786634160 (US e-book) | ISBN 9781786634153 (hardback)
Subjects: LCSH: Human ecology. | Global warming – Social aspects. | Climatic changes – Social aspects. | Nature. | Capitalism – Environmental aspects. | BISAC: POLITICAL SCIENCE / History & Theory. | PHILOSOPHY / Political. | NATURE / Environmental Conservation & Protection.
Classification: LCC GF50 (ebook) | LCC GF50 .M345 2018 (print) | DDC 304.2/5 – dc23
LC record available at https://lccn.loc.gov/2017036839

Typeset in Adobe Garamond by Biblichor Ltd, Edinburgh
Printed and bound by CPI Group (UK) Ltd, Croydon, CR0 4YY

Contents

The two heads had already fused to one
and features from each flowed and blended into
one face where two were lost in one another

. . .

Each former likeness now was blotted out;
both, and neither one it seemed – this picture
of deformity.
Dante, in the eighth circle of hell

Nature does not produce on the one hand owners of money or commodities,
and on the other hand men possessing nothing but their own labour-
power. This relation has no basis in natural history, nor does it have a
social basis common to all periods of human history. It is clearly the result
of a past historical development, the product of many economic revolu-
tions, of the extinction of a whole series of older formations of social
production.

Karl Marx, *Capital, Volume 1*

The sky's changing.
A roaring storm is coming.
A howling mist,
a growling downpour.

. . .

All the money men who close their eyes
and pretend
that this rumble
must be low planes.
Kate Tempest, *Let Them Eat Chaos*

Introduction:
Theory for the Warming Condition

NEVER IN THE HEAT OF THE MOMENT

Is there any time left in this world? In an essay published in *New Left Review* in 2015, Fredric Jameson restated his thirty-year-old diagnosis of postmodernity as the 'predominance of space over time'.[1] We continue to live on a stage where there is nothing but the present. Past and future alike have dissolved into a perpetual now, leaving us imprisoned in a moment without links backwards or forwards: only the dimension of space extends in all directions, across the seamless surface of a globalised world, in which everyone is connected to everyone else through uncountable threads – but time has ceased flowing. Or, as Jameson originally put it in *Postmodernism, or, The Cultural Logic of Late Capitalism*: 'We now inhabit the synchronic rather than the diachronic, and I think it is at least empirically arguable that our daily life, our psychic experience, our cultural languages, are today dominated by categories of space rather than by categories of time, as in the preceding period of high modernism.'[2] This shift of dimensions,

---

1 Fredric Jameson, 'The Aesthetics of Singularity', *New Left Review* II: 92 (2015): 105. For an inventory of Jameson's thesis and its fortunes over the three decades, see the special issue of *Social Text* 34 (2): (2016).

2 Fredric Jameson, *Postmodernism, or, The Cultural Logic of Late Capitalism* (London: Verso, 1991), 16; see further Fredric Jameson, 'The End of Temporality', *Critical Inquiry* 29 (2003): 695–718.

more than anything else, marks the onset of postmodernity: and here we are, still.

The diagnosis hinges on the eradication of nature. Jameson's argument runs something like this: in the modern era, vast fields of old nature remained spread out between the bustling new centres of factory and market. A short drive would take the modernist back to the rural village where she was born; ancient ways of life dotted every horizon, the modern mode speeding up within a landscape tied to the natural and immemorial. It was this contrast that made the modernists *feel* the movement of time – from the old to the new, towards the future – that so fundamentally structured their culture. Now the foil is gone. Peasants, lords, artisans, costermongers have vanished from sight and, along with them, 'nature has been triumphantly blotted out'.[3] In place of villages, there are suburbs; no matter how far the postmodernist drives, she will encounter inhabitants of the same cultural present, watching the same programmes or – to update the analysis – posting pictures on the same networks. The new is the only game in town, and by the same token it loses its meaning and lustre, and instead of moving onwards we seem to be forever stuck in the automated marketplace of the monotonously novel. Postmodernity, then, 'is what you have when the modernization process is complete and nature is gone for good'; without 'the idea of nature and the natural as some ultimate content or referent' there can be no sense of time, and we are stranded in the mega-city where glass surfaces mirror each other, where images and simulacra rule over night and day, where the free play of masks and roles goes on and on without any real, material substance.[4]

But towards this city a storm is on the move.

---

3 Jameson, *Postmodernism*, 309.
4 Ibid., ix, 392. For this analysis of the end of nature as the end of temporality and historicity, see further e.g. 35, 49, 307–11, 365–6; Jameson, 'End', 699; Fredric Jameson, *Late Marxism: Adorno, Or, The Persistence of the Dialectic* (London: Verso, 2007), 95–6; Fredric Jameson, *The Cultural Turn: Selected Writings on the Postmodern, 1983–1998* (London: Verso, 2009), 54–70.

The condition of Jameson's postmodernity is recognisable in life in New York City as depicted in Ben Lerner's fine novel *10:04*. Fabrication and semblance seem to govern the protagonist's every step. He is working to forge a correspondence with renowned authors. A friend asks him to become the father of her child, but not through sexual intercourse; instead he embarks on a laborious process of watching porn flicks, masturbating and handing over his semen to artificial insemination. His head spins from a twenty-four-hour installation called *The Clock*, a montage of clips from thousands of movies integrated in a rolling sequence, so that a scene of lightning staged at 10:04 in *Back to the Future* is replayed at exactly that moment in the real time of the audience, and so on throughout night and day, performing 'the ultimate collapse of fictional time into real time'.[5]

Lerner's New York, however, is under siege. The novel begins with the approach of 'an unusually large cyclonic system' and ends with the cataclysmic landfall of another. 'Houses up and down the coast had been obliterated, flooded, soon a neighborhood in Queens would burn. Emergency workers were fishing out the bodies of those who had drowned during the surge; who knew how many of the homeless had perished?' A point of irrefutable reality pierces the narrative. It submerges the protagonist in a flow of very palpable time: he looks back on 'six years of these walks on a warming planet'. When Union Square turns 'heavy with water in its gas phase, a tropical humidity that wasn't native to New York, an ominous medium', ordinary time is shut down, the air 'like defeated time itself falling from the sky'.[6] The protagonist sinks into obsession with temporality, as he ruminates over what he believes to be the source of all these storms: climate change.

Recent efforts in 'event attribution' corroborate the belief. Every particular storm is the unique outcome of a chaotic mix of weather components, but global warming alters the baseline where these are

5   Ben Lerner, *10:04* (London: Granta, 2014), 54.
6   Ibid., 16, 231, 7, 18, 220.

formed. 'The climate is changing: we have a new normal', one team of researchers submits: 'The environment in which all weather events occur is not what it used to be. All storms, without exception, are different.' Thus superstorm Sandy, which knocked out large parts of New York in October 2012, rode forth on sea levels elevated by some 19 centimetres; high sea surface temperatures sent extraordinary amounts of water vapour into the air as ammunition for the clouds.[7] Similar factors beefed up supertyphoon Haiyan – the strongest recorded storm ever to strike land, up to that point – as it ripped through the Philippines in November 2013, killing more than 6,000 people and leaving bodies bobbing on the sea for weeks.[8] 'No single event can be attributed to climate change', runs a popular media refrain, but a spurt of observation and modelling is now confirming the common intuition that all of this extreme weather would not have happened without it. Individual incidents may very well be pinned on the rise in temperatures, with a scientific accuracy improving by the year. Already when the earth had warmed as little as $0.85°C$, three out of four recordings of extreme heat on land could be derived from the general trend, and as temperatures continue to climb, it will claim an even larger share of the causation.[9] The experience is becoming well-nigh universal: a majority of the human population has been exposed to abnormally

7   Kevin E. Trenberth, John T. Fasullo and Theodore G. Shepherd, 'Attribution of Climate Extreme Events', *Nature Climate Change* 5 (2015): 725–30; quotation from 729. Cf. Andrew R. Solow, 'Extreme Weather, Made by Us?', *Science* 349 (2015): 1445–5; Friederike Otto, Geert Jan van Oldenborgh, Jonathan Eden et al., 'The Attribution Question', *Nature Climate Change* 6 (2016): 813–16; Peter Stott, 'How Climate Change Affects Extreme Weather Events', *Science* 352 (2016): 1517–18.

8   Izuru Takayabu, Kenshi Hibino, Hidetaka Sasaki et al., 'Climate Change Effects on Worst-Case Storm Surge: A Case Study of Typhoon Haiyan', *Environmental Research Letters* 10 (2015).

9   E. M. Fischer and R. Knutti, 'Anthropogenic Contribution to Global Occurrence of Heavy-Precipitation and High-Temperature Extremes', *Nature Climate Change* 5 (2015): 560–5; Peter Stott, 'Weather Risks in a Warming World', *Nature Climate Change* 5 (2015): 516–7.

warm weather over the past decade.[10] Such man-made weather, however, is never made in the present.

Global warming is a result of actions in the past. Every molecule of CO_2 above the pre-industrial level resides in the atmosphere because humans have burnt trees and other plants and, preponderantly, fossil fuels over the course of time. In the beginning, the carbon in coal, oil and natural gas was locked into the crust of the earth; then at some point, those reserves were located and exploited and the fuels delivered to fireplaces, whence the carbon was released as CO_2. At any given moment, the excess of heat in the earth system is the sum of all those historical fires, of the cumulative emissions, the pulses of CO_2 stacked on top of each other: the storm of climate change draws its force from countless acts of combustion over, to be exact, the past two centuries. *We can never be in the heat of the moment, only in the heat of this ongoing past.* Insofar as extreme weather is shaped by basal warming, it is the legacy of what people have done, the latest leakage from a malign capsule – indeed, the air is heavy with time.[11]

When Walter Benjamin roamed the cities of interwar Europe, he jotted down a signpost for further investigation: 'On the double meaning of the term *temps* in French': *temps* as in weather and time.[12] Most likely, the semantic overlap is rooted in the primordial experience of the seasonal cycle drawing the calendar of labour, the olden days when sun, cloud, rain and snow set the rhythm of hunting, sowing, reaping and all sorts of other activities. Then came an era when (some) people lived as though insulated from the weather – 'our seasons', Jameson notes, 'are of the post-natural and post-astronomical television and media variety' – but slowly or

10   Flavior Lehner and Thomas F. Stocker, 'From Local Perception to Global Perspective', *Nature Climate Change* 5 (2015): 731–5.

11   On cumulative emissions and related temporalities of climate change, and for references, see further Andreas Malm, *Fossil Capital: The Rise of Steam Power and the Roots of Global Warming* (London: Verso, 2016), 4–8.

12   Walter Benjamin, *The Arcades Project* (Cambridge, MA: Harvard University Press, 2002), 106.

suddenly, the connotation is reinserting itself in everyday life.[13] This time, however, the weather presents anything but a reliable clock. It tends to upset schedules and routines by dint of the weight it carries from the past. The tempest has a twisted, multiplex temporality, as registered by Lerner's protagonist, who compulsively reports days of 'unseasonable warmth' when walking down October streets:

> The unusual heat felt summery, but the light was distinctly autumnal, and the confusion of seasons was reflected in the clothing around them: some people were dressed in T-shirts and shorts, while others wore winter coats. It reminded him of a double exposed photograph or a matting effect in film: two temporalities collapsed into a single image.[14]

Even more apposite might be his sensation of 'having travelled back in time, or of distinct times being overlaid, temporalities interleaved', for every impact of climate change is, by physical definition, a communication with a human past.[15]

But the links do not only run backwards. The shadow of anthropogenic CO_2 covers the foreseeable and extends into the unfathomable future. A team of the most prominent scientists working on this particular aspect point out that 2100, the year where most scenarios and projections abruptly end – there will be this or that much sea level rise until 2100, this or that much extreme heat – has no real terminal status. The widespread usage of the benchmark is an accident of computer technology, early models having been unable to carry scientists any further. Graspable and convenient, it creates, the team argues, the illusion that the future now in the balance is a relatively short one, a headache for the

---

13 Jameson, *Cultural*, 59.
14 Lerner, *10:04*, 63. Cf. e.g. 107, 153, 206, 231. On the etymological association of tempest and temporality, see Bronislaw Szerszynski, 'Reading and Writing the Weather: Climate Technics and the Moment of Responsibility', *Theory, Culture and Society* 27 (2010): 24.
15 Lerner, *10:04*, 67.

twenty-first century, when in fact the bulk of the rise in temperature and practically all sea level rise produced by any given amount of cumulative emissions will hang on – if it is left to the earth system to work out the consequences – for at least the next 10,000 years, the seas potentially peaking at a level around 50 metres higher than today. Much of this can still be avoided. That possibility supercharges our moment with time. 'The next few decades', the team concludes, 'offer a brief window of opportunity to minimize large-scale and potentially catastrophic climate change that will extend longer than the entire history of human civilization thus far.'[16] An eternity is determined now.

For every year that total decarbonisation of the world economy is postponed – not to speak of every year when emissions are stable or increasing – the shadow of committed warming extends further into the future.[17] For every such year, more impacts become unavoidable. There have already been many years of that kind. Hence, a string of scientific papers coming out in 2014 and 2015 indicated that the main section of the West Antarctic ice sheet has been pushed over its tipping point and is destined to undergo irreversible meltdown, while, even more spectacularly, an equally large glacier on the eastern part of that continent – long believed to be safe from warming – may likewise be sliding towards the sea.[18]

16   Peter U. Clark, Jeremy D. Shakun, Shaun A. Marcott et al., 'Consequences of Twenty-First-Century Policy for Multi-Millennial Climate and Sea-Level Change', *Nature Climate Change* 6 (2016): 360–61.

17   See e.g. Patrik L. Pfister and Thomas F. Stocker, 'Earth System Commitments Due to Delayed Mitigation', *Environmental Research Letters* 11 (2016).

18   E. Rignot, J. Mouginot, M. Morlighem et al., 'Widespread, Rapid Grounding Line Retreat of Pine Island, Thwaites, Smith, and Kohler glaciers, West Antarctica, from 1992 to 2011', *Geophysical Research Letters* 41 (2014): 3502–9; Ian Joughin, Benjamin Smith and Brooke Medley, 'Marine Ice Sheet Collapse Potentially Under Way for the Thwaites Glacier Basin, West Antarctica', *Science* 344 (2014): 735–8; J. S. Greenbaum, D. D. Blankenship, D. A. Young et al., 'Ocean Access to a Cavity Beneath Totten Glacier in East Antarctica', *Nature Geoscience* 8 (2015): 294–8; Fernando S. Paolo, Helen A. Fricker and Laurie Padman, 'Volume Loss from Antarctic Ice Shelves is Accelerating', *Science* 348 (2015): 327–31.

'Whatever we do now', popular magazine *New Scientist* announced, probably with some exaggeration, 'the seas will rise at least 5 metres'.[19] The motion of glaciers being proverbially slow, the scientific consensus has long held that it would take several millennia for a sea level rise of such a scale to materialise, but one of the most sensational papers in recent years contends that ice equivalent to 'several meters' could, in the worst-case scenario, plunge into the oceans *already this century*, much of it during the lifetimes of plenty of young people now in streets near shorelines.[20] With all of these figures, constantly revised and updated, scientists seek to represent the assault from some past curse or ancestral sin ever more difficult to escape. Lerner's protagonist imagines the city soon underwater.[21]

Some history, then, is back: the panic that climate change so easily induces is really a panic in the face of history, our reaction when it dawns on us what they – those who once lit the fossil fires, spread them and still keep them burning – have done to us and our children. Sometimes that history makes a lunge at the present. In December 2015, at the conclusion of COP 21 in Paris, the leaders of 195 nations declared with much fanfare that they would limit the temperature increase to 'well below 2°C above pre-industrial levels' and 'pursue efforts' to stop it at 1.5°C.[22] That year was the first to reach the landmark of 1°C.[23] Hardly had the leaders stopped cheering and congratulating themselves on their achievement and flown home from Paris before the warming took a sudden leap: in February 2016, the average temperature on earth stood at an

---

19   Michael Le Page, 'Five Metres and Counting', *New Scientist*, 13 June 2015.

20   J. Hansen, M. Sato, P. Hearty et al., 'Ice Melt, Sea Level Rise and Superstorms: Evidence from Paleoclimate Data, Climate Modeling, and Modern Observations that 2°C Global Warming Could be Dangerous', *Atmospheric Chemistry and Physics Discussion* 16 (2015): 3761–812.

21   Lerner, *10:04*, e.g. 40, 107–8, 153.

22   United Nations Framework Convention on Climate Change, 'Adoption of the Paris Agreement', 12 December 2015, 22 (available from unfccc.int)

23   World Meteorological Organization, '2015 Is Hottest Year on Record', public.wmo.int, 25 January 2016.

estimated 1.5°C above pre-industrial levels – exactly where it should not be, according to the pledge of two months earlier.[24] Scientists were left scrambling for superlatives to convey the bizarre weather. In the northernmost Arctic, anomalies of 6°C were detected, adding to the impression that the climate system was careening deep into the heat COP 21 had vowed to forestall.[25]

Come July 2016, *Nature* published a paper claiming to demonstrate that both Paris targets were likely beyond reach. Some of the heat generated by an excess of CO_2 in the atmosphere is drawn down by the oceans and stored in their depths for several decades before being released into the air, and because of this time lag, the full realisation of the warming commensurate to any CO_2 concentration is deferred. With current levels – even if no more CO_2 were ever to be emitted – the planet is already doomed 'to a mean warming over land greater than 1.5°C' and quite possibly 'greater than 2.0°C', according to this particular study.[26] Come November, December and the first anniversary of the Paris agreement, temperatures in the Arctic were no longer 1.5 or 2 or 6 but a dizzying 20 degrees hotter than normal.[27] 2016 ended as yet another hottest year on record, on average 1.3°C above pre-industrial levels in one estimate, 1.1°C in another.[28] Clearly, the world was already

24 Glen Peters, 'The "Best Available Science" to Inform 1.5 °C Policy Choices', *Nature Climate Change* 6 (2016): 646–9.

25 Chris Mooney, 'Scientists Are Floored by What's Happening in the Arctic Right Now', *Washington Post*, 18 February 2016.

26 Chris Huntingford and Lina M. Mercado, 'High Chance that Current Atmospheric Greenhouse Concentrations Commit to Warmings Greater than 1.5°C Over Land', *Nature Scientific Reports* 6 (2016): 5.

27 John Vidal, '"Extraordinarily Hot" Arctic Temperatures Alarm Scientists', *Guardian*, 22 November 2016.

28 Copernicus Climate Change Service: 'Earth on the Edge: Record Breaking 2016 Was Close to 1.5°C Warming', https://climate.copernicus.eu, 5 January 2017; WMO, 'WMO confirms 2016 as hottest year on record, about 1.1°C above pre-industrial era', https://public.wmo.int, 18 January 2017; Damian Carrington, '2016 Hottest Year Ever Recorded – and Scientists Say Human Activity to Blame', *Guardian*, 18 January 2017.

brushing the threshold set up one year earlier in Paris. Now, none of these developments were in any way the products of *what happened immediately after COP 21*. The stunning heat records of 2016 were not due to emissions made in the meantime, but the delayed detonation of fuels burnt much earlier. If the Paris pledges were so quickly ground to dust, as it seems at the moment of this writing, it was indeed the past that overtook the present, in a manner that seems rather like the new normal; by the time this book is printed, these records will in all likelihood be obsolete, and so on.

More storms, then, are to be expected. On the cover of E. Ann Kaplan's thoughtful study *Climate Trauma: Foreseeing the Future in Dystopian Film and Fiction*, a red-haired woman stares at a large cyclonic system rolling in from the horizon. Before turning to the flood of apocalyptic films inundating screens in recent years, Kaplan tells the story of how she herself was caught up in Hurricane Sandy and at one point, as she tried to return to her apartment by climbing dark stairs, suffered a panic attack. The experience led her to develop the syndrome of 'pretrauma' – not the usual post-traumatic stress disorder, in which people suffer past wounds, but rather 'fear of a future terrifying event of a similar kind'. Our culture as a whole, Kaplan suggests, is now developing pretrauma. With more and more film, television, literature, journalism inflected by the creeping insight that catastrophic climate change is approaching, consumers of popular culture make up 'a pretraumatized population, living with a sense of an uncertain future and an unreliable natural environment'. In the film from which the cover shot is taken, the protagonist has a series of nightmares and violent hallucinations about monster storms, descends into a spiral of angst and lashes out at his friends: '"There's a storm coming and not one of you is prepared for it."' If this growing genre is obsessed with the future, it is only, Kaplan argues, on the basis of an 'awareness of a traumatic past' that has stacked the deck against the time to come.[29]

---

29 E. Ann Kaplan, *Climate Trauma: Foreseeing the Future in Dystopian Film*

That past, about which nothing can by definition be done, is the source of the future storm.

Now contrast this with Jameson's diagnosis of postmodernity as a condition of synchronic space devoid of time and nature. There is no synchronicity in climate change. Now more than ever, we inhabit the diachronic, the discordant, the inchoate: the fossil fuels hundreds of millions of years old, the mass combustion developed over the past two centuries, the extreme weather this has already generated, the journey towards a future that will be infinitely more extreme – unless something is done *now* – the tail of present emissions stretching into the distance . . . History has sprung alive, through a nature that has done likewise. We are only in the very early stages, but already our daily life, our psychic experience, our cultural responses, even our politics show signs of being sucked back by planetary forces into the hole of time, the present dissolving into past and future alike. Postmodernity seems to be visited by its antithesis: a condition of time and nature conquering ever more space. Call it *the warming condition.*

SOME TASKS FOR THEORY

The history circling back in the warming condition is not of the buoyant modernist kind, not a bristling flow of events linked by purpose and direction, anything but a bandwagon to jump on: rather it is frozen. Nor is the nature now returning of the intact variety Jameson finds in the interstices of modernity: rather it appears to be melting. Yet history and nature they seem to be, and society looks like it is beginning to reel under them. The warming condition is still, however, far from constituting a total 'cultural logic' in Jameson's sense. Indeed, climate fiction (or cli-fi) in film and literature notwithstanding, one might argue that most culture still *ignores* the facts of global warming and that *denial* is the real hallmark of the present, stretching from the quotidian suppression

and Fiction (New Brunswick: Rutgers University Press, 2016), xix, 53, 12.

of the knowledge of what is going on, across the topographies of social life up to the man who won the United States presidential election in November 2016, just as Arctic temperatures went completely off the charts. As for politics in advanced capitalist countries, climate change is utterly overshadowed by issues of immigration and the nation. We shall save some words on that order of priorities for later. As for the panoply of cultural expressions, it would be a tough assignment to show that the changing climate is profoundly altering the way we write, communicate, build, plan, view, imagine as Jameson holds that postmodernity did. Nor does the latter explode like a bubble the moment it comes into contact with the rising temperatures – to the contrary, it is proving very resilient and inflatable indeed.

The age of the omnipresent screen can, of course, be seen as the highest stage of postmodernity, an ever-expanding house of mirrors in which illuminated surfaces reflect each other, free of any outside, shadow, memory or long-term expectation. Permanent connectivity enacts 'the final capitalist mirage of post-history', Jonathan Crary writes in his searing *24/7: Late Capitalism and the Ends of Sleep*: it is the consummation of a homogeneous present, a space where the past has been erased and everything can be accessed on demand, in an instant. Not only does it negate natural rhythms, such as the need for sleep; it also offers a cloister away from the new *temps*. 'The more one identifies with the insubstantial electronic surrogates for the physical self, the more one seems to conjure an exemption from the biocide underway everywhere on the planet.'[30] The more one withdraws into the virtual cocoon, the more one detaches from things taking place in nature. If this assessment is correct, and if the technologies of electronic immersion continue to advance, which seems a certainty, then the postmodern condition is still eminently capable of protecting and even expanding its territory.

---

30   Jonathan Crary, *24/7: Late Capitalism and the Ends of Sleep* (London: Verso, 2013), 9, 100.

It is hard not to interpret the plague that descended on the Western world in the summer of 2016 as a case in point. There were moments when one could not have an evening stroll through a park without feeling that nearly everyone roamed around – faces expressionless, eyes glued to phones – chasing some target that only existed in the virtual realm. How many walks on this warming planet were now conducted in the quest for Pokémon, including in New York and other cities threatened by rising seas? Rarely had the condition of digital life – a sphere without time or nature – invaded so much public space, even kicking off marches, stampedes, gatherings and other forms of collective pseudo-action for the joy of being in the world while not being there. In a dense, suitably bleak riff on Theodor Adorno titled 'Media Moralia: Reflections on Damaged Environments and Digital Life', Andrew McMurry stipulates that 'the new media ecology roars in to fill the void left as old nature exits'. Lending new meaning to 'sleepwalking', the postmodern condition has sunk more deeply than ever into the mind *in step with* the warming. 'The external world', the one where that warming takes place, McMurry continues, 'is now obscure, mostly irrelevant, and, when sensed at all, sensed remotely': between it and us, digital media stand as impenetrable 'veils'.[31] Or, in the words of Kate Tempest: 'Staring into the screen so / we don't have to see the planet die.'[32]

But if the postmodern condition in its digital stage can wrap people up in mental clothing that protects them from contact with the biocide, it is locked in struggle with a formidable enemy. For the warming condition has a whole set of biogeochemical and physical laws on its side. They ensure that its incursions will become deeper and more frequent over time; by force of the nature of the process, climate change has an inbuilt tendency to worsen and

---

31 Andrew McMurry, 'Media Moralia: Reflections on Damaged Environments and Digital Life', in Greg Garrard (ed.), *The Oxford Handbook of Ecocriticism* (Oxford: Oxford University Press, 2014), 493, 497.

32 Tempest, *Let Them Eat Chaos* (London: Picador, 2016), 67.

swamp pretty much everything else. How many will play augmented reality games on a planet that is 6˚C warmer? Moreover, denial, particularly in its suppressive and obsessive forms, is a negative confirmation. It suggests that the thing is there, everywhere, only just below the surface, a distressing presence in the collective subconscious – perhaps global warming is, to use another term of Jameson's, a political unconscious that already pervades culture. Perhaps its intolerable implications are in themselves so many incentives to flee into something like augmented reality. Be that as it may – and we shall return to the phenomenon of denial – when climate change seeps into consciousness, it brings with it a realisation that *more and worse is coming*. Truly at the cutting edge, the warming condition is directed towards the future, like the woman on the cover of *Climate Trauma*. It will make itself felt. If postmodernity is a malaise of amnesia and displacement – as though time and nature had in fact disappeared – we might think of the warming condition as a *realisation*, in the dual sense of the term, of a more fundamental illness or wrongness in the world.

Three pathways are competing to be that realisation. 1.) Business as usual continues to run amok, the 1.5˚C as well as the 2˚C targets are missed, temperatures rise towards 3, 4, 6 degrees of warming within this century, and the material foundations for human civilisation crumble one after another. 2.) The fossil economy is knocked down, preferably within a few decades, warming slows down and then ceases, and civilisation proceeds apace. 3.) There is geoengineering. Intermediate and mixed paths are conceivable – particularly combinations of 2 and 3, or 1 and 3 – but the enormous forces unleashed into the earth system and the long postponement of genuine mitigation now rule out a smooth ride to renewed climate stability. The space for moderate outcomes and half-measures has receded. In the event that path 2 is pursued with maximum global determination and the worst scenarios safely averted, the transformations – technological, economic, political, surely also cultural – will have to be on such a scale as to seal the victory of climate over pretty much the rest of human life, at least for some time, until its destabilisation becomes a memory. Such is the logic of Naomi Klein's theorem 'this changes everything', whatever course it takes.

Needless to say, global warming is only one facet of the biocide, but among the many ongoing processes of environmental crisis, it has a special inner propulsion and potential for generalised destruction. With its dependence on the past and future directionality, its temporal logic contradicts hyper-spatial postmodernity head on. It represents history and nature falling down on society; it clouds the horizon. A theory for the present should home in on it as an unfolding tendency and learn how to track this storm. It ought to probe the emerging condition and the basic parameters for acting within it: what, for a start, is this nature that is now returning? Does it still deserve that name? Is it not so mixed up with society as to disqualify the very notion? If it is indeed nature, how has it ended up in this terrifying shape? Who or what has whipped up this storm system – the forces of matter, or of humanity, or some agent fusing or straddling the two? By what route does history move into something once thought to be so timeless as the climate of the entire planet?

Great blender and trespasser, climate change sweeps back and forth between the two regions traditionally referred to as 'nature' and 'society'. As it happens, contemporary theory is intensely preoccupied with precisely that escalating interpenetration and churns out books, articles, special issues, conferences, all sorts of scholarly conversations on some critical general questions: whatever is this thing called nature? How does it relate to society? Who are the genuinely powerful players in the drama that weaves the two together; how do humans attach to material objects; are technologies or relations running the show; what constitutes an ecological crisis; what can we ever know about any of all this? Here we find various forms of constructionism, actor-network theory, new materialism, posthumanism, the metabolic rift, capitalism as world-ecology and a host of other conceptual apparatuses, all trying to come to grips with the imbroglio between the social and the natural. Can any of them provide a map of the path the storm is taking? This essay sets out to scrutinise some of the theories circulating at the nature/society junction in the light of climate change. Now, theory does not seem like the most exigent business in a rapidly warming world. There is that itching feeling that the only meaningful thing to do now is to let go of everything else and physically cut off fossil fuel combustion, deflate the tyres, block the runways, lay siege to the platforms, invade the mines. Indeed, the only salubrious thing about the election of Donald Trump is that it dispels the last lingering illusions that anything else than organised collective militant resistance has at least a fighting chance of pushing the world anywhere else than head first, at maximum speed, into cataclysmic climate change. All has already been said; now is the time for confrontation. This essay presents no arguments for restraining such impulses. It is, however, written in the belief that some theories can make the situation clearer while others might muddy it. Action remains best served by conceptual maps that mark out the colliding forces with some accuracy, not by blurry charts and foggy thinking, of which there is, as we shall see, no shortage. Theory can be part of the problem. If everything is up for re-evaluation in a warming world, this must apply to it as well: theory too is called to account, required to demonstrate its relevance and declare its contributions, even if some of its producers and consumers would never consider joining some direct action against fossil fuels.

The present essay does not invent this trial; as we shall see, the theories under scrutiny are moving towards agreement on the climate issue as their shared litmus test, the concrete question each must answer to prove its worth.[33] Some more specific criteria could then be set up. An adequate theory should be able to grasp the problem as *historical*, as it has arisen through change over time – the birth and perpetual expansion of the fossil economy – and causes change over time on earth. It should make sense of the very

---

33 On climate as a litmus test, cf. McKenzie Wark, *Molecular Red: Theory for the Anthropocene* (London: Verso, 2015), e.g. 169, 180.

act of digging up fossil fuels and setting them on fire. Even if the theory is formulated from within the capitalist heartlands, it should, not the least importantly, take heed of the circumstance that global warming makes early landfall in places where the modernisation process has not been completed. People who lack the most basic amenities, who cannot afford to take up residence inside any house of mirrors, who continue to subsist on the kind of nature that Jameson found blotted out from the American cities of the 1980s stand first in the firing line. Most of the bodies fished out from the rising seas belong to them.

A place like New York City can bounce back from a storm and switch on its screens again, but the warming condition is hard to shake off in the Philippines. Hence the much-reported results from a survey by the Pew Research Center in 2015: 79 percent of the inhabitants of Burkina Faso claimed to be 'very concerned' about climate change, compared to only 42 percent of the Japanese, who were far more afraid (72 percent) of the Islamic State.[34] Burkina Faso is being wrecked by climate change *in this moment*, storms of dust and sand – known locally as 'the red winds' – burying what crops remain on land parched from ever more erratic rain.[35] The pattern of greater concern in developing countries is persistent. GDP correlates negatively with the feeling: to a far higher degree than their conspecifics in the US or UK, people in countries like Brazil and Bangladesh tend to view the problem as *very serious*, although the unease is surely domestically stratified as well.[36] As a

34   Laetitia van Eeckhout, 'Winds of Climate Change Blast Farmers' Hopes of Sustaining a Livelihood in Burkina Faso', *Guardian*, 7 July 2015.

35   Ami Sedghi, 'Climate Change Seen as Greatest Threat by Global Population', *Guardian*, 17 July 2015.

36   Hanno Sandvik, 'Public Concern Over Global Warming Correlates Negatively with National Wealth', *Climatic Change* 90 (2008): 333–41; So Young Kim and Yael Wolinsky-Nahmias, 'Cross-National Public Opinion on Climate Change: The Effects of Affluence and Vulnerability', *Global Environmental Politics* 14 (2014): 79–106; Alex Y. Lo and Alex T. Chow, 'The Relationship Between Climate Change Concern and National Wealth', *Climatic Change* 131 (2015): 335–48.

double realisation, the warming condition arrives first among masses possessing no significant property, primarily in the peripheries of the capitalist world-economy. It is an old truth that the human condition is expressed in its most concentrated, ominous form among such masses: hence any theorisation should have its antennas directed towards them. An event like Hurricane Sandy is so significant because it sends the signal home.

What, then, can theory for the warming condition inspire, other than despair? Put differently: if both the 1.5°C and 2°C guardrails turn out to have been breached, should we conclude that the storm is raging uncontrollably and that we might just as well start playing the fiddle? No. We should conclude, first of all, that building a new coal-fired power plant, or continuing to operate an old one, or drilling for oil, or expanding an airport, or planning for a highway is now irrational violence. The case can be made that large-scale fossil fuel combustion has always constituted violence, as it inflicts harm on other people and species, and that it has been plainly irrational since the wide diffusion of the basics of climate science, but surely it reaches a new level of demented aggression when temperatures have increased by 1.5°C or a sea level rise of several metres has been locked into the earth system. If the resistance against fossil fuels has been feeble up to that point, it ought to become ferocious after it: *even after all this, you still go on.* The fight is to minimise the losses and maximise the prospects for survival. What, more concretely, can it achieve? We shall offer only some very brief and provisional reflections on this question towards the end. For now, we shall begin from the premise that any theory for the warming condition should have the struggle to stabilise climate – with the demolition of the fossil economy the necessary first step – as its practical, if only ideal, point of reference. It should clear up space for action and resistance.

DISCOVERING COAL ON LABUAN

But to theorise this present, we need a picture of the sort of past that is weighing on it.

In the second quarter of the nineteenth century, the British Empire deployed steamboats to extend its control over territories and accelerate its appropriation of resources from around the world. They required coal. Agents of the imperial machine – officers, engineers, merchants – were instructed to keep their eyes open for coal seams wherever they sat foot, such as on Borneo, where a missionary happened upon some outcroppings in 1837. His discovery touched off a rush for the black gold on that far-flung island, positioned right on the highway between India and China, potentially a perfect fuel depot for the steamboats now frequenting their shores. The most exciting reserves were located on a small island called Labuan. Off the northern tip of Borneo, a most suitable port of call, Labuan was covered by luxuriant tropical forests, and right in their midst, thick veins of coal protruded.[37]

The lieutenant in the Royal Navy leading the expedition later reconstructed the scene in a lithograph. It shows two puny white men pointing at a seam of coal standing out between high trees and a stream of water. The man in the right corner is dressed in the uniform of a Royal Navy officer: he represents the military power by which the Empire has landed in this jungle. With a wondrously erect posture, his eyes turned towards the officer, the other man gesticulates wildly and enthusiastically at the finding; most likely, he envisions the coal as a source of fortune, a material his business can extract and sell to steamboats, not the least those operated by the Navy.[38] The scene exudes excitement, a sense of mastery and proprietary right. It registers the moment when foreign shores are integrated into the fossil

---

37 For details on the British exploitation of coal on Labuan, see Andreas Malm, 'Who Lit this Fire? Approaching the History of the Fossil Economy', *Critical Historical Studies* 3 (2016): 215–48.

38 Cf. the reading of the picture in Andrew Francis, *Culture and Commerce in Conrad's Asian Fiction* (Cambridge: Cambridge University Press, 2015), 1.

economy – a distinctly British invention, most simply defined as an economy of self-sustaining growth predicated on the growing consumption of fossil fuels and therefore generating a sustained growth in CO_2 emissions.[39] The coal of Labuan had never before been connected to any such pursuits. The native population knew about it, but had left most of it untouched: only with the arrival of the British was the coal hauled into a circuit that expanded by setting it on fire.

First the fuel was in the ground, still and unstirred; then someone came to the scene and, eyeing profit and power, commenced its exploitation. In this regard, the lithograph provides an *Urbild* of the fossil economy. It is, if you will, a picture of the Fall (and downwards like a fall, into a shaft the ground, is the fundamental movement of that economy). The uncountable repetitions of the same act over the past two centuries form the defeated time now pouring down from the sky. How can we apprehend that process?

---

39 For more on the fossil economy and the British invention of it, see Malm, *Fossil.*

1

On the Building of Nature: Against Constructionism

AN EPIC CASE OF BAD HISTORICAL TIMING

In *This Changes Everything: Capitalism vs the Climate*, Naomi Klein spots an 'epic case of bad historical timing': just as scientists awakened to the magnitude of global warming and called for a drastic change of course, governments, under neoliberal sway, surrendered the very idea of interfering with the self-driving market.[1] Another case can be added. Just as the biosphere began to catch fire, social theory retreated ever further from sooty matter, into the pure air of text. The introduction to an issue of *Theory, Culture and Society* devoted to climate change registers a late awakening: 'The world of culture and virtuality has met its match; the material world apparently does matter and can "bite back".'[2] Almost as disarmed as governments, a social theory sequestered in the cultural turn long faced climate change with an ingrained refusal to recognise – let alone intervene in – extra-discursive reality: no wonder it looked the other way.

As the atmospheric concentration of CO_2 climbed towards the 400 ppm mark, postmodernist philosophers advanced the view

---

1   Naomi Klein, *This Changes Everything: Capitalism vs the Climate* (London: Penguin, 2014), 201.

2   Bronislaw Szerszynski and John Urry, 'Changing Climates: Introduction', *Theory, Culture and Society* 27 (2010): 1–8.

that what historians do is little more than invent images of the past. The real past, says Keith Jenkins, 'doesn't actually enter into historiography except rhetorically': when the historian purports to relay events, what she is actually doing is giving a passionate speech embellished with cherry-picked data. All interpretations of the past are 'fabricated', 'invented', 'metaphorical', 'self-referencing' – having no basis outside of themselves – and hence equally valid; the sole ground for choosing one over the other is personal taste.[3] In his already classic rebuttal of such historiography, *In Defence of History*, Richard J. Evans deploys Auschwitz as an overwhelming master-case; *mutatis mutandis*, we can expect global warming to be similarly used. To paraphrase Evans: global warming is not a discourse. It trivialises the suffering it generates to see it as a text. The excessive temperatures are not a piece of rhetoric. Global warming is indeed inherently a tragedy and cannot be seen either as a comedy or a farce. And if this is true of global warming, then it must be true at least to some degree of other past happenings, events, institutions, people as well.[4]

One premise of the postmodernist philosophy of history is incontrovertible: the past is gone forever and cannot be retrieved for sensory perception. Historians have access only to shards and fragments that happen to have survived the flames of time, and their representations of the past cannot be taken at face value. Consider the picture of the two British men in the rainforest of Labuan. Supposedly painting a scene that once took place in reality, how can we rely on it to correctly depict what happened? From this sceptical attitude – the stock and trade of historians, as so many have pointed out – postmodernists draw the eccentric conclusion that documents like this offer no peephole into the real past, for they are saturated by the power of discourse blocking the sight.

3 Keith Jenkins, *On 'What Is History?': From Carr and Elton to Rorty and White* (London: Routledge, 1995), 19–20, 37, 151, 178–9; Keith Jenkins, *Refiguring History: New Thoughts on an Old Discipline* (London: Routledge, 2003), 41, 56–60.
4 Richard J. Evans, *In Defence of History* (London: Granta, 2000), 124.

And surely, the picture is overlaid with a set of discursive constructs: white men in virginal nature, picking out what belongs to them, finding the path to progress 'savages' have neglected, preparing to tame the raw. But it also appears to have a material substratum. We have reasons to believe that it refers not only to other images – of men, nature, progress, order – but likewise to *an actual identification of the coal seams of Labuan by British imperial agents.*[5] Among those reasons is global warming itself. If the temperature on the earth is rising, it must be because myriad scenes such as in the Labuan forest have played out in the past: for 'the causes of real effects cannot be unreal.'[6] Present warming suggests that neither commanders of the Royal Navy nor latter-day historians can possibly have cooked up all these mountains of evidence for the consumption of fossil fuels in the past. To the contrary, the fossil economy must have been there for quite some time, before it became visible as a historical entity, existing independently of ideas about it – or else we would not be living on this warming planet. A generalised abnegation of the real past guarantees that the history of that economy cannot be written, or written only as free-wheeling fiction, which would scarcely be of any help.

Just as global warming is only one additional, particularly urgent reason to break with the neoliberal political paradigm, so it is but another nail in the coffin of anti-realism. But postmodernist disavowal dies hard. Much social theory continues to dispute the actuality not only of the past, but of *nature.* In *Making Sense of Nature: Representation, Politics and Democracy*, summing up decades of research, Noel Castree first subscribes to a common-sense definition of nature as that which antedates human agency and endures, even if in altered form, when human agents have worked on it.[7] Then he builds an elaborate case for rejecting its existence. Since

---

5   For a highly effective elaboration of historiographical realism, see Murray G. Murphey, *Truth and History* (Albany: SUNY Press, 2009).

6   Ibid., 14.

7   Noel Castree, *Making Sense of Nature: Representation, Politics and Democracy* (Abingdon: Routledge, 2014), 10.

there are so many ways of thinking about nature, so many variegated meanings attached to it, so many powerful 'epistemic communities' – including geographers such as Castree himself – earning a living from representing it, so long a tradition of governing people through spurious reference to it, nature really 'doesn't exist "out there" (or "in here", within us) waiting to be understood', independent of mind, available for experience. 'I thus regard "nature" as a particularly powerful fiction.' Or: 'nature exists only so long as we collectively believe it to exist' – it 'is an illusion', 'just what we think it is' – or simply: 'there's no such thing as nature'.[8] Its only reality pertains to its power as a figment of discourse.

In one of his extended case studies, Castree reads pamphlets from a timber company and the environmentalists fighting its plans to cut down the British Columbia forest of Clayoquot Sound in the 1980s. The former portrayed the forest as a resource to be harvested, the latter as a wildlife sanctuary to be protected for its own sake. Did either side represent it more accurately than the other? Impossible to say. There was no 'pre-existing entity ontologically *available* to be re-presented in different ways', no '"external nature"', no forest as such prior to its being described; asking if Clayoquot Sound *is* a rare ecosystem is to pose a meaningless question.[9] All natures are constructed within the social world; the one storyline is as fabricated as the other. One cannot reach beyond the filter of ideas, affects, projects to touch or smell the trunks and the moss *as they really are*.

What could this mean for global warming? Castree is consistent. 'Global climate change is an *idea*' – emphasis in original – 'rather than simply a set of "real biophysical processes" occurring regardless of our representations of it.'[10] The ontological status of global warming is that of an *idea*. So when the villages in a valley in Pakistan are swept away by a flood, or a monarch butterfly

---

8   Ibid., 6, 12, 282, 318, 320.
9   Ibid., 114, 142. Emphasis in original.
10   Ibid., 236.

population collapses, or cities in Colombia run out of water due to extreme drought, it is not a real biophysical process but an idea that strikes them. The way to stop climate change would then be to give up that idea. Perhaps we can exchange it for global cooling. If we take Castree at his word – climate change is not a process in biophysical reality that occurs regardless of our representations of it, but an invention of the human mind: for such is all nature – these corollaries follow by necessity. It is unlikely that he would endorse them, which suggests that his argument about nature makes rather little sense of it, drawn as he is into the most banal form of the epistemic fallacy: just because we come to *know* about global warming through measurements and comparisons and concepts and deductions, it *is in itself made up* of those things.[11] We seem to be at a serious methodological disadvantage if we cannot reject that fallacy and affirm that there was in fact nature on Labuan – not in the sense of an idea, but of some objective, extra-discursive reality – in which the British found coal to burn, likewise in nature, with equally real consequences down the road. Understanding the historical phenomenon appears to require realism about the past *and* about nature.

Now Castree is far from the first to express the view that nature is fiction. Back in 1992, in the heyday of postmodernism, Donna Haraway pronounced that nature is 'a powerful discursive construction': it is 'a trope. It is figure, construction, artefact, movement, displacement. Nature cannot pre-exist its construction', and neither can organisms or bodies, which emerge out of discourse.[12] This was a staple of postmodernism, and it remains a popular notion – among certain academics, that is – until this day. In *Living through the End of Nature: The Future of American Environmentalism*, Paul

---

11 On the epistemic fallacy, see Roy Bhaskar, *A Realist Theory of Science* (London: Verso, 2008), e.g. 16, 30, 36–7, 38, 44, 250; Andrew Collier, *Critical Realism: An Introduction to Roy Bhaskar's Philosophy* (London: Verso, 1994), 76–85.

12 Donna J. Haraway, 'The Promises of Monsters: A Regenerative Politics for Inappropriate/d Others', in Lawrence Grossberg, Cary Nelson and Paula A. Treichler (eds), *Cultural Studies* (New York: Routledge, 1992), 296–8.

Wapner asserts that nature is 'not a self-subsisting entity' but 'a contextualized *idea*', 'an ideational canvas', 'a projection of cultural understandings', 'a social construction' – a view he finds both 'solipsistic' and 'compelling'.[13] We shall come across plenty of other cases. That such a cloistered doctrine survives in the age of global warming must be deemed remarkable. It is even more so for the devastating refutations the doctrine has suffered.[14] The fact that all sorts of ideas about nature whirl in and around human minds does not justify the conclusion that these cannot be distinguished from that which they are about: as a matter of course, *conceptions* of nature are culturally determined, but the referent is not thereby similarly constituted. Ten herders can draw very different portraits of the same goat, but that does not mean that the goat *is* a painting. If three hikers come down from a mountain with discrepant impressions – the first found it an easy trip; the second is heavily pregnant and could barely make it; the third is mostly struck by the novelty of snow – we do not thereby infer that they must have climbed three different mountains. We believe that the mountain is one,

---

13   Paul Wapner, *Living Through the End of Nature: The Future of American Environmentalism* (Cambridge, MA: MIT Press, 2013), 7, 126, 19. Emphasis in original.

14   This critique of constructionism is most brilliantly developed in Kate Soper, *What is Nature?: Culture, Politics and the Non-Human* (Oxford: Blackwell, 1995). See further e.g. Holmes Rolston III, 'Nature for Real: Is Nature a Social Construct?', in T.D.J. Chappell (ed.), *The Philosophy of the Environment* (Edinburgh: Edinburgh University Press, 1997), 33–64; Ian Hacking, *The Social Construction of What?* (Cambridge, MA: Harvard University Press, 1999), e.g. 36, 66–7; David Kidner, 'Fabricating Nature: A Critique of the Social Construction of Nature', *Environment and Ethics* 22 (2000): 339–57; Val Plumwood, 'The Concept of a Cultural Landscape: Nature, Culture and Agency in the Land', *Ethics and the Environment* 11 (2006): 115–50; Dave Elder-Vass, *The Reality of Social Construction* (Cambridge: Cambridge University Press, 2012), 234–52. For overviews of the long debate over the social construction of nature, see James D. Proctor, 'The Social Construction of Nature: Relativist Accounts, Pragmatist and Critical Realist Responses', *Annals of the Association of American Geographers* 88 (1998): 352–76; David Demeritt, 'What is the "Social Construction of Nature"? A Typology and Sympathetic Critique', *Progress in Human Geography* 26 (2002): 767–90.

and that it has certain features, such as height, gradient, and extent of the snowpack, that exist in themselves regardless of how the hikers have perceived them. As humans, we cannot say what a storm is like without deploying language, but that does not mean that the storm is a linguistic entity or consists of speech acts.[15]

In fact, it is a trivial observation that ideas about nature are products of social life – so are all ideas – and a mysterious proposition that nature equals these ideas and change as they do. That would mean, for instance, that the sun once rotated around the earth and then swapped place with it. Either the actually existing forest contains a rich wildlife or it does not; either the biosphere is warming up or it is not – and how we come to *regard* the wildlife and the warming is another matter entirely. What Castree espouses, and others with him, is a form of *constructionism* about nature; although it might depart from the innocent insight that we think and talk when we think and talk about nature, it slides into the proposition that nature is thereby *constructed*, coming into the world through our ideas, and that no other nature exists.[16] It is a constructionism of the idealist, neo-Kantian, distinctly postmodernist brand.[17]

It seems unable to inspire the kind of theory we need. Temperatures are not rising because people have thought about coal or made mental images of highways: that is not how environmental degradation happens. 'In short', in Kate Soper's famous formulation, 'it is not language that has a hole in its ozone layer', not a text that is heating up, 'and the "real" thing continues to be polluted and degraded even as we refine our deconstructive insights at the level of the signifier' – what some social theory, even

---

15   An example adapted from Dale Jacquette, *The Philosophy of Mind: The Metaphysics of Consciousness* (London: Continuum, 2009), 149.

16   On this slide, cf. Tim Newton, *Nature and Sociology* (London: Routledge, 2007), 22–4.

17   As for the Kantian roots of constructionism, Noel Castree explicitly evokes them in Noel Castree, 'The Return of Nature?', *Cultural Geographies* 19 (2012): 549. For a careful reconstruction of the genealogy, see Elder-Vass, *Reality*, 244–7.

when it professes to deal with nature, continues to obsess about.[18] What would an alternative view of nature look like? In *What Is Nature?: Culture, Politics and the Non-Human*, surely the most incisive inquiry into that question ever written, Soper defends the following answer: nature is 'those material structures and processes that are independent of human activity (in the sense that they are not a humanly created product), and whose forces and causal powers are the necessary conditions of every human practice, and determine the possible forms it can take.'[19] That definition deserves to be read again and memorised. Many others have been proposed – we shall inspect some of them below – but we shall treat this *realist definition* as capturing the essence of the realm we know as nature. The very existence of that realm thus defined, however, is hotly disputed.

THE PRODUCTION OF NATURE?

Can we really say that the climate of planet Earth, as a major component of nature, is independent of human activity – *not* created by humans? Is it not precisely the other way around now? This would seem to be a case for the theory of 'the production of nature'. Laid out by Neil Smith in *Uneven Development: Nature, Capital, and the Production of Space*, it says that nature is anything but independent; it might have been so in some distant pre-human mist but no longer. Nowadays, nature is produced to the core, from within, in its totality, as the forces of capital reshuffle and rework matter in accordance with *their* logic. When did primeval nature succumb to such awesome social power? Smith is unclear on this

---

18   Soper, *What*, 151.

19   Ibid., 132–3. See also Kate Soper, 'Nature/"nature"', in George Robertson, Melinda Mash, Lisa Tickner et al. (eds), *FutureNatural* (London: Routledge, 1996), 22–34; Kate Soper, 'Disposing Nature or Disposing of It: Reflections on the Instruction of Nature', in Gregory E. Kaebnick (ed.), *The Ideal of Nature: Debates about Biotechnology and the Environment* (Baltimore: Johns Hopkins University Press, 2011), 1–16.

point. In some passages, he seems to argue that the production of nature is indeed a phenomenon specific to capitalism; in others, he hints at a much earlier date of human annexation. Unproduced nature ceases to exist wherever one species has set foot: 'Human beings have produced whatever nature became accessible to them' – not only over the past few centuries, but as long as they have cuddled in caves and foraged in forests.[20] Here, the purpose of the theory seems to be not so much to track a historical shift as to collapse the natural into the social altogether, irrespective of dates and epochs, a priori as it were. Indeed, Smith posits 'a social priority of nature; nature is nothing if it is not social.'[21] One geographer who has often stood up for his theory, Noel Castree, states that it 'is intended to oppose the idea of an independent, non-social nature', postulating a fusion '*from the very start*'.[22]

What are the analytical gains of this move? In the first edition of his classic from 1984, Smith precociously mentions anthropogenic climate change as one instance of the production of nature, but in the afterword to the third edition from 2008, he has something else to say: we cannot know to what extent the climate is changing due to human activities.[23] Even trying would presuppose the false separation.

> The attempt to distinguish social vis-à-vis natural contributions to climate change is not only a fool's debate but a fool's philosophy: it leaves sacrosanct the chasm between nature and society – nature in

---

20   Neil Smith, *Uneven Development: Nature, Capital, and the Production of Space. Third Edition* (Athens, GA: University of Georgia Press, 2008), 81.

21   Ibid., 47.

22   Noel Castree, 'Marxism and the Production of Nature', *Capital and Class* 24 (2000): 25; Noel Castree, 'The Production of Nature', in Eric Sheppard and Trevor J. Barnes (eds), *A Companion to Economic Geography* (Oxford: Blackwell, 2000), 278. Emphasis in original. Cf. Noel Castree, 'Capitalism and the Marxist Critique of Political Ecology', in Tom Perreault, Gavin Bridge and James McCarthy (eds), *The Routledge Handbook of Political Ecology* (London: Routledge, 2015), 285–8.

23   For the early mentions, see Smith, *Uneven*, 80, 88; cf. Neil Smith, 'The Production of Nature', in Robertson et al., *Future*, 50.

one corner, society in the other – which is precisely the shibboleth of modern western thought that 'the production of nature' thesis sought to corrode.[24]

This sounds like an admission that the theory would not, after all, be very relevant for the study of global warming. If we must refrain from saying that it is caused by social and *not* by natural factors – distinguishing the two: singling out one, ruling out the other – how could we acknowledge its existence, let alone investigate it as a result of *history*?

In *Alienation and Nature in Environmental Philosophy*, the most illuminating piece of work to emerge from that subdiscipline since Soper, Simon Hailwood underscores that the very notion of anthropogenic causation requires one of independent nature. 'If it is important to say that *humans* made this, caused that, are responsible for such and such, then we need to run the idea of at least some occurrences as *not* of our doing' – as that which, in our case, preceded the fossil economy and would have continued without it: the typical Holocene climate.[25] As Smith himself admits, one cannot catch sight of global warming if one has removed the background of non-social nature (hence, in his logic, only a fool would try).[26] It seems to follow that some sort of distinction between 'society' and 'nature' remains indispensable, both for research on the history of the fossil economy and for climate science as such; in the field of event attribution, incidentally, simulation of recent storms is contrasted to models of what the weather would have been like

---

24   Smith, *Uneven*, 244. See further the confused arguments on 245–7.

25   Simon Hailwood, *Alienation and Nature in Environmental Philosophy* (Cambridge: Cambridge University Press, 2015), 39. Emphases in original. Cf. Plumwood, 'Concept', 144.

26   Smith's statements notwithstanding, it is evidently possible for scholars committed to his theory to write sensibly about climate change. See Susan W. S. Millar and Don Mitchell, 'The Tight Dialectic and the Capitalist Production of Nature', *Antipode* 49 (2017): 75–93. The problematic implications of the theory are here simply elided.

in the absence of human influence.[27] That is how the historical imprint is detected.

But still: is not the climate of today precisely *produced*? Retaining a nature without human influence in counterfactual computer models is certainly not a way to prove its continued existence. Might the theory be useful if restricted to the past two centuries? To explore this possibility, we must turn to some other attempts to pursue the intuition that nature is now social all the way down.

THE END OF NATURE?

In 1990, one year after Jameson's *Postmodernism* was published, Bill McKibben proclaimed 'the end of nature' in a book of the same name, today regarded as the first popular book on climate change. Before almost everyone else, he sensed that the altered composition of the atmosphere turns everything inside out: the meaning of the weather, to begin with. A sudden downpour can no longer be shrugged off or an Indian summer enjoyed as a caprice of nature. *All* weather must now be distrusted as an artefact of 'our ways of life', including on a Svalbard mountaintop or an Atacama sand dune, in areas that pass as remote wilderness: with CO_2, the human fingerprint is everywhere. 'We have produced the carbon dioxide – we have ended nature' – or: 'By changing the weather, we make every spot on earth man-made and artificial. We have deprived nature of its independence, and that is fatal to its meaning. Nature's independence *is* its meaning; without it there is nothing but us.'[28]

Under what definition has nature disappeared? It might seem, at first glance, that McKibben is operating with a definition akin to Soper's – 'independence' being the key term – but he pushes it one crucial notch further. He is not referring to nature as a set of

27   Gabriele C. Hegerl, 'Use of Models and Observations in Event Attribution', *Environmental Research Letters* 10 (2015). See further references in notes 7–9 above.

28   Bill McKibben, *The End of Nature* (London: Viking, 1990), 43–4, 54. Emphasis in original.

material structures and processes with causal powers of their own, not to the end of photosynthesis or respiration or cloud formation; all such things, he affirms, are here to stay. Rather, *'we have ended the thing that has, at least in modern times, defined nature for us – its separation from human society'*, meaning its purity, its condition of being perfectly pristine, untouched, unaffected by people.[29] Only under this definition can nature possibly be said to have ended. But is it a reasonable one?

If I mix my coffee with sugar, I do not thereby come to believe that the coffee has ended. I believe it has shed one condition and assumed another: it is no longer black coffee, but sweet. Normally, in our daily lives and languages, we do not hold that when A comes into contact with B it ceases to exist – a private company remains a private company as it parleys with the state; a lake stays a lake even if tons of sediment pour into it. This should be an idea particularly commonplace to anyone familiar with Marxist dialectics: capitalist property relations do not vanish the moment they become entangled with feudal or socialist ones; capital can only expand by constantly relating to its arch-foe labour, and so on, throughout a world in which a unity of opposites is an unsurprising state of affairs. Should we proceed differently with nature? Is there any reason to build a certain condition – namely, absence of social influence – into the definition of this particular thing, as a touchstone of its *very existence*?

We might call this the *purist* definition. McKibben presents no justification for it; he simply takes it for granted. But if we consider nature on a slightly smaller scale, it does seem difficult to uphold. Take the oceans. They are now marred by plastic waste swirling around in giant gyres, acidification, overfishing and other human impacts that extend into the deepest, darkest recesses – so can we say that they *ipso facto* are no more? Hardly. The oceans are in a different state, but they are with us as much as ever – and if this applies to the oceans, which form a fairly significant component of

---

29 Ibid., 60. Emphasis in original.

what we know as 'nature', why not also to that majestic totality? There seem to be two possible solutions here. Either one injects sacredness, some form of (ironically) supernatural value into the definition of nature, or one holds on to an extreme form of dualism, which would allow for the belief that the essence of nature is its *absolute segregation* from human society.[30]

Now, if we conclude, as we should, that the purist definition is analytically untenable, it does not follow that McKibben is wrong to lament the end of a *certain condition* of nature.[31] I might have reason to cry out in distaste when someone pours sugar in my coffee; there might be a good deal more compelling reasons to mourn the loss of every pristine place on earth. The point here, however, is that McKibben's sad tidings are analytically unhelpful for our purposes. On the purist definition, the coal the British uncovered on faraway shores belonged to nature prior to their arrival, but as they (or rather their workers) began to dig and heave it, the material somehow fell out of nature, into the sphere of humans. But if the coal had already exited nature, how could the CO_2 then possibly have a lethal impact on it? The antinomies of dualism would reappear at every stage of such a history.

IS ALL ENVIRONMENT BUILT ENVIRONMENT?

If climate change signifies the *end* of nature, we would be forced to conclude that it sets the postmodern condition in stone. In another sign of the times, McKibben published his book the year after Francis Fukuyama wrote his essay 'The End of History?'; while the latter thesis has since become the laughing stock of theory, the

---

30   For similar criticisms of the purist definition and the ensuing proclamation of the end of nature, see Keekok Lee, 'Is Nature Autonomous?', in Thomas Heyd (ed.), *Recognizing the Autonomy of Nature* (New York: Columbia University Press, 2005), 54–5; Val Plumwood, 'Towards a Progressive Naturalism', in ibid., 41–3, Mark Woods, 'Ecological Restoration and the Renewal of Wildness and Freedom', in ibid., 174; Plumwood, 'Concept', 135.

31   The reasons for this lamentation will be inspected in a subsequent essay.

former is held in the highest regard. McKibben himself has moved on to more productive pursuits, as perhaps the single most important leader of the global climate movement, but his obituary of nature has stuck in the intellectual climate despite the reasoning behind it being, as we have seen and shall see more of, questionable. It serves as the point of departure for Wapner's discussions of the dilemmas of environmentalism, as well as for the most recent instalment of the most philosophically advanced attempt at defending constructionism about nature: that of Steven Vogel.

In his first book *Against Nature: The Concept of Nature in Critical Theory*, Steven Vogel spins a constructionist programme out of an idiosyncratic reading of the Frankfurt School canon. Here, he points to four senses in which 'nature is a social category': one can never step into a nature outside of human preconceptions; the nature scientists claim to study is a product of their own practices – postmodernist stock-in-trade, so far – natural objects are integrated into social life; and they are built by labour.[32] Only the last sense, the most original of the four, is retained in *Thinking Like a Mall: Environmental Philosophy after the End of Nature*. Although he backtracks on his earlier idealism, Vogel here takes constructionism farther than ever before. He sets out from the assertion that McKibben was right: nature has indeed ended, most obviously because of the rising temperatures. Accepting the purist definition, however, Vogel takes McKibben's thesis to the next step and claims that if nature expires the moment humans touch it, then it must have been dead and gone long before any CO_2 plumed from chimneys.[33] Not linked specifically to global warming, 'the end of nature might be something that, in the Heideggerian phrase that seems relevant here, has *always already happened*'; by axiomatic necessity, nature 'ceased to exist at the moment the first

32   Steven Vogel, *Against Nature: The Concept of Nature in Critical Theory* (New York: State University of New York Press, 1996), 35–9.
33   Steven Vogel, *Thinking Like a Mall: Environmental Philosophy after the End of Nature* (Cambridge, MA: MIT Press, 2015), ch. 1.

human appeared on the scene' – 'so long ago that we cannot even fix the date'.[34]

So what is it that seems to surround us now? Not discourses or the ooze from epistemic communities; this is not what Vogel is getting at any longer. We are surrounded by a solidly real environment, but it is a *built* environment, one that humans have literally, physically constructed from the ground up. Since there is no way humans can 'encounter a landscape at all without transforming it', every landscape humans have encountered must be classified as built, far-flung islands as much as conurbations, the deserts as much as the highways, the atmosphere every bit as much as – this is the gist of the book – the shopping mall.[35] Not quite the deduction McKibben had in mind, it does follow a quirky but inexorable logic. Paraphrasing Aldo Leopold's classic injunction to 'think like a mountain' so as to get closer to the land, Vogel advises environmentalists to rather think like a shopping mall, for a mall is just as much a piece of the environment as the mountain and no less deserving of protection and awe.[36]

The variety of constructionism fleshed out here is different from the idealist type: as Vogel stresses repeatedly, he is using the word 'construction' in the literal sense, exactly as he would in front of the pyramids. We may thus distinguish between idealist and literalist constructionism about nature; Vogel and Smith have both moved to the latter, while Castree has drifted from the latter to the former.[37]

---

34 Ibid., 8, 29. Emphasis in original.

35 Ibid., 8. This deduction is repeated throughout the first chapters of the book, see e.g. 44, 58, 90.

36 Ibid., particularly ch. 5.

37 On this distinction, cf. e.g. Anna Peterson, 'Environmental Ethics and the Social Construction of Nature', *Environmental Ethics* 21 (1999): 343. In a text written in 1996, Smith 'incorporates material with conceptual construction'; in his book from the same year, Vogel says that '"nature" must itself be seen as discursively and practically constituted.' Smith, 'Production', 50; Vogel, *Against*, 170. Both men later resolved to leave the conceptual-discursive aspects aside and focus on the material-practical. Indeed, they have both rejected idealist constructionism on grounds similar to those offered above: see Neil Smith, 'Nature at the Millenium:

Neither, it is important to note, is a straw man. Vogel really means what he says. 'There is nothing in our environment that we have not, in some sense or other, had a hand in producing', nothing physical or chemical around us originating outside labour, 'no raw materials, no "natural resources," that have not themselves already been the object of prior practices of construction' – statements on repeat throughout the latest opus.[38] All indications are that Vogel wants us to take them seriously. Let us do so. They are not true. Coal is disproof enough: we know that it formed when vegetation slumped into bogs, whose water protected it from oxidation; as the dead plants sank deeper, temperatures and pressure rose; slowly, gradually, the matter solidified into coal, mostly during the Carboniferous era some 286–360 million years ago, when no humans could possibly have assisted in the process. Finding coal in a Borneo jungle is to open a culvert to that past and *draw in what no humans had a hand in producing*, and the same holds for the extraction of any bit of fossil fuel from the bowels of this planet.[39]

Very easily – so easily as to court ridicule, but such is now the state of this theory – literalist constructionism can be shown to be empirically false. Fossil fuels are no trifling matters in our environment; neither are the sun, the earth's crust, oxygen, the element of fire . . . One would have to go to extraordinary lengths of sophistry to present a case for these as in any sense 'constructed' or 'built' by humans, and yet they constitute the *mise en scène* and the *sine qua non* and whatnot of a warming world. The only way to

Production, and Re-enchantment', in Bruce Braun and Noel Castree (eds), *Remaking Reality: Nature at the Millenium* (London: Routledge, 1998), 274–6; Vogel, *Thinking*, 34–6, 57.

38 Vogel, *Thinking*, 41, 63. Cf. e.g. 61–2, 73, 94.

39 See e.g. Jeffrey S. Dukes, 'Burning Buried Sunshine: Human Consumption of Ancient Solar Energy', *Climatic Change* 61 (2003): 31–44; Vaclav Smil, *The Earth's Biosphere: Evolution, Dynamics, and Change* (Cambridge, MA: MIT Press, 2003), 131–4; Smil, *Energy in Nature and Society: General Energetics of Complex Systems* (Cambridge, MA: MIT Press, 2008), 206; David Beerling, *The Emerald Planet: How Plants Changed Earth's History* (Oxford: Oxford University Press, 2007), 42–52.

buttress constructionism against them would be to insist on an extreme version of the purist definition: by *any* contact whatsoever with humans – be it falling on them or carrying them or passing through their lungs – solar radiation and sedimentary rocks and the air and everything else magically become their products. And when Vogel talks about 'buildings' and 'construction', he does seem to presuppose something like this metamorphosis. To affect something is to build it. 'There is nothing we do that does not change, *and therefore build*, the environment', Vogel spells out his generous extension of the term.[40] With this usage, I could make a rightful claim to have built a pyramid in Giza merely by scaling and throwing black paint on it.

When humans come into contact with a landscape, they necessarily change it; by changing it, they build it; therefore humans have built all landscapes on earth (and logically this should extend to the moon and Mars and other celestial bodies as well). The conspicuous Achilles heel of this syllogism, propping up the whole argument, is the use of 'build' as a synonym for 'affect' or 'change'. Vogel defends the conflation by averring that 'to build something *is* to "affect" some material and thereby transform it into something new – wood into a bookcase, clay into a pot, silicon into a memory chip.'[41] Sure, but this is not what is at stake here. If I cut and mould wood into a bookcase, I have undoubtedly built that bookcase – but if I cut a branch off a tree, have I also built *that tree?* This is what Vogel's argument amounts to: not that to build is to affect matter, but that *to affect matter is to build it*. In the common idiom, this is not what the word refers to. The consequences would be enormous if we were to subscribe to Vogel's proposed redefinition: look at the marks I have left in my apartment – see, it is I who have built this condominium. Or, as Val Plumwood has pointed out: I affect the

40 Vogel, *Thinking*, 44. Emphasis added.
41 Ibid., 244. Emphasis in original. The same deduction is offered in Steven Vogel, 'Why "Nature" Has No Place in Environmental Philosophy', in Kaebnick, *Ideal*, 197.

persons close to me, indeed change their lives quite thoroughly; hence I could make a claim to have built or produced or constructed them.[42] Verily, constructionism runs wild here.

So what does it mean to have built or produced – literally constructed – something? Kate Soper again provides the most convincing answer: the crucial criterion is 'to inaugurate a product which previously did not exist.'[43] When we say that pharaoh Khufu built the great pyramid of Giza, we mean that it did not exist at first, but then this man set in motion a process of construction some 4,600 years ago *that brought the structure into being* and there it has stood ever since. The human constructor gives rise to an entity. Something like a watch or a computer is indeed built or produced, for it owes its existence to human actions – by affecting select matters in specific ways, humans have created them *de novo* – but coal and oceans and the carbon cycle fall into another category. So, it seems, does the climate. Earth had it before it had humans.

WHAT IS CONSTRUCTED AND WHAT IS NOT

The metaphor of construction should indeed be taken quite literally: when building something, you do not merely change or affect it but call the structure into existence.[44] Ironically, building is the human praxis around which Vogel builds his argument, while entirely missing the quick of it. One could turn instead to William H. Sewell, who delineates the real utility of the metaphor with precision in his *Logics of History: Social Theory and Social Transformation*. In contradistinction to synchronic thinking so typical for postmodernity,

> the construction metaphor implies a very different, thoroughly diachronic, temporality. Construction is a noun formed from a verb;

---

42 Plumwood, 'Concept', 137.
43 Soper, *What*, 135. See further 136–7, 141–2.
44 Cf. Hacking, *Social*, 47.

it signifies a *process* of building, carried out by human actors and stretched out over time. (Rome, as the proverb puts it, was not built in a day.) The social or cultural construction of meaning is also, by implication, a temporally extended process that requires the sustained labor of human actors. Social construction also implies that when a meaning has been built it has a strong tendency to remain in place: socially constructed gender relations or scientific truths often become naturalized, accepted, and enduring features of the world, just as buildings, once built, continue to remain as an enduring feature of the physical environment.[45]

In none of these senses would the climate be a good fit for the metaphor. *But in every one of them, the fossil economy would.*[46]

If the term 'social construction' is to be meaningful, it must refer to some X that has come about 'in consequence of a sequence of social events', to follow Ian Hacking's *The Social Construction of What?* A constructionist typically believes that the X in question 'need not have existed' had it not been for those events.[47] Applied to the realm of nature, such a belief has something absurd about it. Three storylines have the potential to turn literalist construction-ism into intelligible propositions: 1.) Human beings were beamed onto an empty planet (or universe) and then constructed nature from scratch, starring in the role of divine non-produced produc-ers. Here it would indeed seem that the X came about through social events. (The question of where the raw materials came from would, of course, remain unanswered.) 2.) Human beings emerged from pre-existing nature, but the moment they did so and started to roam the planet, they annulled it. Fresh from that feat, they then proceeded to build all environments on earth. This is Vogel's logic, which begs a few questions, including how humans could be at

---

45   William H. Sewell Jr., *Logics of History: Social Theory and Social Transformation* (Chicago: Chicago University Press, 2005), 360. Emphasis in original.

46   Except that it is not 'a meaning'.

47   Hacking, *Social*, 9, 2.

once the direct offspring and the instant annullers of nature (a storyline only conceivable on the basis of the purist definition). 3.) Humans lived for a very long time among pre-existing nature, but in recent years, they have come to wield such detrimental and pervasive influence over it that it no longer is what it was. This seems to be an activity rather different from construction – more like *de*struction – but the storyline does at least render the earth and everything on it as outcomes of social events. Other questions then arise. If nature ended with late human influence – read: anthropogenic climate change – what forces and causal powers now determine the possible forms that influence can take? Where do *they* come from? Were the channels into which CO_2 emissions run built by humans just now?

The absurdity extends to both varieties of constructionism about nature.[48] Perhaps this is why their proponents, who are no fools, cannot avoid slips of the tongue. All of a sudden, Castree mentions 'a biophysical world that at some level exists' and 'knows nothing of the values and goals according to which we discuss, respond to and intervene in it.'[49] Smith gives away just the distinction he seeks to corrode: 'unlike gravity, there is nothing natural about the law of value; no society has lived without experiencing the operation of gravity, but many have lived without the law of value' – nature in one corner, society in the other.[50] Vogel, for his part, posing as the sternest enemy to any use of the term, says things like 'we human beings are ourselves natural.' In fact, halfway into his book he

48   Cf. the brilliant Hailwood, *Alienation*, 40; Plumwood, 'Concept', 135.

49   Castree, *Making*, 141. Cf. 7, 137–40. Castree is the lead author of an article in the preeminent journal of climate science that starts off by paying tribute to a very realist endeavour: 'The science of global environmental change (GEC) has played a vital role in alerting humans to the extraordinary biophysical effects of their activities.' Noel Castree, William M. Adams, John Barry et al., 'Changing the Intellectual Climate', *Nature Climate Change* 4 (2014): 763. Cf. Noel Castree, 'Unfree Radicals: Geoscientists, the Anthropocene, and Left Politics', *Antipode* 49 (2017): 52–74.

50   Smith, *Uneven*, 82 (cf. 54).

spends a whole chapter reflecting on the fate of artefacts at the hands of nature. Every edifice is subject to precipitation and oxidation and entropy and heat and other 'processes whose fundamental character – whose *nature*, I might even be willing to say – is not and cannot be fully known to us', since they 'are currently [sic] operating independently of humans', not 'something we *produce*'.[51] Claims such as these might be intended to provide nuance to arguments sorely lacking in that quality, but the effect is rather to betray some damning inconsistencies.[52] Sometimes constructionists appear to insert them as caveats of common sense, allowing them to wash their hands of the implications of their argument – but *of course* we do not believe that the earth is a fairy-tale! Who could be so crazy? Before and after such brief parentheses, whether composed deliberately or by accident, however, they continue to bracket, relegate, dismiss and exclude nature in their actual accounts of the ways of the world.[53] Until inevitably, at some point, they step out into that world and have to repeat the admission. Not even its most militant detractors can dispense with the category of nature, and that must be because no one can.

Similarly for those who grieve its end: McKibben cannot help talking about a 'new' nature that behaves differently, but is still, so it seems, that which was supposed to have ended.[54] In *After Nature: A Politics for the Anthropocene*, Jedediah Purdy offers yet another variation on McKibben's necrology, declares that nature is gone for good – 'in every respect, the world we inhabit will henceforth be the world we have made' (in every respect!) – and adds, for good measure, that nature 'is not the sort of thing that has a meaning'.[55]

---

51 Vogel, *Thinking*, 43, 110–12. Emphases in original.

52 A more nuanced case for constructionism is made by Manuel Arias-Maldonado, 'Let's Make It Real: In Defense of a Realistic Constructivism', *Environmental Ethics* 33 (2011): 377–392, but it is nuanced exactly in proportion to its concessions to realism.

53 As argued by Newton, *Nature*, 24–5.

54 McKibben, *End*, e.g. 88–9.

55 Jedediah Purdy, *After Nature: A Politics of the Anthropocene* (Cambridge

And then, without even noticing it, he spends page after page making statements like 'our control over nature seems a precarious fantasy', 'there is no separating human beings from ecological nature', 'we are less distinct from the rest of nature than we often imagine', 'trying to build a peaceful and humane world means finding a way to live peacefully with nature'.[56] After nature? It does not sound like it. Not even its necrologists can write about the corpse without mentioning its movements, and that must be because it is still quite alive.[57]

The category cannot be stamped out from human vocabularies. It refers to the part of the inhabited world that humans encounter *but have not constructed*, created, built or conjured up in their imagination, and that part is very prevalent indeed.[58] It preceded us, surrounds us and will succeed us; it was, is and will be spontaneously generated without us; it may be under all sorts of influence, but that does not put an end to it, any more than a continent ceases to be because it has skyscrapers standing on it. When the British made their way through the jungle of Labuan, they did not produce but precisely *encountered* nature. The moment captured on the lithograph is not the moment when they made the sunlight and the water and the plants and the coal: all these things were there before them, belonging to the part of the world in whose absence they could not have been present. What they resolved to *do* with that nature was, however, up to them. Here supervened the moment of construction: they began to map, test, sell and buy the coal as material for their fossil economy, their Rome, built not in a day but over the course of the nineteenth century. We should reserve talk about

---

MA: Harvard University Press, 2015), 3; Jedediah Purdy, reply to respondents, *Boston Review*, 11 January, 29.

56 Purdy, *After*, 16, 42, 271, 288. See further e.g. 21, 46, 146, 232, 238–9, 277, 286–7.

57 For yet another example of this performative contradiction, see yet another 'after nature' text, a classic in the field: Arturo Escobar, 'After Nature: Steps to an Antiessentialist Political Ecology', *Current Anthropology* 40 (1999): 1–30.

58 Rolston III, 'Nature', 43.

'construction' for that entity and demarcate it from the climate – throw constructionism back into society, as it were, and accept nature as a category *sui generis*. But that presupposes, of course, that the two can be distinguished from one another.

2

On Combined Development: Against Hybridism

THE HYBRIDIST MESH

Much contemporary theory cannot get enough of proclaiming that society and nature have become impossible to tell apart because in fact they are one and the same thing. The main source of inspiration for this way of thinking is Bruno Latour. A quantitative indication of his influence appeared when *Times Higher Education* ranked the writers most cited in the humanities in 2007: topped by Michel Foucault, the list put Latour in tenth place, one notch above Sigmund Freud, 16 notches above Benjamin and a full 26 above Karl Marx.[1] Ten years later, one of his greatest fans proclaimed that 'Latour is starting to look like Michel Foucault's eventual replacement as the default citation in the humanities – he is quickly approaching that point in the social sciences.'[2] And indeed, Latour's sway over contemporary thinking on the relationship between society and nature is probably without equal. He will occupy a central place in what follows.

The foundational text is *We Have Never Been Modern*, which begins with Bruno Latour waking up one morning and reading the

1 Times Higher Education, 'Most Cited Authors of Books in the Humanities, 2007', timeshighereducation.com, 26 March 2009.

2 Graham Harman, 'Demodernizing the Humanities with Latour', *New Literary History* 47 (2016): 249.

newspaper and being taken aback by the blurring of the lines between the social and the natural: first there is a story about the ozone layer (this is written in 1991). Atmospheric scientists warn that the hole is growing, while manufacturers and politicians prevaricate on phasing out the depleting substances. 'The same article mixes together chemical reactions and political reactions': a most remarkable admixture.[3] Reading on, the author finds a story about the progress of the AIDS epidemic and the procrastination of medical companies; another one about a forest with rare species going up in smoke; yet another about frozen embryos, and so on – the entire paper is a blur. Wherever Latour turns his eyes, he sees *hybrids*. There is no way of telling where society ends and nature starts and vice versa; everything happens across the spheres or in the no man's land between them; the world is composed of bastard breeds and trying to cut it in halves – one social, one natural – can only be done with a sword our better judgement must now sheathe.

At the core of Latour's project and prestige, this argument requires some closer consideration.[4] It has, to begin with, a quantitative, historical component. It says that the unions have recently proliferated to such an extent that the social and the natural can no longer be distinguished. In the early days of modernity, there were perhaps a few vacuum pumps around, but now the hybrids fill every horizon:

> Where are we to classify the ozone hole story, or *global warming* or deforestation? Where are we to put these hybrids? Are they human? Human because they are our work. Are they natural? Natural because they are not our doing . . . There are so many hybrids that no one knows any longer how to lodge them in the old promised land of modernity.[5]

---

3 Bruno Latour, *We Have Never Been Modern* (Cambridge, MA: Harvard University Press, 1993), 1.

4 It remains at the core of Bruno Latour, *An Inquiry into Modes of Existence: An Anthropology of the Moderns* (Cambridge, MA: Harvard University Press, 2013), see e.g. the statements on nature and society on 320, 352.

5 Latour, *We*, 50, 131. Emphasis added. Cf. Bruno Latour, *The Pasteurization of France* (Cambridge, MA: Harvard University Press, 1988), 205–6.

Ostensibly an admission of intellectual confusion – I have no idea how to understand something that is at once a product of human work and not – this is a rhetorical way of puncturing the modern illusion of a sharp demarcation between nature and society. Latour believes, of course, that the two have *never* been separated in any way, shape or form: hence 'we have never been modern'. What is new is the sheer ubiquity of the crossbreeds, or the 'quasi-objects' or the 'collectives', which makes the fantasy impossible to sustain any longer: and once we realise this, we also come to see that 'Nature and Society have no more existence than West and East.'[6] The terms 'do not designate domains of reality'. They are utterly arbitrary poles on a mental map, nothing more. 'I am aiming', Latour declares in *The Politics of Nature: How to Bring the Sciences into Democracy*, 'at blurring the distinction between nature and society *durably*, so that we shall never have to go back to two distinct sets.'[7] Let the categories dissolve in the real fluid.

We may take this to be the cardinal principle of *hybridism*, a general framework for coming to terms with the cobweb of society and nature by means of denying any polarity or duality inside it. Hybridism holds that reality is made up of hybrids of the social and the natural and that the two terms therefore have no referents any longer, if they ever did. In his *Bruno Latour: Reassembling the Political*, Graham Harman, Latour's faithful squire, confirms the collapse of the 'difference' between society and nature as the pith of his thinking and restates the fix: 'we must start by considering all entities in exactly the same way.'[8] As we shall see, hybridism comes in other forms, with diverging emphases and points of attack, but they are all united in the conviction that 'society' and 'nature' are two words for an identity, hence superfluous (and noxious) signifiers – and Latour is never far away from them. In

---

6   Latour, *We*, 85.

7   Bruno Latour, *The Politics of Nature: How to Bring Sciences into Democracy* (Cambridge, MA: Harvard University Press, 2004), 53, 36. Emphasis in original.

8   Graham Harman, *Bruno Latour: Reassembling the Political* (London: Pluto, 2014), viii. Cf. Latour, *Pasteurization*, 206.

Environments, Natures and Social Theory, a recent survey of hybridist approaches, Damian F. White et al. recycle their basic rationale from his 1991 manifesto:

> And all the while that this debate is going on, we become more and more aware that we live in worlds of multiple hybrid objects. They keep on popping up: from ozone layers to genetically modified crops, prosthetic implants to histories of modified landscapes. Are they social? Are they natural? Attempts to understand this hybrid world through the purification of objects and subjects into boxes labelled 'society' or 'nature' has limited utility.[9]

Note here a claim fundamental to hybridism: *because natural and social phenomena have become compounds, the two cannot be differentiated* by any other means than violence. Being mixed means being one.

A theoretical *zeitgeist* of sorts, the claim is on repeat in the writings of all the thinkers we have inspected so far. To take but two examples: due to anthropogenic transformation of the earth culminating in climate change, 'it is impossible to now distinguish where humanity ends and nature begins', writes Wapner; producing a similar list again headed by climate, Purdy charges that 'the contrast between what is nature and what is not no longer makes sense.'[10] It is the same epiphany as McKibben's, coming in two versions: 1.) because they are so thoroughly mixed, society and nature do not exist (call this ontological hybridism); 2.) because of this level of admixture, there is no point, no use, no wisdom in telling the one apart from the other (call this methodological hybridism). Regularly overlapping, they share some significant problems.

---

9   Damian F. White, Alan P. Rudy and Brian J. Gareau, *Environments, Nature and Social Theory* (London: Palgrave, 2016), 199. To their credit, White et al. identify several problems with hybridism and offer a number of well-thought criticisms of several approaches: see further below. They do, however, subscribe to the general hybridist project.

10   Wapner, *Living*, 134; Purdy, *After*, 15.

HYBRIDISM IS A CARTESIANISM

Observers of the world often come across combinations. Consider students of religion. Syncretism is a rampant phenomenon in the history of faiths, hiding in the depths of most of them and sometimes brought to the surface in the shape of, say, the Druze belief system, in which doctrines of Hindu, Shi'ite, Platonic, Gnostic, Christian, Pythagorean, Jewish and other provenances are drawn together. Now, a scholar of the Druze faith will wonder at the distinctive *unity* this people has forged out of these fantastically disparate elements. She will study how they have been recombined into a novel totality; how they relate to each other in there; how they entered the faith over time; what particular Druze belief can be traced back to what source, and so on. But she will probably not say this: the Druze faith is a hybrid thing and so we must not try to sift out the Platonic from the Shiite components, whose traces have been lost in this blend; it is impossible to say where the one ends and the other begins; this is a common occurrence in the world of religion, so let us scrap the categories of Platonism and Shi'ism and the rest of it altogether. Saying something like that would not be considered an attempt to *understand* the Druze faith. It would be more like a surrender of the task.

In medicine, one studies the effects of substances on the human body: say, tobacco on the lungs. Where would such research have been led by the pronouncement that since tobacco and lungs are mixed in the bodies of smokers, the categories have become obsolete (if they ever were relevant) and hence the effects of one on the other cannot be meaningfully distinguished? Or consider how etymologists study languages. Does Spanish cancel out Arabic and Latin? Or the field of international relations: the European Union mixes Germany with Greece . . .

Hybridism as a guide to the world would certainly have some interesting political consequences. When Leon Trotsky scanned Tsarist Russia and distilled 'the law of *combined development* – by which we mean a drawing together of the different stages of the journey, a combining of separate steps, an amalgam of archaic with more contemporary forms', he could perhaps have inferred that capitalism was now so deeply enmeshed in Tsarism that it had become pointless to track what parts of Russian social dynamics stemmed from it, let alone single it out for special treatment.[11] Then surely anti-capitalist revolution would have been an idle venture. Or, someone might point out that the very physical makeup of the territories occupied in 1967 is patterned by the commingling of Zionist and Palestinian matter – the air in Gaza hums with the sounds of drones and *muezzins*; houses in al-Khalil have settlers living on top of local families; toxic waste from colonies mix with water in the valleys of the West Bank – and hence purifying this situation into boxes labelled 'the Zionist project' and 'the Palestinian people' has limited utility, for the contrast between them no longer makes sense.

Now, a hybridist might object that these analogies are unfair. Platonism and Shi'ism are, after all, *the same sort of thing*. Air adulterated by cigarette smoke and pure air are modalities of the exact same substance. Germany and Greece are but two nations, capitalism and Tsarism two social forms, Zionists and Palestinians two groups of people – their combinations should provoke no surprise. They do not call for a revision of our ontologies or methods; they do not imply that reality is mongrelised to an extent few have seen; the unification of such similar components does not cancel out their difference. But such an objection would only reveal the problem at the root of hybridism. *Only by postulating nature and society as categories located a universe apart does their combination warrant their collapse.* Only with an implicit conception of them as more *substantially unlike each other* than any other two things can one conclude that their admixture, in contradistinction to so many humdrum alloys, disproves their existence. The revelation betrays itself – oh, so nature and society were not

---

11   Leon Trotsky, *The History of the Russian Revolution, Volume One* (London: Sphere, 1967), 23. Emphasis in original.

self-contained galaxies after all! Then we cannot talk about them any longer!

In the background lurks, again, the legacy of an extreme form of dualism. Latour likes to refer to it as 'the modern constitution'; a more common genealogy derives it from the philosophy of René Descartes. He held that the mind and the body are two 'distinct substances'. The body is extended in space and constituted of parts that can be sliced off and removed like cogs from a machine, in starkest possible contrast to the thinking mind. If a heart is cut out from a body, that body loses a vital component and ceases to be – but where is the heart of the mind? Where are its arms, its legs, its constituent parts potentially separated from each other? They are nowhere, Descartes argued, for the mind is a thing one and whole, indivisible, indestructible; it does not possess a corporeal shape. The body is a physical substance, but the mind is an ethereal, spiritual sort of thing. This is why the mind can live on and prosper without the body; after death and decomposition, it survives because it is made of *utterly different stuff*. 'Two substances are said to be really distinct', Descartes lays down his central criterion, 'when each of them can exist without the other': and here such is the case, Descartes being 'certain that I am really distinct from my body and that I can exist without it'.[12] His philosophy is a *substance dualism*.

In the debate on nature and society, critics of Cartesianism are in the habit of mapping that philosophy onto the pair.[13] Descartes himself did not speak in terms of these categories – his concern was the problem of body and mind – but many observers have found in Western worldviews the fingerprint of that philosopher, his dualist model simply extended to the analogous realms. And, indeed, the all-too-common conceptual segregation of nature and

---

12 René Descartes, *Meditations and Other Metaphysical Writings* (London: Penguin, 2003), 15, 86, 62.

13 A key work in this anti-Cartesian genre is Val Plumwood, *Feminism and the Mastery of Nature* (London: Routledge, 1993), although she traces the problem further back to the philosophy of Plato.

society can be seen as its logical continuation. If only by default, rather than some explicit alignment with Descartes, a characteristically Cartesian view of nature and society treats them as distinct substances fundamentally detached from each other. There might be occasional interstellar traffic between them, through some tiny pineal gland, but their essences are of opposite kinds and move in separate orbits.

Now, hybridism screams out its hostility to Cartesianism from every page it commands. It poses as the absolute negation of that obnoxious philosophy, since it refuses to countenance any distinction whatsoever between nature and society, to the point of *denying their existence*. That latter move, however – that rush to jettison the categories as soon as the extent of their entanglement comes into view – is, at a closer look, merely the flipside of substance dualism. Descartes himself spelled out its corollary: 'to conceive of the union of two things is to conceive of them as one thing'.[14] Anyone who believes that the body and the mind form a union would, he argued, be forced to recognise them as an undifferentiated oneness. By taking observations of their combination as so many reasons to expunge nature and society from the map of the world, hybridism updates this logic for our times. Moreover, it draws all of its rhetorical force from centuries of Cartesian thinking, to which the quantitative, historical component stands in exact proportion, the surprise at the proliferating combinations emanating from the legacy of extreme dualism: of this thinking, hybridism is not so much a rejection *as a consequence*. It is a negation of it only in the way the hangover is a negation of the binge. It is post-Cartesian in the sense that some scholars are post-Keynesian or post-Kantian: they carry the code of the original creed within themselves, if only in diluted form. Hybridism is to Cartesianism what e-cigarettes are to cigarettes.

---

14   Descartes, *Meditations*, 152.

HISTORICAL MATERIALISM IS A PROPERTY DUALISM

The mind, according to Descartes, is nowhere. It does not occupy any location in space. The substance of which it is made is not the kind that sits on a stool or lifts a weight or kicks a stone; it is defined precisely by *not* having extension, of being altogether otherworldly, cut off from mortal flesh. This philosophy gives rise to a well-known problem: that of causal interaction. If a stone is kicked down a path, it is because some foot has come into contact with it at a place. The foot has imparted motion to the stone, causing it to run over the ground; the two objects have interacted at the site of the collision, and that is how all causation occurs. For one thing to cause the behaviour of another, it must strike, brush, bump into, tickle or in some other way touch that thing at a shared location. But if the mind resides nowhere or only on its own numinous plane, where can it exert impact on the body? If the soul has no spatial position, how could it make contact with something physical? How do the two ever meet? It would be rather more occult than a concept hitting a billiard ball. Neither Descartes nor any other proponent of substance dualism has come up with a minimally satisfactory solution to this problem, and since one of the most conspicuous features of the relation between mind and body is that the two act upon one another, modern philosophy has written off that position as indefensible.[15]

But the cognate substance dualism is alive and well in conventional perceptions of society and nature. It is there whenever someone thinks or behaves as though society need not care about what happens in nature, however much the body of nature may bleed – as though it could exist without it. We can easily accept the critique of this version of Cartesian dualism developed by Val

---

15 This follows Jacquette, *Philosophy*, 15–20. For good introductions to the problem, see also William Jaworski, *Philosophy of Mind: A Comprehensive Introduction* (Chichester: Wiley-Blackwell, 2011), 56–9; John Heil, *Philosophy of Mind: A Contemporary Introduction* (New York: Routledge, 2013), 25–9.

Plumwood in her two books *Feminism and the Mastery of Nature* and *Environmental Culture: The Ecological Crisis of Reason*: such dualism is there whenever humans put it in their heads that they live in a region levitating somewhere above the biosphere, independent of it, free and able to bracket it off as an inferior order unrelated to theirs, except as a storehouse of resources they can use up in perpetuity.[16] Not so much a philosophical programme declared by avid preachers, more a syndrome than a credo, this dualism is present in everything from neoclassical economics to climate change denial and sheer indifference to issues of ecology. Devised for negligence, it has its own causal interaction problem: it has no idea about how society can cause a crisis in nature or vice versa.

To realise that there is an ecological crisis with great potential to affect humans is to break with substance dualism. We are, it turns out, of exactly the same substance as nature, inhabit the same planet and constantly touch each other all over the place. In terms of the philosophy of mind, this is a commitment to *substance monism*. From here, however, there are two paths to choose between. One can go on to argue that the social and the natural not only share substance, but that they have no significant properties that tell them apart – a substance monism *and property monism*. This is the position of the hybridists, of Bruno Latour and, as it happens, of Val Plumwood: there is only one substance, and everything made of it has the same essential attributes (we shall soon see what these are). Then there is the view that society is made up of the same substance as nature, but has some highly distinctive properties – what in the philosophy of mind is known as substance monist *property dualism*.[17] To tease out this position, we may first turn to Dale Jacquette's *The Philosophy of Mind: The Metaphysics of Consciousness*, a masterpiece in defence of it.

---

16 Plumwood, *Feminism*, e.g. 47–55, 69–71; Val Plumwood, *Environmental Culture: The Ecological Crisis of Reason* (London: Routledge, 2002), 51, 98, 107–09, 120–21.

17 Property dualism is sometimes also referred to as 'dual-attribute theory' or 'dual-aspect theory'; it overlaps in some respects with 'non-reductive physicalism'.

The quandary of mind and body that Descartes struggled with to such unsatisfactory effect has not gone away. My brain is a physical entity. It contains cells, tissue, fluid, neurons, synapses, blood vessels, matter white and black and grey. But do these things also make up my *mind*? 'My mind', Jacquette writes, 'on casual inspection contains memories, desires, expectations, immediate sensations, embarrassments, likes and dislikes. But my brain on casual inspection contains none of these things.'[18] Brain events have weight and colour, but thoughts seem not to. What colour is my thought that Donald Trump is a racist? How much does it weigh? Does it swerve if I turn my car sharply to the right? How could the physicality of that thought *as thought* be pinpointed and measured? Suppose I attend a concert with Run the Jewels, and suppose the intensity of the performance is heightened by a jury having just acquitted a white policeman for shooting and killing a black man, and suppose a neuroscientist at this moment drops in to subject my brain to observation. She will see neurons firing and flaring like firecrackers, but she cannot possibly inspect or capture *my conscious experience as such*, the quality of taking in the musical furore or the feeling of shared fury. These subjective states appear nothing at all like the features of a material object. As such, they are not available for third-person observation in the way a microphone or a T-shirt is, nor can they be read off from neuroscientific instruments or described in a strictly physical language.[19]

---

18 Jacquette, *Philosophy*, 8.

19 This follows ibid., 8–9; John Searle, 'Reductionism and the Irreducibility of Consciousness', in Mark A. Bedau and Paul Humphreys (eds), *Emergence: Contemporary Readings in Philosophy and Science* (Cambridge, MA: MIT Press, 2008), 69–80; O'Connor and Churchill, 'Nonreductive Physicalism or Emergent Dualism? The Argument from Mental Causation', in Robert C. Koons and George Bealer (eds), *The Waning of Materialism* (Oxford: Oxford University Press, 2010), 279; Michael Jubien, 'Dualizing Materialism', in Koons and Bealer, *Waning*, 338; Heil, *Philosophy*, 3, 19 (Heil ends up concluding, in line with his neutral monism, that this third-person observation problem is in fact no problem at all. Heil, *Philosophy*, 239–40.)

At a first introspective glance, one may indeed be tempted to infer that the mind is something quite disparate from the body. But, then again, we have no hard evidence of disembodied thoughts, no knowledge of minds unattached to brains, no data to suggest that some sort of souls live on after their bodily beds have perished. We have, on the other hand, a surfeit of experiences of the mind directing the body to perform various deeds and of the body interfering with the workings of the mind; as for the latter causal route, anyone who has been under the influence of alcohol or psychoactive drugs can testify to its existence, and the assault on the senses during a concert must surely be the ignition of the mental fireworks. The relation appears to be one of dependence *and* difference. How can the two be reconciled?

The solution of substance monist property dualism – or just 'property dualism', more conveniently – begins with the recognition that the brain is the seat of all mental occurrences. The latter must come to an absolute, impassable end when the former ceases to be. But this suggests that the physical entity of the brain, and the human body as a whole, is a bearer of *mental properties*, which cannot themselves be reduced to sheer materiality or equated with physical components. They are lodged in the body and inextricable from it: hence they belong to the exact same substance. They are non-physical properties of the body, the sum of which makes up the mind.[20] Its signal marker is what Jacquette and other philosophers call 'intentionality'. A thought is always *about* something. It points to an intended object, be it the daughter I long for, the food I crave, the argument I develop, the God I doubt, the storm I expect, the stomach pain that troubles me or the fascistisation of society that frightens me. In this context, 'intentionality' refers to an abstract relation between a mental state and an object, a link by which the former is directed towards the latter. It is an aspect *of the thought itself* – it is not this or that capillary or cortex that is about

---

20 Cf. Penelope Mackie, 'Property Dualism and Substance Dualism', *Proceedings of the Aristotelian Society* 111 (2011): 181–99.

something; considered as a purely material entity, the brain is not turned towards a daughter or a dinner. It gives rise to the mental property of intentional thought, which is distinct from any physical property of the brain and inexpressible in the language pertinent to that underlying level. No one has yet explained how one could possibly scan the brain and pick out the neurochemical state that is about Donald Trump and not about Daenerys Targaryen.[21]

Moreover, when I think about Daenerys Targaryen and ponder her next move in the campaign for seizing Westeros, my thought is about a person who does not exist. Since she is a fictional figure, she cannot be physically connected to the material objects that make up my brain. Here it will not do to say that I am really thinking about the book by George R. R. Martin or the HBO series, since my thought concerns none of these things, but precisely Targaryen herself and her next tactical manoeuvre. I can think of many other things that do not exist in the here and now, inter alia a world that is six degrees warmer. This ability to engage with things that do not (yet) exist – something the brain and nervous system could never do, considered *strictly as such* – establishes a peculiar orientation towards the future, an openness to various options, the art of formulating a goal, faculties such as imagination and creativity and cunning. It follows that 'the mind is a new category of entity in the material world.'[22] Property dualists like Jacquette are adamant that there is nothing miraculous about this appearance – after all, science teaches us that life, with its amazing properties, evolved spontaneously once matter had organised itself into sufficiently complex patterns.[23] So why should not life at a certain stage of its evolution

---

21 Jacquette, *Philosophy*, 9, 59, 135, 218; Jubien, 'Dualizing', 339–43.

22 Jacquette, *Philosophy*, 136.

23 On the emergence and properties of life, see the wonderful Pier Luigi Luisi, *The Emergence of Life: From Chemical Origins to Synthetic Biology* (Cambridge: Cambridge University Press, 2006). The non-mysteriousness of mental properties is emphasised by Jubien 'Dualizing', 343, and strongly disputed by William G. Lycan, 'Is Property Dualism Better Off Than Substance Dualism?', *Philosophical Studies* 164 (2013): 535.

be able to develop the wonder of the mind? Intentionality is *an emergent property* that cannot be reduced to the bedrock on which it supervenes, and cannot exist without it. All thought is actualised by events in the brain, and all thought has at least one property the matter of the brain cannot have *sensu strictu*.[24]

Property dualism, then, admits of only one substance – matter – but considers the human body a species of that substance in possession of uniquely mental properties. The beauty of this solution is that it avoids the Cartesian impotence in the face of the causal interaction problem *while preserving the distinction between body and mind*. As much as substance dualism fails on the former count, substance *and* property monism – or double monism – fails on the latter. Jacquette clinches his case with a particularly powerful example:

> What if a history of the Watergate scandal were to be given in a book filled with nothing but chemical formulas describing the brain and other physical events that took place at the time involving participants in the break-in, wire-tapping and cover-up? . . . Would such a chemical history explain these social-political episodes, even to the neurophysiologist well-versed in understanding chemical symbolism? If anything, it appears that property monist explanations suffer from an explanatory disadvantage in comparison with property dualist accounts of social and psychological phenomena.[25]

And here we are right back at the relation between society and nature.

While Cartesians spread their intellectual toxin, there was an alternative position: nature and society are material substances *tout court*, but the one cannot be equated with the other. We have never been in need of being told that we have never been modern, if by this is meant the insight that society and nature cannot be

---

24 Jacquette, *Philosophy*, e.g. 23, 32, 43, 144, 207, 239–40.
25 Ibid., 36–7.

extricated from one another.[26] The tribe of historical materialists has always preached as much – indeed, in its very name is inscribed the insistence on human beings as made up of matter, while 'historical' implies that social relations cannot be deduced from it. Such relations are exactly as material in substance and utterly unthinkable outside of nature, but they also evince *emergent properties different from that nature*. Picture a tree. It grows out of the soil, draws nourishment from it, expires the moment it is cut off from it: yet it cannot be reduced to it. Nature is a soil for society, the fold out of which it grew and the envelope it can never break out of, but just as a tree can be told from its soil, society can be differentiated from nature, because it has shot up from the ground and branched off in untold directions over the course of what we refer to as *history*.[27]

Bruno Latour, for one, knows this. He is aware that historical materialism has been in permanent opposition to Cartesianism, but he considers it the worst abomination of all – 'those modernists *par excellence*, the Marxists' – because it retains a notion of society and nature *as a pair*. The error is to perceive a contrast where none exists. 'The dialectical interpretation changes nothing, for it maintains the two poles, contenting itself with setting them in motion through the dynamics of contradiction' – worse, it makes ignorance of hybridity 'still deeper than in the dualist paradigm since it feigns to overcome it by loops and spirals and other complex acrobatic figures. Dialectics literally beats around the bush.'[28] The bush, the thorny web of everything, is all there is. One must give Latour credit here for correctly identifying the difference between his approach and that of

---

26   Cf. the critical comments on Latour's sweeping dismissal of all modernist currents in White et al., *Environments*, 131–2.

27   Cf. Arias-Maldonado, 'Let's', 382–3.

28   Bruno Latour, 'Agency at the Time of the Anthropocene', *New Literary History* 45 (2014): 258; Latour, *We*, 55 (and see further 57). Cf. e.g. Latour, *Pasteurization*, 180; Bruno Latour, *Facing Gaia: Six Lectures on the Political Theology of Nature*, bruno-latour.fr/, 2013, accessed 29 February 2016 (link since disabled, lectures to be published by Polity Press), 78.

historical materialism: yes, dialectics is the dance of opposites and requires at least a dyad. Absolute monism rules out dialectics. Only property dualism can capture a dialectics of society and nature.

But what is this 'society' we are talking about? We already have a working definition of 'nature'; one for its counterpart is needed too. A pithy, common-sense equivalent can be readily extracted from the *Grundrisse*: 'Society does not consist of individuals, but expresses the sum of interrelations, the relations within which these individuals stand.'[29] That thing has developed properties that cannot be found in nature per se. It should now be clear how the matrix of positions in the philosophy of mind maps onto the nexus of nature and society: historical materialism is a substance monist property dualism. It is opposed to both Cartesian substance dualism and hybridist double monism (considering them two sides of the same coin).[30] We shall stake out the position in more detail below; for now, let us simply reiterate that there is nothing strange about two things being of the same substance and having distinct properties. Exactly as material, the tree and the chainsaw inhabit the same forest: that is why one can fell the other. But they also follow different laws of motion. That, also, is why one can fell the other.

And so it turns out that double monism has a very pressing causal interaction problem all of its own. If society has no properties that mark it off from the rest of the world – what we insist on calling nature – *how can there possibly be such an awful amount of environmental destruction going on?*

THE URGENCY OF PROPERTY DUALISM

Substance monist materialist property dualism about society and nature – or 'property dualism', for short – implies that there is nothing surprising about the combination of the realms. Rather, it

---

29   Karl Marx, *Grundrisse* (London: Penguin, 1993), 265.

30   Cf. Richard Evanoff, 'Reconciling Realism and Constructivism in Environmental Ethics', *Environmental Values* 14 (2005): 71, 74.

is to be expected as the norm. Following Hailwood, we can say that the entwinement of social and natural relations is made not only possible but inevitable, given that the two are continuous parts of the material world 'rather than utterly distinct orders of being'.[31] What changes is *how* the combinations develop. Some might be innocuous and inconsequential, others benign and productive, others yet malign and destructive, but as such, they will be there for as long as humans with societies stick around. If combinations abound, however, by what procedure do we sift out their components? We may begin by applying a crude test: have humans constructed the component, or have they not? If it is social, then it has arisen through relations between humans as they have changed over time, and then it can also, in principle, be dismantled by their actions; if it is natural, it is not a humanly created product but rather a set of forces and causal powers independent of their agency, and hence it cannot be so disassembled (precisely the distinction Latour is out to erase: between a society 'that we create through and through' and a nature 'that is not our doing').[32] Incidentally, it is often rather easy to conduct this test.

Consider the hole in the ozone layer, a favourite case of Latour's.[33] One obviously social component of that unity is (or was) the manufacturing of chlorofluorocarbons for refrigerators and aerosol cans and other products sold by companies such as DuPont. One no less obviously natural component is the way the chlorine atoms of those substances react with ozone molecules in the stratosphere: breaking them down in the tens of thousands. The one component is just as material as the other, which is why they were able to interact. As a unity of opposites, the process of ozone depletion can be further analysed in its many other social

---

31 Hailwood, *Alienation*, 47.

32 Latour, *We*, 36–7. On this distinction, cf. Jacques Pollini, 'Bruno Latour and the Ontological Dissolution of Nature in the Social Sciences: A Critical Review', *Environmental Values* 22 (2013): 37.

33 Popping up again in e.g. Bruno Latour, 'On Technical Mediation: Philosophy, Sociology, Genealogy', *Common Knowledge* 3 (1994): 55.

and natural components, identified with our simple criteria – and as it happens, this is *the indispensable premise for any solution to such a combined problem.* Only after a process of isolating the social from the natural, hard on the heels of the discovery of their dangerous material combination, could the Montreal Protocol ban companies from producing any more chlorofluorocarbons. It was, in this regard, a bit like Trotskyism and Palestinian resistance. Spurning hybridist paralysis, it attacked the combination at the source of the danger.

Exactly contrary to the message of hybridism, it follows that *the more problems of environmental degradation we confront, the more imperative it is to pick the unities apart in their poles.* Far from abolishing it, ecological crises render the distinction between the social and the natural more essential than ever. Think of an oil spill. A company unleashes the liquid into a delta. There is a novel unity in place – oil and water are mixed – but this gives us no reason to treat the two elements of the situation as identical, or (the same thing) declare that one has devoured the other. Rather, we would want to know more about their specific properties. On the one hand, we have the biological diversity of the delta, the birthing seasons of the dolphins, the birds migrating in and out, the food chain, the wave action; on the other, the operating procedures of the corporation, the workings of the profit motive, the level of competition in the oil industry, the function of petroleum in the wider economy. To fateful effect, after an event in time, the two sets now lap the same shores, lending *urgency* to the study of their difference-in-unity – we need to know how they interact, what sort of damage the one does to the other and, most importantly, how the destruction can be brought to an end. This, as Alf Hornborg has recently argued, is the truly vital theoretical task: to maintain the *analytical* distinction so as to tease out how the properties of society intermingle with those of nature.[34] *Only in this way can we save the possibility of removing the sources of ecological ruin.*

---

34 Alf Hornborg, 'Technology as Fetish: Marx, Latour, and the Cultural

And only thus can we conceive of the fossil economy as a historical phenomenon. Turning someone like Neil Smith inside out, Hornborg writes:

> It is possible *in principle* to trace the interaction of factors deriving from Nature and Society. It should be feasible, for instance, to estimate what the concentration of carbon dioxide in the atmosphere would have been today, if the additions deriving from human social processes had not occurred [indeed it is eminently feasible: the concentration would have been around 280 ppm, rather than the current 400+]. Human societies have transformed planetary carbon cycles, but not the carbon atoms themselves. If the categories of Nature and Society are obsolete, as it is currently fashionable to propose, this only applies to images of Nature and Society as bounded, distinct realms of reality.[35]

Substance dualism makes environmental degradation that originates within society and loops back towards it inexplicable. *So does double monism.* Transcending the Cartesian legacy requires an abandonment of its philosophy, but by no means does it imply an endorsement of ontological or methodological hybridism, in which the dynamic interpenetration of the social and natural again becomes invisible and, as a consequence, unalterable. It is rather achieved through the development of a property dualism, which recognises that everything is connected to everything else (the Alpha of ecological science) and that some parties behave disruptively within that web (the Omega).

Foundations of Capitalism', *Theory, Culture and Society* 31 (2014): 119–40; Alf Hornborg, 'The Political Economy of Technofetishism: Agency, Amazonian Ontologies, and Global Magic', *HAU: Journal of Ethnographic Theory* 5 (2015): 35–57; Alf Hornborg, 'The Political Ecology of the Technocene: Uncovering Ecologically Unequal Exchange in the World-System', in Clive Hamilton, François Gemenne and Christophe Bonneuil (eds), *The Anthropocene and the Global Environmental Crisis: Rethinking Modernity in a New Epoch* (Abingdon: Routledge, 2015), 57–69. Cf. Pollini, 'Bruno', 36–9.

35   Hornborg, 'Technocene', 59. Emphasis in original.

Thus relations of production are material and social but not natural. The carbon cycle is material and natural but not social. Through some events in time, the former moved to take up residence within the latter (like a chainsaw in a forest) – the historical moment depicted in the lithograph from Labuan. Only by seeing the British imperialists as agents on a very, very special mission, cutting their path through a nature whose ways were unknown to them, can we understand the causes and import of their actions. Nature did not impel them to search for coal; society did not set up the atmosphere. The fallout materialised at the intersection.

SOME PROBLEMS IN PROPERTY DUALISM

There is something unfortunate about Descartes and the philosophy of mind setting the terms of this debate. The mere positioning of society as analogous to the mind suggests an idealist baggage. Furthermore, a thought does not *consume* synapses or neural networks in order to live. No one has heard of a person who has exercised her mind so expansively and gluttonously that she has scooped out half of her brain, in the way it is possible for a human community to, say, deplete its soil through over-intensive farming. Thoughts are not metabolising creatures; their relation to the brain is not absorptive, dissipative, potentially exhaustive like that between humans and the rest of nature. Hence there is a risk of going astray along the parallel, and it is increased by certain problems in property dualism as a philosophy of the mind, on which its critics hammer hard. To be sure, it is difficult to imagine how a mental substance and a physical substance can interact. But why should it be any easier to see how mental and physical *properties* could do so? If something has a non-physical character – a thought, for instance – how could it exercise influence on something as resolutely physical as the movements of a body? Property dualism, say the critics, has applauded itself for ejecting Descartes' causal interaction problem only to invite it in through the back door. Positing any sort of mental causation of the behaviour of physical objects – notably human bodies – merely restates the insoluble riddle on another level.[36]

Against this wounding charge, property dualists have devised several defences. Some retort that physical and mental properties are linked together in this particular kind of causation, the two sets not mutually exclusive but rather interdependent and jointly efficacious. Some suggest that certain physical events are 'enabled' by states of mind, while others posit the existence of 'psychophysical laws' whose inner workings we have yet to understand, but the traces of which we come across constantly.[37] If the conundrum has not to this date received a satisfactory and widely accepted solution, there is one very compelling reason to believe that some sort of solution must exist: the phenomenon of human action, topic of the next chapter. If I want to raise my arm in a salute, I do it. If I am subject to an electric shock or epileptic convulsion, my arm might swing upwards in the same movement, but only the former event counts as an action. The readily ascertainable fact that actions happen in this world strongly indicate that mental properties *can* have causal impact on bodies, even if we do not yet know exactly how they go about doing it. The prices to be paid for accepting any

---

36 A clear statement of this critique is Lycan, 'Is Property'. Heil formulates it from the position of neutral monism in Heil, *Philosophy*, 192–3, Jarowski from that of hylomorphism in Jarowski, *Philosophy*, 58–9, 240–2. A related attack on property dualism from the position of substance dualism (purportedly of the non-Cartesian variety) is waged in Dean Zimmerman, 'From Property Dualism to Substance Dualism', *Proceedings of the Aristotelian Society Supplementary Volume* 84 (2010): 119–50, against which Mackie, 'Property' 2010 is an effective defence.

37 See e.g. Tim Crane, 'The Mental Causation Debate', *Proceedings of the Aristotelian Society* 69 (1995): 1–23; Joseph Almog, 'Dualistic Materialism 1', in Koons and Bealer, *Waning*, 349–64; O'Connor and Churchill, 'Nonreductive'; Jubien, 'Dualizing'; Chiwook Won, 'Overdetermination, Counterfactuals, and Mental Causation', *Philosophical Review* 123 (2014): 205–29; Thomas Kroedel, 'Dualist Mental Causation and the Exclusion Problem', *Nous* 49 (2015): 357–75. An excellent survey of the debate is Sophie C. Gibb, 'Mental Causation', *Analysis Reviews* 74 (2014): 327–38. She concludes: 'which position to adopt in this debate is still very much an open question'. Ibid., 335.

of the two main alternatives – substance dualism, which clearly rules out interaction, and physicalism, which eradicates everything mental – seem prohibitive, leaving us with property dualism as the lodestar with the greatest promise for further explorations.[38]

But here we shall halt and not go any deeper into the labyrinth of the philosophy of mind. Instead, we shall reformulate property dualism as a specific position on nature and society. The simplest way to understand the category of substance, for our purposes, is to think of an answer to the question 'what *kind* of a thing is this?' A property, on the other hand, is that described by an answer to the question 'what is this thing *like*?' Thus we can say that a flag is a physical thing, made up of atoms and other particles, and so is the stone. But the flag is red and flaps in the wind, whereas the stone is grey and falls to the ground almost as soon as it has been thrown. The two entities are of the same substance, but they have different properties pertaining to colour, shape, mass and weight, and this presents us with no mystery.

Now we can specify four tenets of our property dualism: 1.) Natural and social properties are distinct types of properties. 2.) Natural and social properties attach to material entities of one and the same substance. 3.) An entity can have both natural and social properties, so that it is a combination of the two. 4.) Social properties ultimately depend on natural properties, but not the other way around.

The distinction is one of reality, not a fancy of classification. It can be confirmed, in line with the above test, by asking a question that must necessarily be aetiological: is this property a result of relations between humans, or of structures and processes independent of human activity? Furthermore, we can now easily see that causal interaction poses no problem commensurate to that in the philosophy of mind, for *social properties are not immaterial or mental* any

---

38 Cf. Crane 'Mental', 17; Paul Humphreys, 'How Properties Emerge', in Bedau and Humphreys, *Emergence*, 111; Gibb, 'Mental', 327, 334; Won, 'Overdetermination', 28.

more than natural ones are.[39] The traffic between the two involves no crossing between the non-physical and the physical. If humans have minds, it must be because their complex bodily constitutions have given rise to them, which means that they have minds *by nature*; hence mental properties are inscribed on the natural side of the coin as much as on the social. It follows that social causation of the behaviour of physical objects is no ontological puzzle.

At this point, we need to take note of another definition of nature: as all that is. Some would say that nature is the cosmos as a whole, the infinite totality in which everything exists, the universe of the physical (and perhaps also the divine). On this view, the gentrification of a neighbourhood is exactly as natural as the rotation of a planet, since both take place within all that is. But using 'nature' in this rather trivial sense would be to miss what is at stake in the debate under consideration; no one questions the cosmos, save perhaps for the most dyed-in-the-wool transcendentalists, and no one juxtaposes the cosmic to the social. It is nature, on the realist definition, that occupies both roles. In no way does that definition imply, however, that the social stands on the side of, runs parallel to or floats somewhere above the natural: to the very contrary. Because it is of material substance, and because the material world is natural at root – nature having been alone until society sprung up in its midst – something social must have something natural as its *substratum*. Being material means being bound up with nature. If relations of production are material, they are also, by definition, built on and maintained through the natural. It is the material that connects the other two in the triangle, but not as a symmetrical or neutral baseline, for matter must fundamentally obey the laws of nature.[40] On the realist as much as on the cosmic definition, there is no being outside of nature. If this sounds paradoxical, it is because it *is* so, in

---

39   The arguments from causal closure and overdetermination, popular in the critique of property dualism in the philosophy of mind, fall equally flat here.

40   Hence we can say that there are non-natural social properties of the material world, whose fundamental properties are natural.

a way eloquently rendered by Soper: 'Nature is that which Humanity finds within itself, and to which it in some sense belongs, but also that from which it seems excluded in the very moment in which it reflects upon either its otherness or its belonging.'[41] We shall try to specify this precarious position more fully and, crucially, return to the notion of 'substratum'. For now, all of this might become a little clearer if we turn to the concept of *emergence*.

The classical example of emergence is water. That liquid can douse flames, even though one of its constituent parts (hydrogen) is highly flammable on its own, while the other (oxygen) makes things burn faster. H_2O freezes at zero degrees, whereas at that temperature H and O would both be gases. As the atoms are fixed in a certain arrangement at the level of the molecule, something novel emerges *at that level*, and the same goes for any number of other molecules, such as CO_2, which has the ability to wiggle in a way that blocks infrared light and sends it back from where it came, notably the earth, trapping heat inside the system. On its own, an atom of C or O could do nothing of the kind. Other famous examples include beehives and anthills: the individual bee or ant has a limited repertoire, often behaving erratically on its own, but the collective system exhibits a marvellously complex division of labour which assigns the member a task.[42] More formally, an emergent property is a property of the system *resulting from the organisation of its parts*. Following recent advances in the studies of emergence – the 'relational' theory developed by Dave Elder-Vass in sociology, the 'mutualist' one by Carl Gillett in the philosophy of science – the source of novelty is precisely the complex *relations* between the components of an entity, be they

---

41 Soper, *What*, 49.

42 Luisi, *Emergence*, 123–4; William C. Wimsatt, 'Aggregativity: Reductive Heuristics for Finding Emergence', in Bedau and Humphreys, *Emergence*, 100–1; Dave Elder-Vass, *The Causal Power of Social Structures: Emergence, Structure and Agency* (Cambridge: Cambridge University Press, 2010), 90; Carl Gillett, *Reduction and Emergence in Science and Philosophy* (Cambridge: Cambridge University Press, 2016), 42.

atoms in a molecule, neurons in a brain or individual human beings in a society.[43] The specific mode by which the collective is composed *shapes the roles* filled by the components. It is more than just a cliché to say that 'parts behave differently in wholes' or that 'wholes are more than the sum of their parts'.[44]

Contrary to prejudice, again, there is no magic in such emergence, no balmy substances or vital forces popping out of hats.[45] It is a prosaic matter of the configuration of parts begetting novel properties, such as heat-trapping in the case of carbon and oxygen. Endowed with that property, the whole – the CO_2 molecule – can then have a causal effect *in its own right* on the rest of the material world. The property is a genuine novelty, not a temporary failure of scientists to locate it in the component parts; it may be explained by the interplay between them but *does not exist in them*; as such, it exists only in the totality.[46] A card-carrying reductionist would object that if we only scratch the surface hard enough, we will eventually realise that there is *nothing but the parts* in any system. All its properties can be described in the language of the lowest-level physics. At most, the continuous aggregation of components – so and so many exemplars of particle X, plus so and so of Z, and Y – generates certain patterns, which can, in principle, always be

---

43   Elder-Vass, *Causal*; Gillett, *Reduction*. For other stimulating takes on emergence, see e.g. Michael Silberstein and John McGeever, 'The Search for Ontological Emergence', *The Philosophical Quarterly* 49 (1999): 182–200; Mario Bunge, *Emergence and Convergence: Qualitative Novelty and the Unity of Knowledge* (Toronto: University of Toronto Press, 2003); Nils Henrik Gregersen (ed.), *From Complexity to Life: On the Emergence of Life and Meaning* (Oxford: Oxford University Press, 2003); Stuart Kauffman and Philip Clayton, 'On Emergence, Agency, and Organization', *Biology and Philosophy* 21 (2006): 501–21; Richard V. Solé and Jordi Bascompte, *Self-Organization in Complex Ecosystems* (Princeton: Princeton University Press, 2006).

44   Gillett, *Reduction*, e.g. 42–3, 195, 202.

45   As repeatedly emphasised by Gillett, who is at pains to distinguish his theory of 'strong' emergence from both the 'weak' and 'ontological' versions.

46   Elder-Vass, *Causal*, e.g. 23, 31, 66–7, 91, 193.

scientifically decomposed.[47] Such reductionism has scored moderate empirical successes against some exaggerated visions of emergence in the natural sciences, but there is one sphere into which it seems unable to make inroads: that of society. Properties of society cannot be derived from the atomistic aggregation of its members. Something like capitalist property relations do not develop through the uniform piling of one body upon another.

Consider Rex Tillerson. As a human individual, he constitutes the lowest-level particle, if that is the right word, in his society. He is also an eminently natural body. Naked and alone, he possesses no power, but as the paterfamilias of his reproductive unit, with four children, he enjoys certain prerogatives; as the CEO of ExxonMobil, he contributed differential power of a very considerable magnitude; and as the secretary of state in the Trump regime, he is equipped with certain authorities and expected to behave according to some protocol or other. In the family, the corporation and the state, the distinctive principles of interrelation confer upon the body of Rex Tillerson (including his mind) a determined repertoire of truly powerful behaviour. He himself influences these relations in turn – this is the essence of Gillett's 'mutualist' theory, according to which the components and the composition mutually condition one another, as well as of Marx's dictum about making history under already existing circumstances – but his body is impotent on its own. Its power is not a function of him being randomly or regularly and cumulatively added to other persons. It is inexplicable without reference to the intricate setup of the relations, for if the body of Rex Tillerson was inserted into some other setting – say, a refugee camp or an assembly line – it would be instantly stripped of its present command over the bodily movements of others. Trying to explain what is going on in these arenas by digging down to the lowest level – Tillerson's physical body, its metabolism, its bumping into others of the kind – would be a category mistake.

---

47 See Gillett, *Reduction*, for a comprehensive account and nuanced treatment of reductionism; on aggregation, see also Wimsatt, 'Aggregativity'.

Society, then, on the *Grundrisse* definition, has, in the very last instance, natural components. But they are arrayed in relations *out of which a society emerges*, as a system with novel properties *that are nowhere to be found in nature* – even laws of motion that no human bodies, not even local relations between two or three of them, have in and of themselves. Which ones exactly? A lattice-work of relations, society is jam-packed with emergent properties. We would be unwise to try to catalogue them here; in what follows, we shall only mention a few. They can exert all manner of causal effects on the rest of the world, notably nature.[48] As all levels with emergent properties, society can exercise *downward causation* on its constituent parts and elemental bases. It has emerged from nature – more immediately, from the biological bodies of members of our species – and it has to stay within that bedrock, much like water can exist solely on a planet with oxygen, but society also has the singular ability to affect aspects of nature so as to touch off a crisis.

On this view of the world, however, the thresholds of emergence seem to count in the millions and billions. In nature, chemistry is filled with them. In biology, Stephen Jay Gould bases his path-breaking 'hierarchical theory of selection' on the levels of gene, organism, population, species and clade, each with its own properties that may become subject to selective pressures: 'In our mother's house – the Earth – are many mansions.'[49] Or, in the architectural simile chosen by Gillett, 'we have different kinds of "towers" of fundamental laws, like a collection of step pagodas rising from the jungle. In this landscape, we thus have an array of different sets of fundamental laws', each leading to the next in a monumental

---

48 Collier, *Critical*, 120, 140; Roy Bhaskar, *The Possibility of Naturalism: A Philosophical Critique of the Contemporary Human Sciences* (London: Routledge, 1998), 31–42.

49 Stephen Jay Gould, *The Structure of Evolutionary Theory* (Cambridge, MA: Harvard University Press, 2002), 700. Cf. Richard Levins and Richard Lewontin, *The Dialectical Biologist* (Cambridge, MA: Harvard University Press, 1985), e.g. 288.

'pyramid of laws'.[50] A list would include everything from quarks and cells to genera and galaxies, passing over the narrower succession of leaf, tree, grove, forest and uncountable others of the kind. In society, one could enumerate household, workplace, corporation, industry, class, nation-state, world-system and quite a few mansions and pagodas in between. In nature *and* in society, emergence operates as though in a progression from the more basic units to the higher – or, in the vertical metaphor preferred by critical realists, from one stratum to another, each with its own defining mechanisms and relative autonomy, up indeed to the cosmos as a whole across an infinity of 'stratification'.[51]

This view of the world is the very antithesis of hybridism, with its urge to flatten ontological hierarchies and efface distinctions.[52] But it also appears at odds with property dualism. For there is, in the words of Andrew Collier, no 'one Great Divide' between society and nature, but rather 'many divisions between mutually irreducible strata', a flow of emergences caring nought for where the natural ends and the social begins.[53] The sophisticated materialist position would then seem to be a property *pluralism*. To this problem, however, there is a straightforward answer. Environmental destruction, including climate change, does not happen at the boundary between droplet and cloud, or between petal and flower, or stone and slope, shop steward and federation, municipality and the United Nations. It happens *right at the interface between society and nature*. We may then treat property dualism as a special case or subdivision of a wider pluralism, as long as we keep in mind that each of the two supertotalities contains many series of totalities nested within them, like Russian dolls. Furthermore, while this view has been formulated in the terminology of 'substances' and 'properties', we may just as well distinguish between natural and

50 Gillett, *Reduction*, 256–7.
51 See e.g. Bhaskar, *Realist*; Collier, *Critical*; Elder-Vass, *Causal*.
52 This conflict is noted by White et al., *Environments*, 139–40.
53 Collier, *Critical*, 242.

social *relations*, dynamics, phenomena, entities or categories, as long as we follow the formulated criteria. With these provisos, property dualism about nature and society sits just where we need it, straddling a juncture of our times.

THE PARADOX OF HISTORICISED NATURE

CO_2 is a trace gas. It is not within the capacity of humans to make it more than a tiny little fraction of the atmosphere. We are talking about a rise so far from 280 to some 400 parts *per million*, and yet that little meddling with the composition – combined with emissions of gases whose concentration counts in the parts per billion and trillion – has been enough to usher in the consequences of climate change experienced so far and put more in the pipeline. This is because CO_2 has a unique function in the climate system, sometimes likened to that of a 'control knob', the turning of which impels a whole range of mechanisms to heat or cool the earth: and now it is 'being turned faster than at any time in the geological record'.[54] Such is the scale of the human interference. Still, it is only a minor reshuffling of grains of sand in a system whose vastness boggles the mind; all the rest is an avalanche of chain reactions, which humans do nothing to bring about (hence turning the knob decreases control). Consider the fact that ice melts above $0°C$. This relation – between water in its solid state and temperature – is utterly anterior and exterior to humans and what they do to one another. Now, a signal is being transmitted through the climate system that sets this relation in motion like a vibrating string, playing out over ice caps and sheets and shelves on and between the poles. Or take the albedo

---

54 Andrew A. Lacis, Gavin A. Schmidt, David Rind and Reto A. Ruedy, 'Atmospheric CO_2: Principal Control Knob Governing Earth's Temperature', *Science* 330 (2010): 359. Cf. Andrew A. Lacis, James E. Hansen, Gary L. Russell et al., 'The Role of Long-Lived Greenhouse Gases at Principal LW Control Knob that Governs the Global Surface Temperature for Past and Future Climate Change', *Tellus B* 65 (2013): 19734.

effect: the power of white surfaces to reflect radiation back into space and the obverse power of dark surfaces to absorb it, store it on earth, convert a retreat of ice to an accumulation of heat in the open ocean, which causes more ice to melt, and so on. That, too, is an entirely *natural* relation, between entities in nature, with no social input whatsoever.

At whatever point one chooses to study global warming as a material process in the biosphere, one finds relations between things in nature not adorning it or adding to the margins of it, but constituting it through and through. Far from receding out of view, thousands of natural relations – between the Arctic sea ice and the jet stream, between the salinity of the water and the deep currents of the ocean, between monsoons and moisture, storm surges and sea levels, habitats and heat, drought and evapotranspiration, corals and acidity, precipitation and oscillation – define the phenomenon in all its bewildering complexity. The combustion of fossil fuels becomes a problem by dint of *its* relation to all those variables, best described not as one of construction or production but *perturbation*. Society having touched off climate change, nature does the rest of the work. In the art of building, the equivalent scenario would be something like turning one screw into one plank and then, as though on signal, watching all the bricks and the beams and the concrete steel and window panes come rushing to the site and spontaneously assemble in the shape of, say, a shopping mall: a magical event, meaning that construction does not happen like that. Global warming is not built but triggered. The climate is not created but *changed*, unhinged, disrupted, destabilised.

And the components of the process can be sifted apart. Large-scale fossil fuel combustion has appeared through a very peculiar human history and may be discontinued, whereas the circumstance that oceans expand when they heat up is beyond the purview of any human. Subsidies to fossil fuel companies are endemic since the twentieth century and could easily be terminated by governments, but there is nothing to be done about the fact that the acidity of the oceans increases when the air contains more CO_2.[55] Hybridism denies that there is anything qualitatively different between UN climate negotiations and the process of photosynthesis, but not only *is there* an evident difference – one constructed by humans, the other not – denial of it also whisks away the significance of the combination. For the problem of climate change is constituted precisely by how social relations *combine* with natural ones that are not of their making. Without the primacy of the totalities of nature, emitting CO_2 and other greenhouse gases would present no problem. When humans decide whether to extract fossil fuels or not, subsidise the industry or not, slash emissions worldwide or not, they take decisions on the material bridge that connects them to all the factors of the earth system, which then pull off the consequences. If the bridge did not span two sides, the decisions would have no meaning.

Climate science advances by bringing to light mechanisms in nature that curve back on politics. Take, for instance, the findings by a team of Yale researchers published in *Science* in April 2016, suggesting that the role of clouds in global warming has been seriously underestimated. In clouds of mixed content, ice crystals reflect more sunlight back to space than do liquid droplets, and hence a cloud with a large proportion of the former will act to cool down the planet – but in climate models, clouds have so far been ascribed an unrealistically large share of ice. In reality, liquid drops make up more than previously thought. This means that for any given amount of emissions, the ensuing rise in temperatures will be higher than projected; indeed, the Yale team concludes that while standard estimates predict that a doubling of the atmospheric concentration of CO_2 over preindustrial levels would result in a warming of between 2°C and 4.6°C, the feedback mechanism of

---

55   In 2012, fossil fuel industries in this world received five times larger subsidies than the renewable energy sector. David Ciplet, J. Timmons Roberts and Mizan R. Khan, *Power in a Warming World: The New Global Politics of Climate Change and the Remaking of Environmental Equality* (Cambridge, MA: MIT Press, 2015), 143.

clouds instead implies a range of 5°C to 5.3°C.[56] *That sheds a new light on what it means to emit another ton of CO_2.* Or take the findings that when permafrost thaws, communities of microbes spring to life and start decomposing the carbon hitherto stored in the soil, releasing it as either methane or carbon dioxide and doing it much faster than previously believed.[57] Again, we have here a causal effect coming from within the realm of nature, which is not a product of society, but which any climate policy should *take into account.* This is the general form of the problem.

It is precisely because they are continuous parts of the overall material world that the social and the natural intertwine, but only by keeping them analytically distinct can we differentiate between those aspects of the world that humans have constructed – i.e., the emergent properties of society – and those generated by forces and causal powers independent of them – i.e., the emergent properties of nature – and examine how these have, at ever more complex levels, become braided. Adapting his project to the age of climate change, Latour maintains that 'there is not a single case where it is useful to make the distinction between what is "natural" and what "is not natural"'.[58] He thinks that this age is the final nail in the coffin of the distinction.[59] In reality, it is precisely the other way around. Maximising the prospects for survival presupposes that we become more alert than ever to the dichotomy between what people create through and through and what is not their doing. That does not mean, of course, that a warming planet can be literally cut in two halves – if that were possible, we wouldn't be in this

---

56 Ivy Tan, Trude Storelvmo and Mark D. Zelinka, 'Observational Constraints on Mixed-Phase Clouds Imply Higher Climate Sensitivity', *Science* 352 (2016): 224–7.

57 Kai Xue, Mengting M. Yuan, Zhou J. Shi et al., 'Tundra Soil Carbon Is Vulnerable to Rapid Microbial Decomposition under Climate Warming', *Nature Climate Change* 6 (2016): 595–600.

58 Bruno Latour, 'Fifty Shades of Green', *Environmental Humanities* 7 (2015): 221.

59 See e.g. Latour, *Facing*, 78–9; Latour 2013, *Inquiry*, 10.

predicament – but the *analysis* of it must execute a similar operation. ExxonMobil in one corner, vulnerable permafrost in another:
and then swing into action.

The driver of climate change is a type of society – the fossil economy – that did not exist before the nineteenth century. If CO_2
emissions form the main conduit from that society into climate, it
is only because a whole array of social relations have been constructed
so that they carry those effluents into the atmosphere; once up
there, they connect to uncounted natural wholes. Global warming
is not a flat, monolithic hybrid or 'quasi-object', but a moving unity
of opposites, a dynamic combination, a process in which social and
natural components tumble over each other: and as the knob is
turned, nature propels it onwards. So very far from ending that
domain, the combustion of fossil fuels activates certain 'material
structures and processes that are independent of human activity (in
the sense that they are not a humanly created product), and whose
forces and causal powers are the necessary conditions of every
human practice, and determine the possible forms it can take'. It is
thus that the storm progresses towards doorsteps around the world.

We can here discern a paradox. *The more profoundly humans have
shaped nature over their history, the more intensely nature comes to
affect their lives.* The more the sphere of social relations has determined that of natural ones, the more the reverse, towards the point
of some breakdown. We may call this *the paradox of historicised
nature.* It structures the warming condition, but in an uneven and
tilted way. The social relations experiencing the most intense dislocation are found at the farthest remove from the densest
concentrations of the relations that brought the process about. But
if poor people in the peripheries suffer the worst fate for now – and
even more in the near future – they stand first in a line that
stretches towards some endpoint. The immense popularity of the
end-of-nature thesis might be a warped reflection of the early stages
of global warming, as the power of social relations first comes into
view; further down the road, the end of society might seem far the
more compelling proposition. Such, in any case, is the sequential

logic of the paradox of historicised nature: we will not get less nature and more society as temperatures rise, but rather the other way around. Six degrees and there may mostly be natural forces and causal powers left.

So E. Ann Kaplan is right when she writes that nature is now 'offering instructions to humankind by its very violent intrusions'.[60] It really is nature that comes roaring back into society in a warming world, and it is time that flaps its wings as it does so. The nature that is knocking on the door of the postmodern condition – occasionally breaking it down, crashing through glass, sweeping away screens, even in its heartlands – is something of a spectral creature, for it is carried forward by a human past. The mad force it possesses is a function of the shafts through which time has flown since the early nineteenth century; more than the revenge of nature, this is the revenge of historicity *dressed* in nature. The larger the cumulative emissions of CO_2, the more uncontrollable the storm; the more society has intruded and intrudes on nature, *the more nature invades society* with a haunted army whose early incursions are now felt. As historical time fell out of view with nature, they now come back together. The fact that nature has been pushed into a negative mode, with relations vibrating so virulently as to threaten to eradicate entire biomes, does not at all diminish its presence (neither would an asteroid impact). Castree charges that talk of independent nature is pure ideology, but it would be more correct to say that independent nature is the only thing that cannot come to an end.[61] The paradox of climate change is that it makes it appear more strangely alive than ever.

---

60   Kaplan, *Climate*, 38.
61   Castree, 'Capitalism', 288.

3

On What Matter Does:
Against New Materialism

AN ASSEMBLAGE OF VARIEGATED SWARMING
MATERIAL ACTANTS

Dissatisfaction with the cultural turn has lately spread in the ranks of theorists. Materiality, many have come to recognise, really does matter and can 'bite back': a corrective to the obsession with discourse is overdue. The avant-garde group calling themselves 'new materialists' aim to sober up theory and shove it back into the physical world where things play a role; in fact, they like to argue, every second on earth must be lived out within the force-fields of the material, from the most mundane object (the phone that wakes you up) to the most cosmic heights (the stars that hover above you) – so 'how could we be anything other than materialist?'[1] Text, language, symbols, semiotics are all fine, and undeniably elements of human existence, but what reason is there to suppose that they matter any more than matter itself, other than some lingering Cartesian prejudice?[2] Worse still – and this is the principal sin of the cultural turn, in the eyes of new materialists – how can we go on pretending

---

1   Diana Coole and Samantha Frost, 'Introducing the New Materialisms', in Diana Coole and Samantha Frost (eds), *New Materialisms: Ontology, Agency, and Politics* (Durham, NC: Duke University Press, 2010), 1.

2   Karen Barad, 'Posthumanist Performativity: Toward an Understanding of How Matter Comes to Matter', *Signs: Journal of Women in Culture and Society* 28 (2003): e.g. 806–7.

that humans are the protagonists of this planet, when it should be obvious by now that matter acts with no less momentous effect?[3] An imperious power seems to inhere in things.

The new ones, however, are not only dissatisfied with what we have called idealist constructionism, but also unhappy with the *old* materialists, who did not go far enough and likewise failed to 'give materiality its due'.[4] Previous cohorts treated matter as a mass of dead objects, which might have suffused and surrounded humans on all sides but still functioned as a stage for their internal dramas, where all the exciting action happened. The accusation is, of course, directed at Marxists: if the 'materialism' signals a farewell to deconstruction, the 'new' flags a distance from the historical variety. Two contributions to the volume *Material Powers: Cultural Studies, History and the Material Turn* clarify the differences. In historical materialism, the relations between people determine how they relate to matter; more specifically, relations of production are the hands that forge and select productive forces as their hammers. Therefore, we learn, this 'is not in any meaningful sense a materialism. Rather, we could think of it as something like a "socialism"', in the sense not of a programme for socialising the means of production, but of a theory privileging *the social* as the dynamo of development.[5] A real – new – materialism must accord that role to matter *qua* matter. Marxists treat matter as an 'outcome', a 'medium', an 'obstacle', and that is outright unfair. Matter is what 'makes things happen; it has' – the shibboleth – '*agency*'.[6]

3　See e.g. Rebekah Sheldon, 'Form/Matter/Chora: Object-Oriented Ontology and Feminist New Materialism', in Richard Grusin (ed.), *The Nonhuman Turn* (Minneapolis: University of Minnesota Press, 2015), 195.

4　Coole and Frost, 'Introducing', 7.

5　John Frow, 'Matter and Materialism: A Brief Pre-History of the Present', in Tony Bennett and Patrick Joyce (eds), *Material Powers: Cultural Studies, History and the Material Turn* (Abingdon: Routledge, 2010), 33.

6　Chris Otter, 'Locating Matter: The Place of Materiality in Urban History', in Bennett and Joyce, *Material*, 43, 45. Emphasis added. For another type of attack on Marxism, whose primary quality is extreme obscurity, see Pheng Cheah, 'Non-Dialectical Materialism', in Coole and Frost, *New*, 70–91. A sort of

80

This is what sets new materialism apart: the contention that matter has agency.[7] If the only point to be made was that matter matters, or that all is matter, or that human praxis is inextricable from environments of matter, then perhaps some old version could do, but that would have been rather timid. Matter is the active shaper of the world. Under this banner, the new brigade leads theory on a 'material turn', whose widely diffusing doxa is precisely that agency has been wrongly conceived as the prerogative of humans and must now promptly be recognised in the things themselves: in worms, fatty acids, dogs, clouds. That turn has found fertile ground in environmental history, a field in which any history of the fossil economy must perforce dwell. Environmental historians – not all, but many – are fond of talking about the agency of dirt, insects, rivers, soil; indeed, some consider the demonstration of natural agency to be the main aim of their research. In typical formulations, we are urged to view 'nature as an active, shaping force'; rallied to the cause of breaking down the dichotomy between nature and culture and distributing agency evenly, so that nature can come across as 'a co-creator of history'; told that environmental historians have proved that beasts and trees and the planet itself 'were in fact authentic actors in the historical drama'.[8] Humans have had enough time in the limelight.

Such codes are given for climate change too. We are enjoined to realise that when it comes to warming the planet, not only elites

rapprochement is hinted at in Jason Edwards, 'The Materialism of Historical Materialism', in ibid., 281–98.

7 Cf. Luigi Pellizzoni, 'Catching up with Things? Environmental Sociology and the Material Turn in Social Theory', *Environmental Sociology* 2 (2016): 312–21.

8 Ted Steinberg, 'Down to Earth: Nature, Agency, and Power in History', *The American Historical Review* 107 (2002): 83; Kristin Asdal, 'The Problematic Nature of Nature: The Post-Constructivist Challenge to Environmental History', *History and Theory* 42 (2003): 61; J. Donald Hughes, *What Is Environmental History?* (Cambridge: Polity, 2006), 16. Cf. e.g. William Cronon, 'The Uses of Environmental History', *Environmental History Review* 17 (1993): 1–22; John Herron, 'Because Antelope Can't Talk: Natural Agency and Social Politics in American Environmental History', *Historical Reflections* 36 (2010): 33–52.

have agency, nor only humans, but 'chemical species and geophysical forces' just as much.[9] In an attack on Marxist analyses of climate politics, Adam Trexler exhorts us to dethrone both capital and humanity and make room for 'the agency of other species, greenhouse gases, Arctic sea ice, glaciers'; to acknowledge the special agency of 'weather' and 'carbon dioxide and methane'; to remember, not the least, 'coal smoke's agency', the agency of 'coal' and 'ovens' and 'coal power plants'.[10] This might seem just the antidote to constructionism that we need. Does not our critique of it imply precisely that nature contributes – in a most active, agitated state: like a ball of fire – to shaping the world? Is this not exactly what it means to say that humans turn the control knob and then the dark surfaces and the liquid drops and the microbes in the tundra do the rest of the work? The material turn appears to give not only materiality but *nature* its due.

The main source of inspiration for this way of thinking is, once again, Bruno Latour. In the double monism of his actor-network theory, agency is the key property of all entities hitherto divided by 'the modern constitution'. Objects, says Latour, have as much agency as persons – for do not hammers *hit* nails? Do not kettles *boil* water, knives *cut* meat, soap *take* the dirt away? Such verbs designate actions that are every bit as real as voting in an election or making love (in which the paper of the ballot, the wood of the box, the sheets and the bed would be as much actors as the voters and the lovers). Things are wont to 'allow' and 'forbid', 'authorise' and 'suggest', 'block' and 'encourage'; there is nothing in their nature that renders them any less agential than our own so often arrogant species. Latour's definition of agency is unconventional but straightforward enough: 'making some difference to a state of affairs'.[11]

---

9   James R. Fleming, 'Climate, Change, History', *Environment and History* 20 (2014): 582.

10   Adam Trexler, 'Integrating Agency with Climate Critique', *symplokē* 21 (2013): 226, 233–5.

11   Bruno Latour, *Reassembling the Social: An Introduction to Actor-Network Theory* (Oxford: Oxford University Press, 2005), 71–2, 52.

The only question we need to ask about Y is if it has some sort of effect on some Z; if the answer is yes, that Y possesses agency. The ability to make a difference is what counts.[12]

Jane Bennett carries the torch forward in *Vibrant Matter: A Political Ecology of Things*, the closest one comes to a philosophical manifesto for the current of new materialism. Building on Latour, she adopts his terminology of 'actants' – substitute for the common 'agents' – who are endowed with the capacity 'to make a difference, produce effects, alter the course of events'; an 'assemblage' of actants is the real source of action in the world. Agency is shared among the actants – humans and nonhumans alike – as they team up to do their parts in bringing about some outcome, forming 'a swarm of various and variegated vibrant materialities'.[13] Now, the category of nature sits uncomfortably in this scheme. Assertive in their hybridism, new materialists seek to dissolve all distinctions between 'natural' on the one hand and 'social' or 'cultural' or 'human' on the other in the boundless ambience of matter. Another prominent exponent, Diana Coole, opines that 'nature may be said to have become so thoroughly imprinted with and destroyed by human projects – projects that are altering the very geology and biosphere of the planet – that it no longer makes sense to refer to any relatively independent domain': nature is over, but matter rules.[14] Yet it is clear that much of what the new materialists speak of as 'matter' or 'materialities' would fall under the realist definition of nature we have defended.

Thus the theory would seem to have potential to illuminate our world. Applied to the early days of the fossil economy, it would imply that, say, the coal in the steamboat, the vapour, the iron of

---

12   As further explicated by ANT scholar Edwin Sayes, 'Actor-Network Theory and Methodology: Just What Does It Mean to Say that Nonhumans Have Agency?', *Social Studies of Science* 44 (2014): 134–149.

13   Jane Bennett, *Vibrant Matter: A Political Ecology of Things* (Durham, NC: Duke University Press, 2010), viii, 96. Cf. e.g. 3, 9, 21, 31–4, 122.

14   Diana Coole, 'Agentic Capacities and Capacious Historical Materialism', *Millennium: Journal of International Studies* 41 (2013): 454.

the boiler, the piston of the engine, the stoker, the captain, the directors of the company, the carbon dioxide in the column of dense smoke made up an assemblage of swarming actants, each with its own 'strivings', none more central or determinant than any other.[15] Indeed, Bennett herself has recently argued that it is precisely on this score that her current proves its superiority over Marxism: the latter cannot offer 'an equally satisfying response' to the 'growing awareness of climate change'.[16] In a warming world, new materialism works better than the historical version. At this moment of writing, Bennett has yet to specify the reasons for why this should be so, but the test that she proposes is also ours, and it is perfectly possible to stitch together the response to the problem new materialism actually offers.

But then consider, again, the picture from Labuan. Does the coal deserve the status of agent – or actant – in what is about to unfold? Is the glade active in the discovery? Do the two men have no special role in the episode? Can we say that the deposit *strives* to be exposed and the carbon to be hauled up from the underground? The coal at Labuan very much made a difference to a state of affairs. So did the hulls of the steamboats. Shall we then say that an assemblage of actants appeared on Labuan, where the humans in question had no agency *qualitatively different* from that of the coal and the hulls and all the other materials present? This would seem to be the message new materialism and the wider material turn would convey about the scene, immediately raising the question of whether they would not rather engulf it in darkness.

---

15 Electricity, in Bennett's analysis, is one thing that deserves recognition for its 'strivings'. Bennett, *Vibrant*, 27.

16 Jane Bennett, 'Systems and Things: On Vital Materialism and Object-Oriented Philosophy', in Grusin, *Nonhuman*, 223.

DOES A RIVER HAVE A GOAL?

The central category we must here drill into is obviously agency. What does it mean to have it? In everyday language and folk psychology, acting is associated with wanting. One who acts is someone who does something because she wants something in the world. The sun does not act when it rises in the morning (although it certainly makes a difference to a state of affairs), for on the lay view, an element is needed which is absent in the daybreak: an agent seeking to accomplish some goal. The parent who wakes up his child when the sun rises has agency, while the morning light does not. Indeed, the child herself will not be old before she understands the difference, detects the intention of the parent and protests and negotiates with him in a way she would not do with the morning light; there is evidence to suggest that this disposition to parse surroundings into intentional agents and non-intentional things is a shared by humans across cultures.[17] The demarcation is not only made by the populace, but also by professional practitioners of philosophy of action, a field of inquiry hitherto as unresponsive to Latour and new materialism as they are aloof from it. *Philosophy of Action: An Anthology*, a recent collection of 37 of the most important papers, establishes this distinction as a sort of lowest common denominator for everyone in the field.

Jennifer Hornsby: 'An event that merits the title "action" is *a person's* intentionally doing something.'[18] Harry G. Frankfurt: 'When we act, our movements are purposive.'[19] Helen Steward: 'Can a wave act? Or a computer? If not, why not?' It all depends on

---

17 Bertram F. Malle, 'Intentional Action in Folk Psychology', in Timothy O'Connor and Constantine Sandis (eds), *A Companion to the Philosophy of Action* (Chichester: Wiley-Blackwell, 2013), 357–65.

18 Jennifer Hornsby, 'Agency and Actions', in Jonathan Dancy and Constantine Sandis (eds), *Philosophy of Action: An Anthology* (Chichester: Wiley-Blackwell, 2015), 56. Emphasis in original.

19 Harry G. Frankfurt, 'The Problem of Action', in Dancy and Sandis, *Philosophy*, 28.

whether 'things may conceivably be settled *by* that entity in the light of what it thinks and wants'.[20] Frederick Stoutland: 'There is no action where there is no *intentional* acting. What distinguishes mere behavior – where things happen but there is no agency – from acting, is that the latter is intentional under at least one description. Acting, that is to say, is *essentially* intentional'; without 'the capacity to act for reasons', there can be no talk of genuine agency.[21] Those philosophers may disagree on any number of other questions – what is the role of desires in the formation of intentions?, does an action have the same kind of cause as any other event?, does the agent bring about her action or its results?, do collective agents exist? – but they start their musings from the shared insight that agency is a sharply delineated property in the world.[22] It does not belong to everything. Only some events deserve to be classified as actions: me raising my arm, for instance, and me raising my arm with a clenched fist, but not me breathing or me sneezing because of a tickle. If I slip on wet leaves and fall on train tracks, it *happens*, but if I seek to end my life and throw myself in front of the train, I act. In the latter scenario, I guide the movements of my body so as to fulfil an intention I have set for myself; in the former, external forces beyond my control initiate those movements; if the wind blows the leaves onto the tracks, no one who could even potentially be an agent is involved. This line cuts rather deeply through the universe, ordering events and entities on either side as we trip through life.

On the popular and philosophical view, then, having agency is intimately tied to *having a mind*. 'To act is first to think. Whatever cannot think cannot act', states Jacquette. Furthermore, the mind of the agent assumes a specific mode of intentionality – not any

---

20   Helen Steward, 'Moral Responsibility and the Concept of Agency', in Dancy and Sandis, *Philosophy*, 390. Emphasis in original.

21   Frederick Stoutland, 'The Ontology of Social Agency', in Dancy and Sandis, *Philosophy*, 166. Emphases in original.

22   See also Lilian O'Brien, *Philosophy of Action* (Basingstoke: Palgrave Macmillan, 2015).

kind of mental directedness towards an object, such as when I think of the dead bird I saw in the forest, but a peculiar aiming at an X that has not yet come about. I intend to wake my child, who is not in this moment awake; I intend to end my life, which has so far not ended. This is, if you will, the Targaryen mode of intentionality, but with the crucial proviso that the agent strives to drag her imaginings into the realm of reality: 'Whenever we act', continues Jacquette, 'we intend to do something, and our intending intends, is directed toward or about *a state of affairs that does not yet exist* – hence actions are 'future-directed, and in some cases fiction-directed', since it may so happen that the state the agent aims at never comes to exist (e.g. utopia).[23] If only dimly, routinely or impulsively, the punctual parent and the suicide candidate make inner pictures of whatever it is they intend and then project them onto the world through their bodily action: and in this precise sense, intentionality is essential to agency.

Now this standard view is embraced not only by plebs and philosophers, but also by historical materialists. A classic enunciation of it appears in the first volume of *Capital*:

> A spider conducts operations which resemble those of the weaver, and a bee would put many a human architect to shame by the construction of its honeycomb cells. But what distinguishes the worst architect from the best of bees is that the architect builds the cell in his mind before he constructs it in wax. At the end of every labour process, a result emerges which had already been conceived by the worker at the beginning, hence already existed ideally.[24]

This is the *differentia specifica* of human labour, that everlasting condition of the existence of our species. In terms from the philosophy of action, Marx posits the 'priority of future-directed intentions' as the trademark of our interaction with the rest of

---

23   Jacquette, *Philosophy*, 258, 262–3. Emphasis added.
24   Marx, *Capital: Volume I* (London: Penguin, 1990), 284.

nature; in the words of biologists Richard Levins and Richard Lewontin, he observes that what is 'unique to humans is the conscious planning, the imagining of the result before it is brought into existence'.[25] Some would object with vehemence to this view. Posthumanists, scholars in critical animal studies, some philosophers of action would argue that animals do in fact possess the consummate minds of architects: beavers are no less deliberate in their construction work than humans; predators make intricate plans before they swoop down on their prey; bees excel in the coordinated behaviour of a planned economy.[26] But we can put such objections to the side for the moment, for new materialists make a much more audacious claim. They are not primarily interested in animals. They hold that *inanimate matter* has as much agency as humans. They would censure Marx for overlooking the agency of the cobwebs as such, their sticky silk, the crust on which they stand and, in the case of the bee, the agency of the honeycomb cells. Hence we can focus on the division between humans and inanimate matter, and affirm that new and historical materialism do espouse opposite views. The latter attributes a type of agency to humans that does not exist in wax. It considers such agency utterly significant for what happens on this planet.

Thus Perry Anderson maintains, in *Arguments within English Marxism*, that the sort of future-directed agency singled out by Marx has animated human history. Almost all people have almost always spent almost all their lives pursuing 'private' goals: cultivating a plot, exercising a skill, finding a partner, building a family, staving off a threatening fate. Prosaic, often monotonous, such projects remain 'inscribed within existing social relations,

25 Michael Bratman, 'Two Faces of Intention', in Dancy and Sandis, *Philosophy*, 131 (emphasis removed); Levins and Lewontin, *Dialectical*, 255.

26 E.g. Jonathan L. Clark, 'Labourers or Lab Tools? Rethinking the Role of Lab Animals in Clinical Trials', in Nik Taylor and Richard Twine (eds), *The Rise of Critical Animal Studies: From the Margins to the Centre* (Abingdon: Routledge, 2014), 139–64; John McDowell, 'Acting as One Intends', in Dancy and Sandis, *Philosophy*, 151; Plumwood, *Feminism*, e.g. 131–5.

and typically reproduce them. Yet they remain *profoundly intentional enterprises*, which have consumed the greater part of human energy and persistence through recorded time.'[27] Indistinguishable from the praxis of labour, this sort of agency builds and rebuilds the material basis of society. It is, in relation to inanimate matter, a signally human property, present whenever this species moves around in the world, one item on the top of the list of property dualism.

Needless to say, the standard view of agency can be at once the common-sense consensus and the Marxist position *and* wrong. It might well be the case that the new materialists have seen something everyone else has missed. No doubt can be cast on their aspiration: this brigade wants (very much a goal) to throw the received wisdom on agency out the window. A first move is to sever the link to intentionality. 'Agency is not aligned with human intentionality or subjectivity', declares Karen Barad, explaining, in what is perhaps a more complicated way of rehashing Latour's definition, that 'agency is a matter of changes in the apparatuses of bodily production'.[28] Berating Hannah Arendt for believing in human intentionality 'as the most important of all agential factors, the bearer of an exceptional kind of power', Jane Bennett advances along two paths: searching for nonhuman forces that 'approximate some of the characteristics of intentional or purposive behavior', and *decoupling* agency from just that sort of behaviour and indeed from any kind of subject at all. The two seemingly divergent paths – a brazen anthropomorphism; an equally bold anti-subjectivism – cross each other in the general project of erasing the boundaries between the human and nonhuman, animate and inanimate matter. Things are as much agents (or actants) as humans are, because they have some humanlike intentionality, and/or because intentionality is not a proper criterion of agency. 'Things' can here comprise almost any

---

27   Perry Anderson, *Arguments within English Marxism* (London: Verso, 1980), 19. Emphasis added.

28   Barad, 'Posthumanist', 826.

entity or event; Bennett suggests that in the case of something like the American invasion of Iraq, one should see 'the process as itself an actant, as itself in possession of degrees of agentic capacity.'[29] The regime of George W. Bush was not the source of the action in 2003. The swarm of the invasion *qua* invasion was.

If matter has agency in new materialism, then, it is because everything and anything can be said to have it. Latour's definition is utterly minimal: the ability to make a difference is hard to tell from the property of existing.[30] Is there any Y in this world that does not have some sort of effect on a Z? But he persists: we should 'direct our common attention to agencies – that is, which real difference does it [sic] make in the world?'[31] Or: 'an agency, an actant, by definition is *what acts*, what has, what is endowed with agency.'[32] That latter statement is circular. It has no discernible meaning. Perhaps this is the logical upshot of depriving the category of agency of any contrastive effect: the new notion cancels all the way through. As the key property in a property monism, sprinkled like unholy water on all that exists, 'agency' appears to lose meaning, the concept not enriched but eviscerated. Whether the strategy favoured for the moment is to see intentionality everywhere (an omni-intentionalist conception of agency) or to deny that intentionality is necessary (an anti-intentionalist ditto), the product really is the night when all cows are grey. More or less by intention, it shuts down attention to the diacritical human property that – most others believe – is a rather important factor in the ways of the world.

But it might still be the case that Latour and his peers are onto something. In an article aiming to demonstrate the utility of his theory of agency in times of climate change, he gives the example

---

29   Bennett, *Vibrant*, 33–4, 29. Latour similarly classifies revolutions as 'actors' in their own right. Latour, *Pasteurization*, 165.

30   As recognised by Sayes, 'Actor-Network', 141.

31   Latour, *Facing*, 11–12. Cf.: '*any thing* that does modify a state of affairs by making a difference is an actor'. Latour, *Reassembling*, 71. Emphasis in original.

32   Latour, *Facing*, 17. Emphasis in original.

of two adjacent rivers, the Atchafalaya and the Mississippi. The mighty Mississippi would pour into the Atchafalaya, whose river-bed is much smaller but also *lower*, were it not for the sturdy engineering works of the Army Corps of Engineers that nail down the giant and prevent it from jumping down the gradient. This, according to Latour, shows that the rivers have goals: the Atchafalaya to swallow the Mississippi, the latter to enter the former. 'The connection between a smaller but deeper river and a much wider but higher one is what provides the *goals* of the two protagonists, what gives them a *vector*' – and 'to have goals is one essential part of what it is to be an agent.'[33] Hence the river is a full-fledged agent. In her urge to overcome Cartesian bigotry, Val Plumwood takes a similar stance: she accepts that intentionality is essential to agency and goes for an all-out omni-intentionalism. A volcano 'preparing to erupt' is '*equally intentional*' as any person in the vicinity. Mountains and trees act with the goal of growing. Photosynthesis has 'intentional structure'; the transfer of pollen is powered by 'intentional capacities'; we should open our ears and eyes to 'speaking matter' – basalt cones speak to the observer who cares to listen – and endorse at least a 'weak panpsychism'.[34] Without allegiance to Latour, and before the explosion of new materialism, Plumwood offers her omni-intentionalism as the cure for the modern callousness towards nature: see, it has as much agency as any of you presumptuous exploiters.[35]

But is it *plausible* to ascribe goals to a river or a mountain? They evidently do not have brains, which means that they cannot have minds, which ought to imply that they lack the ability to form intentions, as the term is commonly used – but intentionality is here rather equated with moving from one location or state of affairs towards another *regardless of whether the agent can draw a*

---

33 Latour, 'Agency', 10. Emphases in original.

34 Plumwood, *Feminism*, 135; Plumwood, *Environmental*, 121, 177–83. Emphasis added.

35 See further e.g. Plumwood, *Environmental*, 26, 46, 56, 99, 109, 175, 215, 263.

mental picture of its goal. On this view, a meteorite falling through space does indeed have agency. There are at least nine senses of what it means to have a goal that are lost here.

Imagine a person who joins a militant political organisation. The new recruit might have the goal to further the aims of the group, but he might also have the goal to infiltrate it on behalf of the authorities: 1.) one and the same action can be performed with different, indeed antithetical goals. The infiltrator will take pains to behave exactly like any other member, but 2.) the real goal might be unavailable for third-person observation since it is a mental state. If others around him have no idea of what is going on, he himself is fully aware of it: 3.) the agent understands his own actions in terms of the goal.

And these are only the basics. Suppose that the agent joins the organisation on 1 January 2020, but that the scheme for infiltrating it was developed over the previous three years: 4.) a goal can be formulated long before the plan for attaining it is set in motion (this is the distinction between prior intention and intention in action). As the infiltrator starts burrowing through the organisation, he adapts to the practices of his fellow members and modifies his comportment so as to maximise the extraction of information: 5.) the agent keeps track of the progress towards his goal and makes sure to alter his line of action as circumstances change. If he makes progress, he might feel pride; if not, shame: 6.) one who has a goal can evaluate his behaviour in relation to it. He might have been sent on the mission and internalised its aim as his own, but for some reason or other, he might never carry it out: 7.) a goal can exist without being put into practice. Or, while he is in the process of carrying it out, the organisation might fall apart because of internal splits and cease to exist, and so he can suspend the infiltration: 8.) an agent halts an action if the desire underpinning the goal disappears. Finally, imagine that the infiltrator is originally bent on destroying the group, but as he devotes his life to participating in its actions, absorbs the radical literature, falls in love with another member, witnesses the brutal repression of the police first-hand, he gradually changes his mind and eventually becomes a truly zealous militant: 9.) the goal as such can be revised and abandoned.[36]

It is not clear that a river can have a goal in any of these senses – possibly in the fifth and seventh, if they are sufficiently strained – since they are indeed predicated on having a mind. They seem to be so many reasons to accept the distinction Lilian O'Brien makes in her excellent survey of the field, *Philosophy of Action*: between agents on the one hand, and things with a *causal profile* on the other. When we speak of hydrochloric acid as a 'corrosive agent', we do not really mean that it has a goal, but that it has a certain way of influencing its surroundings (making a certain type of difference, one could say).[37] Goal-having presupposes the emergent stratum pinpointed by the standard view: 'to speak of goals is to speak of what an agent *has in mind*'.[38] This capacity or property cannot be found in an island. But it can be eminently present in the men who make their way through its jungle, after having told the natives that they have come to spread progress and lift them out of ignorance and penury. And then something might happen that is of far-reaching import, which would not have happened without this one-of-a-kind agency.

THE QUESTION OF UNINTENDED CONSEQUENCES

In an article that has, for this current, the uncommon quality of being fairly lucidly argued, Timothy James LeCain spells out the case Bennett has only asserted: new materialism is the best theory for making sense of global warming, as well as other environmental crises associated with 'the Anthropocene'. 'It is evident', LeCain writes, 'that humans did not set out to cause such global geochemical changes.

---

36 This list draws on arguments in O'Brien, *Philosophy*, 137–45; G. E. M. Anscombe, 'Intentions', in Dancy and Sandis, *Philosophy*, 109; Donald Davidson, 'Intending', in ibid., 119; Bratman, 'Two', 146–9.

37 O'Brien, *Philosophy*, 136–7; cf. 4.

38 Arthur W. Collins, 'Action, Causality, and Teleological Explanation', in Dancy and Sandis, *Philosophy*, 321. Emphasis added.

Instead, they were largely the unanticipated and *unintended conse-quences* of the large-scale use of hydrocarbons, fertilizers, and other modern technologies.' For this reason – because something like climate change was never intended by anyone who dug up or set fire to fossil fuels – it is incorrect to see humans as the agent behind the process. To 'conclude that humans alone were responsible for the course of events that resulted from burning coal' is outright 'nonsen-sical': coal *itself* bears responsibility. Fossil fuels have acted to 'shape humans and their cultures in all sorts of unexpected ways'; indeed, 'coal shaped the humans who used it far more than humans shaped coal' (which is, from one angle, tautologically true, since humans never shaped coal). New materialism teaches us that 'humans and their cultures are best understood not as the creators of their destiny and environment, but as products of a material world that is constantly creating and recreating them' – warming up their planet, for instance.[39]

Latour is of the same mind. The microorganisms and plants that provide the feedback loops of the climate system give the lie to the standard view – 'and more often they come back with a vengeance! Each of these loops registers the *unexpected reactions of some outside agency* to human action.'[40] The tacit postulate here is that inten-tional human agency terminates at the point where unintended consequences materialise. Then some other agency takes over, namely that of the entity which *causes* those consequences. This is a way of saving the idea of ubiquitous non-human agency in a warm-ing world, without necessarily having to attribute mature intentionality to a piece of coal or a molecule of CO_2. Their contri-bution is the sum of the unintended consequences, which proves that they have at least as much agency as do humans, whose share of that property ends when they irrupt.

So imagine I partake in a riot. Stone in hand, I advance towards

---

39   Timothy James LeCain, 'Against the Anthropocene: A Neo-Materialist Perspective', *International Journal for History, Culture and Modernity* 3 (2015): 20, 4, 21, 23. Emphasis added.
40   Latour, *Facing*, 133–4. Emphasis added.

the front, aim at the police and, determined to knock one of them out, throw the projectile with all the force I can muster. It slams into a lamppost I had not seen in the turmoil and bounces back right onto the eye of one my comrades. On the new materialist and Latourian view, it is now the lamppost that is the agent of the event, my own agency having ceased at the moment of the collision. And, indeed, the lamppost does 'alter the course of events', following Bennett – but, on the standard view, it is not the agent behind the wound that my comrade sustains. The agent is the person who *instigates* the sequence, authors the event, is 'the source of some input into the world', the one who brings something about or makes it happen through guided bodily movements, such as those I perform when I pick up and throw a stone.[41]

What would be achieved by drawing the line around my agency where unintended consequences show up? It would, for a start, inaugurate a conception of human agency as definitionally incapable of ever having anything other than *intended* consequences, since whatever else happens is the doing of some other agency (or actor or actant). Every human agent would then essentially become omnipotent inside her sphere of action. The moment her throw-in on the field veers off its course, she no longer exercises agency; some other lump of matter does. Thus humans may have located and extracted fossil fuels, but the fossil fuels and all the matter they connect to are, as LeCain proposes, the true agents of the ensuing climatic disruption. The notion of 'unintended consequences' – so critical for all issues of ecological crisis – here crumbles away, for it presumes the centrality of one agent who acts with a certain intention and thereby unleashes a chain of events that are *her* doing, although not one with her initial goal.

Imagine that the police respond by shooting massive amounts of teargas towards the crowd. So much of it rains down, and so strong is the wind, that gas enters the bedroom of an infant and asphyxiates

---

41 Helen Steward, 'Moral Responsibility and the Concept of Agency', in Dancy and Sandis, *Philosophy*, 385.

her. In one elaboration of the standard view, Helen Steward stresses that 'moral responsibility is reserved to agents – and so a world which excludes agency is also a world which excludes moral responsibility.'[42] Likewise, a theory that partitions agency so that unintended consequences are seen as the outcome of some material actant is also a theory that evacuates the world of recklessness, improvidence, liability, responsibility and a whole range of other moral parameters. The parents of the dead infant would be asked to vent their anger on the wind. We shall return to the ethical and political implications of this theory.

John McDowell beautifully captures the alternative: to act is like

> dropping a stone in a pool, causing ripples that spread out in all directions. One's intentions in action, *qua* happenings in objective reality, have effects that radiate out in time and space from the initial intervention. There seems to be no principled way of drawing a limit to the possible extent of the causal reverberations of a bit of acting. They are bound to outrun the agent's capacity for foresight, let alone her capacity to include them in what she intends,

not because the reverberations or their additional causes are endowed with the property of agency, but because *she is a material being situated in a fully material world*. Hence the outcome, however unintended, 'generates a truth about what one has done'.[43] But the one that has done the doing remains the human agent.

This applies to the stone-thrower, to the police forces, to the explorers and extractors and burners of fossil fuels: in all these cases, 'what one is doing or has done is determined by what alterations in the objective world *can be traced to one's intentional interventions in it*, independently of whether the alterations were intended or even foreseen.'[44] If acting is like throwing a stone into a pool (or towards

---

42   Ibid., 384.
43   McDowell, 'Acting', 155.
44   Ibid. Emphasis added.

a line of policemen), then an action is likely to take on a life of its own and collect more characterisations as it sails through the world (also becoming the injuring of a comrade – or the killing of a child, or the warming of a planet). It might then be discovered that the agent has done something she had never dreamed of. She owns the action no less for that. Neither the stone nor the canister nor the coal is the agent; the outcomes to which they contribute are integral aspects of the original action as stretched out over time.[45] Global warming is an integral aspect of consuming fossil fuels, not *another* action performed by others. This, McDowell points out, is what allows us to 'distinguish the special sort of difference-maker an agent is from the sort of difference-maker that, for instance, a meteorite can be'.[46] The meteorite makes some difference to a state of affairs, but that is a definition of *causal impact* – not agency, which is a subclass of things that make a difference.[47] This is the exact opposite of Latourian new materialism, and by far the more cogent view.

Note that the analytical problem here is not solved by talking about the 'distribution of agency' or 'relational agency' in some vaguely egalitarian fashion. If half of the stone-throw would be assigned to me and half to the lamppost, we would be back where we started, and the same applies to any other principle of allocation. Latour asserts that 'far from trying to "reconcile" or "combine" nature and society, the task, the crucial political task, is on the contrary to *distribute* agency as far' as possible: a safe recipe for blotting out this factor.[48] The paradox of historicised nature would,

---

45 See further Donald Davidson, 'Agency', in Dancy and Sandis, *Philosophy*, 15–18; Jonathan Bennett, 'Shooting, Killing, and Dying', in ibid., 21–5; Maria Alvarez and John Hyman, 'Agents and their Actions', in ibid., 40; Hornsby, 'Agency', 55.

46 McDowell, 'Acting', 157.

47 Cf. Alf Hornborg, 'Artifacts Have Consequences, Not Agency: Toward a Critical Theory of Global Environmental History', *European Journal of Social Theory* 20 (2017): online first, 98–9.

48 Latour, 'Agency', 15. Emphasis in original. Cf. the very similar formulations in Latour, 'Fifty', 221–3; Bruno Latour, *Reset Modernity!* (Cambridge, MA: MIT

for instance, be obscured. It would become ungraspable if the agency were to be fairly apportioned between humans and ice, between which there is no equality or symmetry. Ice is ripe with *consequences*, which is precisely why certain actions of humans can be so fateful. When Latour writes that, in a warming world, 'humans are no longer submitted to the diktats of objective nature, since what comes to them is also an intensively subjective form of action', he gets it all wrong: there is nothing intensively subjective but a lot of objectivity in ice melting.[49] Or, as one placard read at a demonstration held by scientists at the American Geophysical Union in December 2016: 'Ice has no agenda – it just melts.'[50] Better to adopt a restrictive notion of agency and accept, with Maria Alvarez and John Hyman, that we must 'leave it to nature to unfold the consequences of our actions'.[51] The fact that humans act within the carbon cycle and other circuits of nature does not in any way diminish our agency. It amplifies it.[52]

ACTION ON FOSSIL FUELS

British imperialists came to Labuan with a clear goal in mind: to find coal. They intended to unearth it, get it out of the ground and deliver it to various furnaces. More precisely, we can, judging from

---

Press, 2016), 168. This latest book of Latour's is a monument of academic narcissism. Here he has edited a sumptuously designed volume of essays covering 550 pages, the unifying theme of which is the greatness of Latour himself: contributors write about how they travel between Latour's lectures and ponder his genius; there is a picture of him laughing together with the deputy mayor of Paris; students have their brows furrowed in workshops organised by him, and so on. In the index of names, 'Latour, Bruno' refers the reader to 158 different pages. Plato has 21. Isabelle Stengers comes in second with 22.

49   Latour, 'Agency', 5.

50   Alan Yuhas, 'Inside the Largest Earth Science Event: "The Time Has Never Been More Urgent"', *Guardian*, 15 December 2016.

51   Alvarez and Hyman, 'Agents', 41. Cf. Davidson, 'Agency', 18.

52   As pointed out by Clive Hamilton, 'In Defence of an Anthropocentrism for the Anthropocene', lecture at Lund University, 7 June 2016.

the lithograph, surmise that the entrepreneur present at the scene hoped to earn money, while the officer saw in the deposits a prop for the steamboat lines in the area. Such profoundly intentional enterprises were anything but spectacular: rather they were trivially typical for the merchant and the mariner trying to reproduce themselves at the time and, if possible, expand their own empires. And yet the fossil economy is unthinkable without precisely that garden variety of agency, deep down in the material base of society. Such, in any case, is the bottom line of climate science. Humans have brought about global warming by locating, removing and setting fire to fossil fuels, and that has not happened through somnambulism or haphazard forays: it has been a persistent project throughout the past two centuries, driven by an everyday agency inscribed within existing social relations and reproducing them anew. That is why we are able to say that humans and humans alone have turned the control knob. Or are we?

Proponents of the material turn have another idea. 'Actor network theory', avers Trexler in *Anthropocene Fictions: The Novel in a Time of Climate Change*, an ambitious attempt to ground a theory of the phenomenon on Latour, 'is not about providing a theoretical account of the single source, but rather provides a means to trace the extraordinary number of actors that together create what is commonly referred to as climate change'. Hence the claim that coal and ovens and glaciers have as much agency as humanity or capital – indeed, Trexler faults a focus on corporations and other social actors for failing 'to account for climate's distinct, nonhuman agency', by which he partly means 'the insistent agency of a global climate' per se (compare the invasion of Iraq).[53] We have inspected two ways of justifying this view – severing the link between agency and (human) intentionality, and drawing a line between (human) agency and its unintended consequences – found that neither holds water, and been drawn towards the conclusion that they shed more

---

53   Adam Trexler, *Anthropocene Fictions: The Novel in a Time of Climate Change* (Charlottesville: University of Virginia Press, 2015), 58, 191, 224. Emphasis added.

obscurity than clarity on the dynamics of a warming world. But there are a couple of other arguments to examine.

A more moderate interpretation would be that the coal reserves of Labuan were '*participants* in the course of action', to quote Latour; engaged in 'the collaboration, cooperation, or interactive interference of many bodies and forces', with Bennett.[54] Such words are chosen to designate other, slightly lower orders of action than prime agency (some hierarchies creep in even here). Yet it is unclear how they would avoid according an inordinately active role to the coal reserves, for there is no evidence of them having participated or collaborated or interfered or done anything else in the 1830s: all indications are that they behaved exactly as they always had – namely, not at all. They just lay there. *Like all fossil fuels always and everywhere*, the coal first exploited by the British was utterly impassive, plucked from underground, removed from its eternal stillness, fuels for the machines of men and fossilised to boot: by definition, instruments for the power of (some) humans.

But here new materialists might fall back on another line of defence. Fossil fuels are a necessary condition for their own combustion. Since it would be impossible to stage a play without lighting, or zap a TV without a remote control, Latour argues, these things are as much actors as the persons performing and zapping.[55] But a condition cannot be equated with the state of affairs for which it is necessary. That would be an illogical guarantee for communicative breakdown: being born a mammal would then mean being born a human; being alive would mean being mortally wounded. Environmental historian Linda Nash is guilty of a related conflation when she defends the material turn by asserting that 'so-called human agency cannot be separated from the environments in which that agency emerges.' 'Nature influences and constraints human actions', she writes, and 'environments shape human

54 Latour, *Reassembling*, 71; Bennett, *Vibrant*, 21 (cf. 103). Emphasis in original.

55 Latour, *Reassembling*, 46, 71.

intentions.'[56] True, but this does not mean that they *are* or *possess* the properties they help to call forth among humans. Spring may be conducive to infatuation, and the darkness of the Arctic winter makes some people depressed, but we do not say that the spring *is* in love or that the darkness *feels* blue, unless we write poetry – a noble enterprise different from critical research – or unless we seek to turn the pathetic fallacy into theory writ large. Something may have all sorts of constraints and spurs and preconditions it cannot be separated from, but it does not thereby fade into them, and they do not thereby attain its character. The existence of coal seams on Labuan was not the act of their exploitation, any more than the computer on which the present book is composed is the book itself or its writing, however necessary a condition it might have been.

One property that even new materialists would hesitate to attribute to an oven or a glacier is the capacity for conscious reflection. In the human kingdom, intentions are often formed through habit, personal character or emotional gut reaction, but there is always also that ability to pause, take a step back, put one's desires and beliefs under a mental microscope and make them objects of deliberation.[57] Perhaps I should act in some other way? With advanced symbolic communication at her disposal, the agent can engage in inner or outer conversations and, for instance, negotiate a conflict between the demands she faces from her surroundings and her goals in life, or between her desires and her values.[58] She might decide that giving up her plot and moving into a convent is better for her wellbeing, or develop a disposition for burning coal instead of wood in the exercise of her skill, or resolve that her cravings to fly off for a weekend in the Maldives cannot be reconciled with her

---

56 Linda Nash, 'The Agency of Nature or the Nature of Agency?', *Environmental History* 10 (2005): 69. The words 'actions' and 'intentions' are emphasised in original.

57 Hornsby, 'Agency', 53–4; Davidson, 'Intending', 120, 122; McDowell, 'Acting', 153.

58 Elder-Vass, *Causal*, 93–7; Vivek Chibber, *Postcolonial Theory and the Spectre of Capital* (London: Verso, 2013), 190–5.

ideal of a sustainable lifestyle, or just be torn on the question. This, also, is part of what it means to be a human and not an anemone.

Hence the native inhabitants of a tropical island might conclude that they will not in any way assist the foreigners in digging coal. The officers of the Royal Navy might convene and discuss whether steam or sail is the most efficient mode of propulsion for their boats, come to a decision and then set about eliminating obstacles to its implementation. Such reflection is, as Margaret Archer has argued, constitutive of human agency in general and its *political* potential in particular: only by reflecting on their situation can humans actively turn to shaping it.[59] The capacity unlocks the second level in Perry Anderson's tripartite scheme of agency – the pursuit not of private but of 'public' goals, in which actions 'acquire an independent historical significance as causal sequences in their own right, rather than as molecular samples of social relations.'[60] Staple examples include political campaigns, military confrontations, religious crusades, the signing of treaties, the erection of monuments, the exploration of distant lands. Such endeavours depart from the private baseline by their intention to leave a mark on the public arena. Here the individual no longer acts to further her own goal, but acts *together with others* to achieve something they have jointly set their minds on.

Philosophers would classify this as a species of 'collective action', and some of them would even go so far as to say that the agent itself is collective, like a stratum with emergent properties. Frederick Stoutland has outlined what is probably the most daring theory in this direction. An individual cannot herself play the anthem 'Feel Like Funkin' It Up': only a brass band can. Only a football team can win the Champions League, only a government proclaim a state of emergency, only something like a trade union threaten a strike, only a corporation disclose a stock dividend. It is wrong to

---

59 Margaret Archer, *Being Human: The Problem of Agency* (Cambridge: Cambridge University Press, 2010), e.g. 263–9, 308.

60 Anderson, *Arguments*, 19.

say that the eight members of Rebirth Brass Band *each* plays 'Feel Like Funkin' It Up', for while all do their part in producing the sound, the rhythm and harmonies and irresistible groove are not divisible or reducible to any of them. It really is *the band* that performs the tune, as an agent with its own ontological reality. When it enters a New Orleans second line parade, it has the intention to play 'Feel Like Funkin' It Up', but that action might also have unintended consequences (someone fainting with excitement). This is not a random collection of individuals, such as those forming a queue, but a collective agent with some coherence and endurance; often it has structures of leadership, formal or informal. The corporation is a prime example. 'A corporation has beliefs and intentions, and while its employees may share the content of some of those attitudes, *they are the corporation's attitudes.*' The corporation might set up a certain goal – say, downsizing to half its present workforce – which then accounts for the unity of action towards achieving it. In that case, 'it is not the actions of its employees that explain the corporation's agents; on the contrary, the corporation's actions explains the actions of its employees.'[61] It plays the beat to which the members conform.

Now there exists a category of corporations that are in the business of making profit from unearthing fossil fuels, getting them out of the ground and delivering them to various furnaces. They repeat the scene from Labuan on a daily basis. These are the corporations that plan for the destruction of villages in the Central European region of Lusatia so as to make room for the expanding lignite mines; that drill for oil inside the Yasuní rainforest of Ecuador, whose biodiversity is believed to be the densest on earth; that seek to overcome the resistance against a pipeline for the transportation of crude oil straight through the lands and waters of the Standing Rock Sioux and other Native American tribes in North Dakota; that look for ways to expand coal mining in Zimbabwe; that prospect for oil in the marine park of the Great Australian Bight; that

---

61 Stoutland, 'Ontology', 167, 174. Emphasis added.

pump oil and natural gas from under the jungles of northern Borneo, sending them to the terminals of Labuan; that frack, bore, dig, hack their way through the crust in the quest for ever more fossil fuels to sell for burning. To get those fuels above ground is their *intention*. To make money from them is their underlying motive and raison d'être; individual employees may or may not feel strongly for it, but this is the course of action of the corporations. To pursue it without blinking is the task of the group agent. Elsewhere, we have called this line of business 'the primitive accumulation of fossil capital' – most simply defined as the generation of profit through the production of coal, oil or natural gas for sale to fire-places – and drawing on Stoutland, we can now say that the fraction of the global capitalist class presiding over it intends, as a matter of fact, to soak the planet in the maximum amount of fossil fuels.[62]

What would happen if that intention were to be realised? According to one estimate, the proven fossil fuel reserves in the ground – excluding any further discoveries, as well as deposits made available by new technologies – are enough to cause a rise in the average temperature by 8°C.[63] According to another, operating on similar assumptions, their combustion would eliminate the Antarctic ice sheet. Sea levels would then rise by some 58 metres, predominantly during the next 1,000 years.[64] Given that these estimates are based exclusively on the reserves already mapped and claimed, they must be considered low bars for what this class fraction exists to accomplish. Some philosophers would conclude that, even if eliminating the Antarctic ice sheet is no part of what the corporations intend – they are only trying to *make money* – the fact that they have knowledge of this consequence and *still* continue to

62   See Malm, *Fossil*, 291, 320–26, 355–61.

63   Katarzyna B. Tokarska, Nathan P. Gillett, Andrew J. Weaver et al., 'The Climate Response to Five Trillion Tonnes of Carbon', *Nature Climate Change* 6 (2016): 851–55.

64   Ricarda Winkelmann, Anders Levermann, Andy Ridgwell and Ken Caldeira, 'Combustion of Available Fossil Fuel Resources Sufficient to Eliminate Antarctic Ice Sheet', *Science Advances*, 11 September 2015.

explore and extract all over the globe means that they are intentionally working to rid the earth of all that ice and warm it up to unliveable levels. Others would merely count these as side effects.[65] In either case, this is what the sum of the intentions in this department of capital accumulation adds up to.

Now the bulk of this action takes place very far from the spotlight. It mostly belongs to Perry Anderson's first level of agency, safely tucked into the routine reproduction of social relations. It is, of course, from that level class as such derives, but occasionally a collective agent ascends from the base and steps onto the public scene to, openly or furtively, advance some goal or other. The bankrolling of climate change denial is a case in point. Another is the systematic campaign to influence climate negotiations undertaken by coal, oil and gas corporations; over the past two decades, they and their associates have engaged in consultations with negotiators, cocktail receptions at summits, drafting of legal texts, sponsoring of side events, all manner of overt and covert lobbying. What have they achieved? In their magnificent exposé *Power in a Warming World: The New Global Politics of Climate Change and the Remaking of Environmental Inequality*, David Ciplet and colleagues summarise the effect: 'government representatives, who are structurally dependent on private sector profitability, may anticipate resistance from powerful business and related interests at home to initiatives that threaten established industries' and, infused with such intentions, turn down proposals for radical emissions cuts. The 'enduring dominance' of this particular capitalist fraction has left a very strong mark indeed on the climate negotiations.[66] No one has done more to water them down to their present state of near futility.

With its consecration of the principle of *voluntary* emissions reductions – nations deciding for themselves if they intend to cut

---

65   See e.g. Alfred R. Mele, 'Intention', in O'Connor and Sandis, *Companion*, 113; Joshua Knobe, 'Intentional Action and Side Effects in Ordinary Language', in Dancy and Sandis, *Philosophy*, 158–60; O'Brien, *Philosophy*, 64–70.

66   Ciplet et al., *Power*, 137, 149.

their own CO_2, when, how much and by what means – COP 21 in Paris attested to the success of the campaign to hollow out international mitigation. But that was nothing like the offensive that came a year later. Through the election of Donald Trump, this particular fraction of the capitalist class – call it primitive fossil capital – has gained direct control of the most powerful state in world history. When these words are written, Trump has been in the White House for a week. He has just signed executive orders for the construction of the Keystone XL and Dakota Access pipelines to be restarted, spitting the popular resistance that suspended both projects in the face. He has instructed the Environmental Protection Agency to remove all content related to climate change from its website and appears hell-bent on shutting the institution down. In short, it looks like he will make good on his promise to dig up the fossil fuels remaining in American ground as fast as possible and turn the most proudly illiterate climate denialism into official state ideology.[67] Aiming his scattergun in all directions, it seems relatively plausible that he might self-destruct faster and destroy more things in the process than any American president has ever done. He has in his hands at least one tool for actually reducing climate change to a comparitive non-problem, in the form of the US nuclear arsenal.

Whether the Trump saga ends with a bang or a whimper, it has already demonstrated one thing conclusively: in the second decade of the twenty-first century, primitive fossil capital is nowhere near becoming a marginalised force. Had it been so, it could not this easily have slipped into the top positions of the state apparatus that functions as the highest representative of capitalism as a whole.[68] Trump has filled his cabinet with men who in one way or another have made fortunes from the primitive accumulation of fossil

---

67   For a recent survey of this American current, see Michael E. Mann and Tom Toles, *The Madhouse Effect: How Climate Change Denial is Threatening Our Planet, Destroying Our Politics, and Driving Us Crazy* (New York: Columbia University Press, 2016), 52–116.

68   For this role of the US, see Leo Panitch and Sam Gindin, *The Making of Global Capitalism: The Political Economy of American Empire* (London: Verso, 2012).

capital, headed by the man who personifies this line of business: Rex Tillerson, whose career at ExxonMobil spans forty-one years, ten of which he served as CEO. He is the main character in *Private Empire: ExxonMobil and American Power* by Steve Coll, a gem of business journalism, where the secretary of state-to-be comes across as a paragon of banal evil: while studying in Austin, he 'evaded the city's blossoming music counterculture' and 'gave over much of his extracurricular charity work to the Boy Scouts of America' and read his favourite book, *Atlas Shrugged*. Under him and his predecessor, ExxonMobil engaged in a series of imperialist ventures in places such as Aceh, Equatorial Guinea, Iraq, Nigeria and Chad; it moved swiftly to benefit from the retreating Arctic ice and drill for more oil to burn. Coll explicates why imperialism is a necessary imperative of this corporation: 'the object of Exxon's business model lay buried beneath the earth. Exxon drilled holes in the ground and then operated its oil and gas wells for many years, and so its business imperatives were linked to the control of physical territories.'[69] It recreates the scene at Labuan on a global scale.

Tillerson has famously opened his heart on the purpose of it all: 'My philosophy is to make money. If I can drill and make money, then that's what I want to do.' Since he has the refinement to talk about philosophy here, we may as well subject that statement to a little bit of philosophical analysis. With the premise 'my philosophy is to make money', Tillerson refers to his prior intention, the goal he has formulated for himself, in his mind, before developing any particular plan of action. 'If I drill and make money' is a conditional clause allowing a certain randomness in the choice of methods – *if* I drill and make money, as though he could be doing pretty much anything else to get rich, but now that he is in this particular line of business 'then that's what I want to do': suggesting that in action, the intention will not veer off course, nor countenance any obstacles. This man will act as he intends, come rain or

---

69 Steve Coll, *Private Empire: ExxonMobil and American Power* (London: Penguin, 2012), 333–5, 20.

shine. This is the sort of intentionality that presently occupies the highest seats of capitalist state power. It burns in the heart of a collective super-agent. Its bearers aim to never cease to be victorious.

Climate politics, in other words, necessarily plays out on Anderson's second level, where public goals are projected and clash, always on the basis of the capacity for collective deliberation. If anything, the uniqueness of human agency is here accentuated. Take the example of a massive earthquake and a military invasion. Both can have the most serious effects on human life, communities, whole nations and biota too: they make a very tangible difference to states of affairs. Yet no one would call for rallies against a fault-line, even if a quake seemed imminent. It is, on the other hand, entirely reasonable to gather in front of a government building and demand that the mobilised troops stay home. Is there an actual difference between the mechanisms of these events? So it seems: the earthquake occurs; the invasion is ordered and implemented; the latter is the result of a decision, and the decision-makers could have chosen otherwise (if the demonstrations threatened the stability of their regime, for instance), while the former is the outcome of mute plate tectonics. Should we uphold this distinction, between physically determined events on the one hand and reflexively intentional collective acts on the other? *In climate change, it makes all the difference.* A superstorm like Sandy occurs and wreaks havoc on a city, but the building of a pipeline like Keystone XL is ordered and rammed through – or not. Only those inclined to pantheism will ask the storm to choose another trajectory; the pipeline continues to be the object of intense contestation. One reason for the resistance to it is that it would contribute on a grand scale to the excess of CO_2 in the atmosphere that so dramatically increases the risk of extreme weather events – but the Trump regime evidently has intentions that care nought for this.

Without the need for any detour through theory, the climate movement has used precisely this landscape of intentionality to set its compass. In recent years, it has focused on targeting primitive fossil capital – or 'the fossil fuel industry' – because that is where the most intense, concentrated and aggressive intention to excavate fossil fuels, with the greatest assets of power, resides. No similar intention can be found in microbes or in the climate *qua* climate. The movement has been doing what it can to thwart that enemy, by mobilising an oppositional intentionality formed in the same way as when the inhabitants of Labuan once gathered around fires and, as the historical evidence suggests, agreed to turn their backs on the new enterprise.[70] Whenever it acts, the movement intends a state of affairs that does not yet exist – all fossil fuels left untouched in the ground – and hence its actions are future-directed, and perhaps even fiction-directed, not on an individual but on a collective scale. This is the level where the fate of the fossil economy is determined. Human and human collectives only may clash over it – or, put differently, *a resistance can be conceived solely by affirmation of the most singularly human forms of agency.* The rest is a matter of consequence.

LEARN TO ACCEPT THE BUMPY PROCESS

Now we need not speculate about what new materialism could do to climate politics, for an intervention from a scholar of that creed makes it abundantly clear. In short order, Jessica Schmidt jettisons nature and society, structure and subject, intentional agency and 'centralised authority' and 'effective decision-making' and other odious categories, leading her straight to the conclusion that climate change is *'neither intelligible nor meaningfully shapeable'*. Just let the mysterious storm rage on. Or, do the most a human being can possibly do and adapt to the thundering matter – and if you fail, then *that* is something for which you must take responsibility. 'If we let ourselves be negatively affected' by climate-induced disasters, 'then this indicates insufficient reorientation in our ways of thinking and attitudes towards ourselves and our relationship with the world, in the sense that we have not yet become aware enough that

---

70   See further below.

disruptions are part of the bumpy process of life.' Victims take heed: 'The experience of harm – having been negatively affected – simply means that *we are to be blamed* for not yet having become sufficiently aware of our attachments'. Now go tell that to the people in Burkina Faso and the Philippines. It is incumbent upon them and us to give up the idea of changing course: what humans are truly 'responsible for is undoing the political and mental structures that encourage decision-making rather than adaptation.'[71] Learn to live with whatever matter sends your way.

In this sort of thinking, it is not a question of whether the resistance is strong enough, if it will succeed or fail dismally in the end, if something could be done to promote it: a priori, the endeavour is ruled out as pointless. It is simply not within the remit of humans to shape climate. But perhaps Schmidt has here fallen prey to an intellectual mishap that does not reflect what new materialism is all about? Alas, it does not appear that way. Timothy James LeCain writes that 'neo-materialist theory pushes us to consider how the planet has made humans rather than the other way around. The earth is not in human hands, it suggests: humans are in the earth's hands.' While others have recently argued that the concept of 'the Anthropocene' imprecisely places the burden for climate change and related ills on humankind as a whole – some have championed 'Capitalocene' as a more adequate designation – LeCain moves in the opposite way. He thinks that the name of the epoch should include no reference to anything human. The 'Carbocene', or with the Greek word for coal 'the Anthrakacene', would better register the 'role played by carbon and hydrocarbons like oil and gas *in creating* our current era.' To illustrate this aetiology, LeCain recounts an episode from *Star Trek* where a team of space travellers descends on a planet covered by lush tropical plants and brightly coloured

---

71 Jessica Schmidt, 'The Empirical Falsity of the Human Subject: New Materialism, Climate Change and the Shared Critique of Artifice', *Resilience: International Policies, Practices and Discourses* 1 (2013): 183, 187, 190–1, 181. Emphases added.

flowers of Edenic charm. As soon as they touch the vegetation, it secrets poisonous acid: the planet turns out to be inhospitable to human life. The same applies to the earth. We are in its hands, and they are malevolent; what climate change reveals is that this terrestrial body is 'hostile to human wellbeing' and 'actually exudes a sort of material acid that is harmful' to our species.[72] Then flying off to another planet must always have been a more realistic course of action than resistance of any sort.

Despite sporadic protestations to the contrary, the tendency of new materialism is to lapse into a determinism of the crudest variety.[73] There are no checks and balances in the theoretical construct to prevent that from occurring; indeed, it stands out for not having anything to say about specifically social, historically contingent drivers of something like global warming. Its core belief is that agential matter 'not only seems to but actually *has* a power of its own'. Guns and landmines have such power '*as against* those who fire or plant them'.[74] Bennett is aiming for a worldview in which matter 'acts as an outside or alien power'; as one of its premises, '"human" agency is *itself* always a radically collective, multi-specied endeavor effect.'[75] If these words are to have any meaning in our case, we really are instructed to believe that deposits have agency as against those who excavate them, that coal and clouds have acted as outside powers, that non-human species were as much endeavouring to consume fossil fuels all along. And verily, in his anti-Marxist demonstration of how matter 'makes things happen', Chris Otter adduces this as an example: 'The consumption of non-renewable fossil fuels, on which contemporary modern energy systems and

---

72   LeCain, 'Against', 4–5, 23.

73   For one such protestation, see ibid., 13.

74   Patrick Joyce and Tony Bennett, 'Material Powers: Introduction', in Bennett and Joyce, *Material*, 10, 5. Emphases added.

75   Jane Bennett, 'A Vitalist Stopover on the Way to a New Materialism', in Coole and Frost, *New*, 47; Jane Bennett, response in Bonnie Washick and Elizabeth Wingrove, 'Politics that Matter: Thinking about Power and Justice with the New Materialists', *Contemporary Political Theory* 14 (2015): 86. Emphasis in original.

petrochemical industries are based, has obviously risen dramatically since 1900.'[76] And it is inanimate *matter* that has made that happen. Global warming is one of Latour's many quasi-objects, and all quasi-objects possess 'action, will, meaning, and even speech'; then it comes naturally for Graham Harman to explain that Latourianism is so much better than any theory of the left, because the latter is 'unable to conceptualize the climate threat as anything but the inevitable side effect of a more encompassing *human* problem called Capitalism'.[77] Unlike what the left believes, the threat is not anthropogenic in origin.

This is the logical endpoint of new materialism: and it slams its head right into the ABC of climate science. It also performs an act of whitewashing. Not only the notion of unintended consequences, but that of responsibility – so critical for climate politics – is toned down or turned off.[78] In her famous study of the North American blackout in August 2003, Bennett baulks at singling out deregulation and corporate greed as the real culprits and accepts the claim of the First Energy corporation that no one really was to blame, for in shutting itself down it was the grid that 'spoke'. The 'federation of actants is a creature that the concept of moral responsibility fits only loosely and to which the charge of blame will not quite stick'.[79] One can imagine how this line of reasoning could enter international climate negotiations. It was not *us* who initiated coal consumption or emitted the CO_2; it was the swarm of actants that caught us in their whirlwind, the coal that strove to be burnt, the cars that sped forwards . . . 'What is lost in the move from historical- to new-materialism', Bennett modestly admits, 'is, perhaps, the satisfaction of having a root cause that is targetable and blame worthy.'[80] But in climate

---

76 Otter, 'Locating', 54.

77 Latour, *We*, 136; Harman, *Bruno*, 144. Emphasis in original.

78 'It is even more difficult to condense the distributed, impersonal causes of global warming into a climate villain.' Trexler, *Anthropocene*, 14.

79 Bennett, *Vibrant*, 36, 28.

80 Bennett, response, 87.

politics, singling out that root cause is not a matter of intellectual satisfaction. It is a matter of life and death. Even after death, when it comes to negotiating who should cough up money for the loss and damage wrought by climate change, it will all be a question of responsibility.

Or consider another star of the material turn, Timothy Morton, who likes to compose sentences such as 'the car winks at me knowingly' and 'what spoons do when they scoop up soup is not very different from what I do when I talk about spoons' – he believes that global warming is a 'hyperobject' endowed with agency, and that oil itself is 'a vastly distributed agent with dark designs of its own'.[81] Oil has dark designs of its own. Since the bulk of theory bid farewell to historical materialism in the 1970s, it has engaged in an endless cycle of turns – cultural, linguistic, affective, cognitive, performative, material, posthuman, nonhuman: turn, turn, turn, turn, turn, turn, turn, turn – and perhaps it is then not so surprising that a certain dizziness eventually ensues.[82] The only sensible thing to do now is to put a stop to the extension of agency.[83] In this warming world, that honour belongs *exclusively* to those humans who extract, buy, sell and combust fossil fuels, and to those who uphold this circuit, and to those who have committed these acts over the past two centuries: causing the climate system to spin out of control, they and they alone instigate the paradox of historicised nature. Popular talk of the warming earth as 'agent

---

81 Timothy Morton, 'They Are Here', in Grusin, *Nonhuman*, 187; 'An Object-Oriented Defense of Poetry', *New Literary History* 43 (2012): 215; *Hyperobjects: Philosophy and Ecology after the End of the World* (Minneapolis: University of Minnesota Press, 2013), 53.

82 This is by no means a complete list: Mark Carrigan has produced a catalogue of 47 turns within the social sciences and humanities, including 'the auditory turn' and 'the insect turn'. Mark Carrigan, 'Can We Have a "Turn" to End All Turns?', https://markcarrigan.net, 13 July 2014.

83 Cf. the call to sanity from an environmental historian exasperated with the trend: Paul S. Sutter, 'The World with Us: The State of American Environmental History', *The Journal of American History* 100 (2013): 97–8.

of history' should be discontinued.[84] The dichotomy between human agency and non-human non-agency underpins the whole of climate science, the barrier on which the material turn must founder.

What of other subfields of environmental history? Agency extension might seem more plausible when nature – un-historicised, with no control knobs having been turned by humans – bursts into society in the guise of a drought, poisons people with disease, opens up a new landscape by depositing sediments or makes some other eventful impact. It is when we reverse the arrow – seeking to account for the role of human life *in nature*, illustrating the impact of human history *on the natural world* (later curving back on society) – that it looks so dubious. Paradoxically, the idea of natural agency works best (or least worst) when naturally caused occurrences in the lives of humans are the historical explananda, whereas a more biocentred history, interested in how nature has been transformed from within the realm of the social, needs to steer clear from anthropomorphism and reserve agency for humans.

At a closer look, however, the extension appears unwarranted even for those other fields. In an essay in *The Economic History Review*, Bruce S. Campbell demonstrates how calamitous climate anomalies and the Black Death conspired to plunge fourteenth-century Europe into crisis, throwing feudal society off course and unleashing a cascade of events that splintered the continent into economic vanguards and laggards. He concludes that nature 'was an historical protagonist in its own right' possessed with 'agencies' – but what he really seems to mean is that it had causal impact.[85] It had dreadful influence and shattering force, just as the asteroid had when it hit the earth of the dinosaurs and just as future climate will have under continued business as usual. But the one

---

84 For one such example, see Latour, 'Agency', 3. Rosi Braidotti sees 'the earth as a political agent.' Rosi Braidotti, *The Posthuman* (Cambridge: Polity, 2013), 64.

85 Bruce M. S. Campbell, 'Nature as Historical Protagonist: Environment and Society in Pre-Industrial England', *The Economic History Review* 63 (2010): 310, 283.

emergent property they lacked, lack and will lack is agency. Some precision on this point will not hurt. The particularities of human agency as a source of – and potential remedy to – ecological destruction should not fall out of sight. All environmental history ought to adhere to property dualism.

A WORD ON POSTHUMANISM

But are we not all hybrids now? We have pacemakers and amalgam fillings and contraceptive implants inside us and use screens as our extended selves. Our bodies consist of more bacteria than human cells and our pets have electronic tags tying them to us. We call ourselves human, but we flow in and out of our presumed opposites: machines, animals, medical technologies, digital circuitry in whose absence we would not be the sort of beings we are.[86] This is the observation at the heart of posthumanism, a sibling of new materialism, chiefly preoccupied with liquefying the wall between the human and the nonhuman. In her classic 'cyborg' and 'companion species' manifestos, Donna Haraway revels in the sight of the boundaries – between organism and machine, physical and nonphysical, dog and master, nature and culture – leaking away: 'nothing', she exults, 'really convincingly settles the separation of human and animal.'[87] In *What Is Posthumanism?*, Cary Wolfe elaborates and answers the question with a technical enough definition: 'posthumanism names a historical moment in which the decentering of the human by its imbrication in technical, medical, informatics, and economic networks is increasingly impossible to ignore.'[88] The human is no longer a centre; it slops and spills in all directions. It scatters into and absorbs its erstwhile margins. We are

---

86 E.g. Lucile Desblache, 'Hybridity, Monstrosity and the Posthuman in Philosophy and Literature Today', *Comparative Critical Studies* 9 (2012): 245–55.

87 Donna J. Haraway, *Manifestly Haraway* (Minneapolis: University of Minnesota Press, 2016), 10.

88 Cary Wolfe, *What Is Posthumanism?* (Minneapolis: University of Minnesota Press, 2010), xv. Even human language is 'essentially non- or ahuman'. Ibid., 120.

witnessing 'a colossal hybridization of the species', with Rosi Braidotti, whose tract *The Posthuman* announces that 'the concept of the human has exploded': and this is a good thing.[89]

It would be hard to imagine worse historical timing for a theoretical proposition, although this one is perhaps less epic than banal. There is nothing posthuman about the warming condition. It is characterised by the repercussions of human history befalling every ecosystem on this planet, rather like how every planet in this solar system bathes in the light from the sun. Just as terrestrial nature is swept up in a maelstrom that exceeds anything that came before it, in terms of all-encompassing ambit *and* strictly centralised provenience; just as human intimacy with nonhuman species is unveiled *in the effects humans have on them*, even though they might never have come physically close to any humans; just as the action one single species can perform – that of combusting fossil fuels – drops like a stone into the biospheric pool, along come some theorists and trumpet that 'humans are losing their place at the ontological center of reality'.[90] It is a bit like saying that the *kaaba* loses its place at the centre of Muslim prayer just when the *tawaf* begins. Or, with Clive Hamilton: posthumanism

> repudiates our uniqueness as world-makers just at the time our world-transforming power reaches its zenith . . . Only in the last two or three decades has the pre-eminence of human agency truly confronted us. No other force, living or dead, is capable of influencing the Earth System and has the capacity to decide to do otherwise. Now *that* is agency; and it is what makes humans the freak of nature.[91]

The warming condition is hyper-human. It might perhaps usher in a posthuman moment, in a slightly different sense, if the average temperature is allowed to increase by 8°C or more and push the last

---

89   Braidotti, *Posthuman*, 65, 1.
90   Harman, *Bruno*, 146.
91   Hamilton, 'Defence'.

sweltering humans – unlikely to forget who brought the demise upon them – off the edge of the planet, but until then the ontological centre will hold. Posthumanists like to quote Foucault's 'wager that man would be erased, like a face drawn in sand at the edge of the sea' as a prophecy, but even if a posthuman world were to transpire, it would take many tens of thousands of years before the face of man is erased from the sea.[92] In the here and now, scientists report accelerated risk of species extinction from climate change.[93] In June 2016, they dispatched news of the first mammal to pass away, the Bramble Cay melomys, a small rodent living on an island in the Australian Torres Strait, far from farmland and cities but literally inundated by the rising sea.[94] At least one thing settles the separation of human and animal: the former can wipe out the latter by means of the type of energy it chooses to use. A pacemaker carries scant weight against that reality.

Posthumanism has yet to come up with anything like a convincing response to the particular problem global warming poses to it, and the same goes for a more general problem identified by Kate Soper. With her characteristic rigour, she points out that every injunction to act in a more sustainable manner is 'clearly rooted in the idea of human distinctiveness. For insofar as the appeal is to humanity to alter its ways, it presupposes our possession of capacities by which we are singled out from other living creatures and inorganic matter.'[95] It bears repeating: *any* call for a more environmentally beneficial practice by necessity puts humans front and centre. This alone should give the quietus to posthumanism, and so

---

92   Wolfe, *What*, xii.

93   Mark C. Urban, 'Accelerating Extinction Risk from Climate Change', *Science* 348 (2015): 571–3.

94   James Watson, 'Bring Climate Change Back from the Future', *Nature* 534 (2016): 437; Michael Slezak, 'Revealed: First Mammal Species Wiped Out by Human-Induced Climate Change', *Guardian*, 14 June 2016.

95   Soper, *What*, 40. Cf. 41, 160–61; Hailwood, *Alienation*, 21; White et al., *Environments*, 141; Alf Hornborg, *Global Magic: Technologies of Appropriation from Ancient Rome to Wall Street* (Basingstoke: Palgrave Macmillan, 2016), 163.

it is no wonder that it remains stuck for an answer. Soper goes further, however, and shows that posthumanists are engaged in one great performative contradiction, for *they too* address humans as they could no other beings.[96] They have yet to be observed trying to convince prokaryotes or plastic bags about the veracity of their claims. All their books, papers and conferences are centred on human audiences, which has the practical effect of highlighting another rather exceptional capacity of this species: that of reappraising its place in the cosmos. The rodents who tell each other 'we are not so special after all, and look what Foucault wrote' remain to be observed. Making this conceptual discrimination is not to give carte blanche for torturing or extinguishing rodents – to the exact contrary, it is to erect, or rather openly acknowledge, the foundation for treating them better. If we want to prevent more tragedies like that of the Bramble Cay melomys, we need to get 'human beings to recognize their unique responsibilities for creating and correcting environmental devastation, both for themselves and for other species' – to become *humanists*, in other words.[97]

Such humanism, being another version of property dualism, attains some urgency in a warming world. No one would ask CO_2 molecules to come down from the heavens or demand that the oil platforms scrap themselves and pay their victims – not even Timothy Morton, for he would not find a way to communicate with the oil. Nor can we expect primates to be of much help in ending the fossil fuel era. Recent posthumanist fetishes – augmented reality, the blades of Oscar Pistorius – will not do the trick either, and if the machines of geoengineering are one day rolled out in an attempt to cool the earth, surely their strings will be pulled by ordinary mortals. Barring the implantation of some ecosocialist chip in

96   Kate Soper, 'The Humanism in Posthumanism', *Comparative Critical Studies* 9 (2012): 375–6. This only gives a taste of Soper's critique of posthumanism. For the full argument, see also Kate Soper, 'Of OncoMice and Female/Men: Donna Haraway on Cyborg Ontology', *Capitalism Nature Socialism* 10 (1999): 73–80; Soper, 'Disposing'.

97   Soper, 'Humanism', 377.

our brains, humans of the classical type are the only ones who could *possibly* rise up and shake off fossil fuels from their economies. It then seems a rather dispiriting and demobilising move to tell them that they are nothing special, that nothing separates them from an animal or a machine, that they have no centrally placed agency on which everything else depends. It is not quite the pep talk for the Herculean task they face. Indeed, if the maximisation of survival prospects now first of all requires that the fossil economy must be dismantled *in toto*, we are lifted straight up to Perry Anderson's third level of agency:

> Finally, there are those collective projects which have sought to render their initiators *authors of their collective mode of existence as a whole, in a conscious programme aimed at creating or remodelling whole social structures* . . . It is the modern labour movement that has really given birth to this quite new conception of historical change; and it is with the advent of what its founders called scientific socialism that, in effect, for the first time collective projects of social transformation were married to systematic efforts to understand the process of past and present, to produce a premeditated future. The Russian Revolution is in this respect the inaugural incarnation for a new kind of history, founded on an unprecedented form of agency.[98]

Less of Latour, more of Lenin: that is what the warming condition calls for.

---

98 Anderson, *Arguments*, 20. Emphasis added. Cf. Bhaskar, *Possibility*, 38.

4

On Unicorns and Baboons:
For Climate Realism

BRUNO LATOUR FACES A CRISIS

So far, we have looked at two aspects of the exuberantly creative thinking of Bruno Latour: his hybridism and his attribution of agency to nonhuman matter. They are of a piece. But we should recall that Latour began his intellectual career by promoting the first current we considered above, constructionism, for which he was a major source of inspiration in the 1980s and 1990s.[1] Drawing on fieldwork in laboratories and forays into the history of science – most famously the medical discoveries of Louis Pasteur – he came to the conclusion that scientists *construct* facts, in a sense that closes or even transcends the gap between idealist and literalist constructionism: scientists call the world they observe into being. Their observations are not solipsistic reveries, not free-floating ideas that invent reality as one might build castles in the air – no, scientists dirty their hands with all sorts of matter they *ally* with, or associate with, or link up to in multifarious networks, which then reorder and reconstitute the world.[2]

To make a little more sense of this theory, we may borrow Latour's example of the tuberculosis bacterium. In the 1950s,

---

1 Thus Latour is the main source of inspiration for the idealist-constructionist arguments in *Against Nature*: see Vogel, *Against*, 7–8, 36–8, 47–8, 130.

2 See e.g. Latour, *Pasteurization*.

French scientists brought the mummy of Ramses II to Paris, examined it and found that the cause of his death had been tuberculosis. But that bacillus was discovered in the nineteenth century, whereas the pharaoh lived three millennia earlier – so how can we really say that he died of tuberculosis? For Latour, that would be 'an anachronism of the same caliber as if we had diagnosed his death as having been caused by a Marxist upheaval, or a machine gun, or a Wall Street crash'. The pathogen had no existence prior to scientists teaming up with it. Ascertaining it as the cause of the pharaoh's death required that his corpse be inserted into a network of hospitals, X-ray machines, lamps, sterilised instruments, white-coat specialists, all of which played their part in constructing the fact of the disease – and such facts 'cannot, even by the wildest imagination, escape their local conditions of production'.[3] And so it was only really *after* the flight to Paris, where Ramses II had the special privilege of being transported through time into the halls of advanced medical science, that tuberculosis entered Egyptian history and the pharaoh started coughing and spitting that particular bacterium.[4] It follows, of course, that no other Egyptians than the pharaoh ever died of tuberculosis, since insertion into the French actor-network was not bestowed upon any of the anonymous masses of farmers, slaves and craftsmen, but that corollary is not of primary concern for us here.

Instead, we are interested in the contrast between a Latourian constructionist and a realist epistemology and how the two equip us for our crisis. A realist would say that microbes were already present in the world before Pasteur lifted the veil on them, but Latour would dispute this; a realist would hold that Venus had its phases before Galileo trained his telescope on them, but Latour would deny this; Latour would claim that scientifically observed reality is an

3   Bruno Latour, 'On the Partial Existence of Existing and Nonexisting Objects', in Lorraine Daston (ed.), *Biographies of Scientific Objects* (Chicago: University of Chicago Press, 2000), 248, 250.

4   Ibid., 266.

assemblage, of which the observations and tools and other objects mobilised by the scientists form necessary components.[5] Tuberculosis, microbes, planetary phases cannot be ascribed real ontological status anywhere but inside these networks. They exist insofar as they accept recruitment into them (where they were prior to that point, or how they go about accepting the invitation, is generally not explained). We can detect the trace of an epistemic fallacy here, but when Latour developed this theory in the 1980s, he was so confident in its integrity that he elevated it into a set of universal philosophical theses, numbered as in a *Tractatus*, in which much of hitherto existing thought was razed to the ground:

There is no such thing as superior knowledge and inferior knowledge.[6]

'Science' is much too ramshackle to talk about. We must speak instead of *the allies* which certain networks use to make themselves stronger than others.[7]

We have to abandon beliefs . . . in the existence of logic, in the power of reason, even in belief itself and in its distinction from knowledge.[8]

No set of sentences is by itself either consistent or inconsistent; all that we need to know is who tests it with which allies and for how long.[9]

---

5   This follows Dave Elder-Vass, 'Disassembling Actor-network Theory', *Philosophy of the Social Sciences* 45 (2015): 103–10; cf. Dave Elder-Vass, 'Searching for Realism, Structure and Agency in Actor Network Theory', *The British Journal of Sociology* 59 (2008): 460–1.

6   Latour, *Pasteurization*, 232.

7   Ibid., 218. Emphasis in original. Cf. e.g. 52.

8   This particular formulation is from the final section of part one of *The Pasteurization of France*, of which the *Tractatus* of *Irreductions* forms the second: ibid., 150.

9   Ibid., 179. Cf. 181.

Nothing is more complex, multiple, real, palpable, or interesting than anything else,

and so on.[10]

This epistemological nihilism boils down to a rather vulgar type of Machiavellianism or Nietzscheanism: what is right is solely a question of might.[11] The networks that successfully resist 'trials of strength' come out on top, and that is where something like truth – another category Latour abhors – takes hold.[12] Producing (what is falsely called) knowledge is the art of bonding with the most potent allies, in whose company the producer can convince his audience that he is right. Harman is happy to draw out some implications: 'We cannot say that neutrons are *more real* than unicorns, only that they are *stronger* than unicorns. After all, neutrons simply have more and better animate and inanimate *allies* testifying to their existence then do unicorns.'[13] Square circles, asteroids, King Lear and Pepsi bottles are separated by the degrees of strength exercised by the networks in which they partake as actants.[14] No scientist is objectively more right than any other, only hooked up with greater or lesser force, and the battlefield extends way beyond the laboratory: there can be no court of appeal, no external standard against which a power can be measured or censured or rejected. Or, in Latour's words: 'We cannot distinguish between those moments when we have might and those when we are right.'[15] Being right without having might is – that rare thing – a contradiction in terms.[16]

---

10   Ibid., 156. Cf. 163.

11   As pointed out in the excellent critique by Benjamin Noys, *The Persistence of the Negative: A Critique of Contemporary Continental Theory* (Edinburgh: Edinburgh University Press, 2012), 91.

12   Latour, *Pasteurization*, 158.

13   Harman, *Bruno*, viii. Emphases in original.

14   These are Harman's examples: Harman, *Bruno*, 41, 90. Cf. Latour, 'Agency', 12.

15   Latour, *Pasteurization*, 183.

16   As confirmed by Harman, *Bruno*, 32, 35–6, 42–3, 119.

Such a theory has a good deal of consequences, including, manifestly, for knowledge about nature. Scientists who claim to study nature never do so – for 'look at them!', Latour exclaims, with all the conviction of a positivist: they are *inside* their laboratories and *inside* the world they have created and will never be able to go anywhere else. It also follows that – his emphasis – *'there is no such thing as prediction'*. As for forecasts about nature, 'Pasteur, Shakespeare, and NASA are indistinguishable' in their prognostic capability.[17] Now having spread this gospel and successfully enlisted a whole bunch of allies in the social sciences, humanities and the extra-academic world, Bruno Latour must have, some mornings in the early twenty-first century, been reading his newspapers, as is evidently his habit, and become positively shocked by the threat of climate change. And not only that: he seems to have been taken aback by the *denial* of the science. In numerous texts from recent years, Latour airs genuine anxiety about global warming and veritable fury at the well-heeled people who still preach that it is all a hoax. One of his most cited essays, 'Why Has Critique Run out of Steam?' from 2004, begins with him reading an editorial in the *Wall Street Journal* railing against emissions cuts and an interview in the *New York Times* with a Republican strategist repeating the line on 'the lack of scientific certainty'. This is clearly a moment of personal crisis for Bruno Latour.

> Do you see why I am worried? I myself have spent some time in the past trying to show *'the lack of scientific certainty'* inherent in the construction of facts. I too made it a 'primary issue.' . . . Was I wrong to participate in the invention of this field known as science studies? Is it enough to say that we did not really mean what we said? Why does it burn my tongue to say that global warming is a fact whether you like it or not? Why can't I simply say that the argument is closed for good?[18]

---

17 Latour, *Pasteurization*, 219, 255.

18 Bruno Latour, 'Why Has Critique Run Out of Steam? From Matters of Fact to Matters of Concern', *Critical Inquiry* 30 (2004): 226–7. Emphasis in original.

Yes, why?

Now, one might expect that after such a mea culpa, Latour would make a clean break with his earlier epistemology, or at least take a clear step away from it towards some form of realism, but that is not his next move. Instead, 'Why Has Critique Run out of Steam?' writes out another prescription: stop questioning things so stubbornly. People who are convinced about the climate hoax or some similarly nutty conspiracy theory have the same mindset as critical scholars who see power, society, empire, capitalism or some other vile behemoth behind false appearances, the same basic attitude of suspiciousness, the same default position of 'critique' that must now be declared defunct – be a little gentler and less harsh with the actants. That is perhaps not the most reassuring route to follow where towering obstacles block action on climate. Critique would not seem like the first weapon to throw into the river just now. Rather, Latour's disposal of it should be read as a sign of the crisis his intellectual project faces in a warming world. In subsequent texts, the signs proliferate and multiply, as Latour wavers between reverting to his old constructionism and groping for a way towards something new.

One avenue Latour follows in his writings on climate is precisely to emphasise scientific uncertainty. In *The Politics of Nature* (also from 2004) and his celebrated Gifford lectures (2013), he makes the hackneyed argument that nature does not exist, and that references to it have the sole function of shutting down political debate.[19] With nature out of the picture, how can he define ecological crisis? As a *crisis of scientific objectivity*.[20] Thus the one outstanding feature of global warming is that

---

19   Latour, 'Agency'; Latour, *Facing*, 114. Cf. e.g. Latour, 'Fifty', 221–2.

20   See Bruno Latour, *Politics*, where this particular argument is admirably summed up on 231. Cf. e.g. Bruno Latour, 'Politics of Nature: East and West Perspectives', *Ethics and Global Politics* 4 (2011), 72. But not even Latour can really shake free of the concept of 'nature'. In the glossary generously appended to this book, nature is defined as 'an unjustified process of unification of public life and of distribution of the capacities of speech and representation in such a way as to make political assembly and the convening of the collective in a Republic impossible.' Latour, *Politics*, 245. We also learn that nature 'does not refer to a domain of reality

the end of nature is also the end of a certain type of scientific certainty about nature. As has often been noted, every ecological crisis opens up a controversy among experts, and these controversies generally preclude the establishment of a common front of indubitable matters of fact that politicians could subsequently use in support of their decisions.[21]

So what really constitutes climate change as a crisis is the debate over its existence and the absence of knowledge on which to base a policy. Now that is some way of losing the plot again. This is vintage Latour, clinging hard to the old position, rehashed by Harman (in 2014): 'knowledge claims are a terrible basis for politics.'[22] And so Latour can blurt out (in 2013): 'let's confess that *we are all climato-sceptics*. I certainly am.'[23]

One hundred and eighty degrees in the other direction, in the very same lectures, and the judge bangs the gavel: 'the menace caused by the anthropic origin of "climate weirding" is probably the best documented, most objectively produced piece of knowledge anyone would ever be able to possess in advance of taking action.'[24] Now, it seems, Latour is reading the newspapers again. It makes him want to wage war on the climate deniers who subvert the objective truth.[25] How is he going to reconcile these positions? One way is to tell the deniers the following: aha, so you are

---

but to a particular function of politics reduced to a rump parliament, to a certain way of constructing the relation between necessity and freedom, multiplicity and unity, to a hidden procedure for apportioning speech and authority, for dividing up facts and values.' Ibid., 133. Among all the many competing definitions of nature, these would be good candidates for the gibberish prize.

21   Latour, *Politics*, 63.

22   Harman, *Bruno*, 119. Cf. e.g. 37, 57–8, 108, 163, 180.

23   Latour, *Facing*, 109. Emphasis in original. 'This is why', he also says, 'I proposed to take *positive* the existence of controversies over climate science.' Ibid., 116. Emphasis in original.

24   Ibid., 113.

25   See also Bruno Latour, 'Anthropology at the Time of the Anthropocene – A Personal View of What Is to Be Studied', lecture at the American Association of

suspicious of the climate scientists because they deploy computer models, send each other emails, organise workshops, apply for money, standardise data sets – but so what? Scientists always 'try to *assemble* a political body'; there's no other way research can be done. And by the way, you deniers merely seek 'to assemble another flock, define other entry tests, police differently spread border lines with new documentations', so you're no better yourselves.[26] With this defence, Latour manages to place his constructionism on the right side of the battle, but with armour like a sponge: the climate scientists are not *right*. They have just been more successful than you in attracting allies. Accept that, and accept that everything is settled in trials – all entities 'have to be *made*, constructed, elaborated, fabricated' – and that your proposition about the world has neither more nor less validity than the present consensus.[27] *An Inquiry into Modes of Existence: An Anthropology of the Moderns*, one of the heftier recent books by Latour, starts with the same gambit: the climate denialist should forget about the question of who is objectively right and instead put his trust in the enormous institutional apparatus of science.[28] Right being a function of might, the denialist ought to surrender to the right-might of the scientific consensus. At the time of this writing, Latour has yet to explain how this assessment is affected by the ascent of climate denialism to the most powerful state apparatus in the world.

But granted, Latour has also been trying out other theoretical trails: resuscitating James Lovelock's idea of 'Gaia', while scientists discuss what to write on its gravestone – it is so attractive to Latour because it implies that microorganisms and vegetation are the fully

---

Anthropologists, Washington, 2014, bruno-latour.fr/, accessed 5 July 2016.

26   Latour, *Facing*, 46–47. Emphasis in original. See further e.g. 48–9, 87, 94. Cf. Latour, *Reassembling*, 89–90; Latour, 'Agency', 2.

27   Latour, *Facing*, 15. Emphasis in original. A similar argument is developed, without reference to climate science, in Bruno Latour, *On the Modern Cult of the Factish Gods* (Durham, NC: Duke University Press, 2010), e.g. 18–20, 71–2.

28   Latour, *Inquiry*, 2–6, 11.

intentional creators of climate, and that 'She [Gaia] follows goals' – or rechristening nature 'OWWAAB', acronym for 'out of which we are all born' (whose existence is 'highly *disputed*'); or suddenly flirting with the notion of the Capitalocene, acknowledging that there's no agency quite like the human and recognising the implausibility of posthumanism in a warming world.[29] He deserves credit and respect for his searching. Rather less so, however, for the guideposts that can be still connected to the core of his programme.

FOR EPISTEMOLOGICAL CLIMATE REALISM

So let us instead propose ten simple theses for an epistemological climate realism without equivocation.

1.) If scientists had never discovered global warming, it would still be happening. The atmosphere would now contain more than 400 ppm of carbon dioxide even if no CO_2 observatory would have been built at Mauna Loa; the ice would be melting in Antarctica even if no researchers had ever bothered to travel there; the Bramble Cay melomys would be extinct in the real, actual world even if no newspaper had reported about it; the temperature on earth would continue to rise tomorrow if all humans – including all academics – were to disappear tonight. To accept climate science *is to believe this*. It is to believe that the costly equipment at Mauna Loa, the research stations on Antarctica, the attention temporarily paid to

---

29   For Latour on Gaia, see Latour, *Facing*; Latour, *Inquiry*, e.g. 176, 486; Bruno Latour, *Reset*, e.g. 107, 111; Bruno Latour, 'Why Gaia Is Not a God of Totality', *Theory, Culture and Society* (2016), online first. Quotation from Latour, 'Politics', 9. For some summaries of the death of Gaia, see Tyler Volk, 'Natural Selection, Gaia, and Inadvertent By-Products', *Climatic Change* 58 (2003): 13–19; Tyler Volk, 'Real Concern, False Gods', *Nature* 440 (2006): 869–70; William H. Schlesinger, 'Requiem for a Grand Theory', *Nature Climate Change* 3 (2013): 697. For OWWAAB, see Latour, *Facing*, e.g. 13; quotation from 20 (emphasis in original). For the Capitalocene, the centrality of humans and the criticism of posthumanism, see ibid., 76–80, 116; Bruno Latour, 'On Some of the Affects of Capitalism', lecture at the Royal Academy, Copenhagen, 2016, bruno-latour.fr/, accessed 5 July 2016, 2, 5–8, 18; Latour, 'Why Gaia', 18.

the rodent, the daily measuring of temperatures across the globe, even the famed computer models in themselves play zero role in constituting the reality of global warming. If climate science is basically correct, it means that it had nothing to do with bringing its referent about (fossil fuels had). Only on the condition that the factuality of a warming world is independent of the science can its claims be intelligible at all; the results of that science register what it *does not* produce. Humans are doomed to expressing their knowledge of climate, as of anything else, in thought, but the object is a different matter, neither allied nor symmetrical nor parallel nor bundled with the thought. In the terminology of critical realism, 'the intransitive dimension' – climate change – is independent of 'the transitive dimension' – the science about it – or, in short, the storm is coming whether the barometer is there or not.[30]

2.) The discovery of global warming entails that the combustion of fossil fuels had the causal effect of increasing the concentration of CO_2 and thereby heating the planet in 1842, in 1857, in 1936, in 1953 and in any other year when the science was not yet conceived or still in its infancy. Had that not been the case, the warming as such would not have happened, and the science about it would not exist. Saying that the process was already ongoing in 1869 is not anachronistic; saying that it started when the Intergovernmental Panel on Climate Change was established in 1988 is incomprehensible. In the words of Roy Bhaskar, 'knowledge follows existence, in logic and in time; and any philosophical position which explicitly or implicitly denies this has got things upside down.'[31]

---

30 Drawing on Bhaskar, *Realist*, e.g. 21–7, 31–7, 47–9, 185, 250; Bhaskar, *Possibility*, 9–14; Roy Bhaskar, *Reclaiming Reality: A Critical Introduction to Contemporary Philosophy* (London: Routledge, 2011), 15; Elder-Vass, 'Disassembling', 106–8; Ernesto Laclau and Roy Bhaskar, 'Discourse Theory vs Critical Realism', *Alethia* 1 (1998): 14; Matthias Lievens and Anneleen Kenis, 'Social Constructivism and Beyond: On the Double Bind between Politics and Science', *Ethics, Policy and Environment* (2017): forthcoming.

31 Bhaskar, *Realist*, 39.

3.) Science is, with Bhaskar, '*work*; and hard work at that'.[32] Climate science is an epic endeavour in protracted, taxing collective work, spanning continents, involving armies of unsung researchers spending uncounted hours on desolate field sites and tedious experiments in laboratories. Some of this work is reflected in Spencer R. Weart's authoritative chronicle *The Discovery of Global Warming*, which tries to restore some value to all the embodied labour time: 'One simple sentence (like "last year was the warmest on record") might be the distillation of the labors of a multigenerational global community.'[33] As the warming proceeds apace, the amount of work grows secularly, but all of it would be in vain if it could not presuppose the existence of the intransitive dimension. That is the dimension Latour finds it so very hard to come to terms with, as even Harman sometimes recognises with a tinge of discomfort: his maestro is unable to 'distinguish the object of knowledge from the means by which it is known.'[34] Distinguishing the two is, of course, the very starting point of critical realism, as laid out in Bhaskar's *A Realist Theory of Science*: on the one hand, there is the transitive dimension, or 'the social production of knowledge by means of knowledge' – think of chains of humans passing instruments from hand to hand, exchanging articles, learning from teachers, even whispering in each others' ears – and on the other, the things to which they, sometimes tentatively and always fallibly, reach out.[35] For Bhaskar, critical realism is not some high-flown philosophical concoction, but a down-to-earth reflection of what scientists actually do and think: climate science could be his perfect example. 'The modelers admitted they still had much to learn', writes Weart. Later: 'Scientists were finding a variety of new evidence that something truly exceptional was happening.' Castree and Latour and

32   Ibid., 57. Emphasis in original. Cf. Bhaskar, *Possibility*, 16–17; Bhaskar, *Reclaiming*, 22.

33   Spencer R. Weart, *The Discovery of Global Warming* (Cambridge, MA: Harvard University Press, 2003), 121.

34   Harman, *Bruno*, 142. Cf. 164.

35   Bhaskar, *Realist*, 185.

scholars of their ilk can go on purporting that global warming is an idea or an assemblage, but on the ground the scientists always 'took it for granted that the future climate is as real as a rock'.[36] Climate science is critical realism in practice.

4.) Climate denialists are wrong. They have far too much might. Had they even more might, or had they less, they would be neither more nor less right.

5.) The fact that it is humans who have released the carbon into the atmosphere does not make climate change subjective. It is as objective and biophysical as any other episode of alteration in the earth's climate – say, the Paleocene–Eocene Thermal Maximum 55 million years ago – only the material agent is different this time (and capable of releasing the carbon much faster than any natural processes ever did).

6.) It is because all humans are material beings possessed with the property of agency that some of them can study the climate which some of them are changing.

7.) Climate science must be questioned, but always from the front, not from the rear. Because it is the result of a process of social production, it has been and will be open to influences from surrounding bourgeois society, impure and questionable.[37] As Weart and a plethora of other sources make clear, the ideology that did most to impede the development of climate science in the twentieth century was *gradualism*, or the dogma that nature evolves in an immeasurably slow tempo – *natura non facit saltum*, in the well-worn maxim of Charles Darwin. It took the work of thousands and thousands of scientists to break through this barrier and adapt assumptions to the reality that climate actually can make leaps. But deep-seated gradualism is still a transitive magnet that pulls scientists in the direction of *underestimating* the speed of

---

36   Spencer R. Weart, *The Discovery of Global Warming: Revised and Expanded Edition* (Cambridge, MA: Harvard University Press, 2008), 159, 180, 201. See further Weart's comments on constructionism on 199–200.

37   Cf. Collier, *Critical*, 56.

global warming: it should be the object of a vigilant critique.[38] There is nothing gradual about the warming condition.

8.) Competing claims about climate – is it changing? warming? cooling? warming up slower or faster than in the 1990s? – can only be assessed by engaging with the intransitive dimension. When one scientist says 'the reduction of ice in Antarctica is a function of mass balance and hence it will be slow' and another says 'no, the glacier dynamics are at least as important and so the melting could happen fast', the two are discussing *the same thing out there*, or else their theories would not be rivals. If the former is rejected and the latter confirmed, it is because the object has a distinct existence that can be observed, and it is by dint of this duality of climate science – it being a social product about something occurring in nature – that progress can occur.[39] One sentence can match the real ice better than another. To borrow a metaphor from Andrew Collier, climate science advances by taking soundings from the intransitive warming world.[40] This is why it is a more reliable source of prediction than climate fiction (though not necessarily more inspiring).

9.) Obviously, climate realism is entirely compatible with a passionate interest in representations of climate change.[41] Cli-fi, for instance, may contribute to a naturalisation of the problem by representing it as an act of God, and it also has the potential to inspire action by tracing the storm to its human roots. For this and other reasons, this discursive practice should command the closest attention – but not because it constitutes or constructs climate

---

38 An attempt at a comprehensive analysis of the obstructive role of gradualism in the development of climate science is made in Andreas Malm, *Det är vår bestämda uppfattning att om ingenting görs nu kommer det att vara för sent* (Stockholm: Atlas, 2007).

39 Drawing on Bhaskar, *Realist*, e.g. 38, 166–7; Collier, *Critical*, 82–4.

40 Collier, *Critical*, 88.

41 As pointed out by Robert J. Antonio and Brett Clark, 'The Climate Change Divide in Social Theory', in Riley E. Dunlap and Robert J. Brulle (eds), *Climate Change and Society: Sociological Perspectives* (Oxford: Oxford University Press, 2015), 346–8.

change through its own literary efforts. A powerful cli-fi novel might hypothetically have an effect on the public so electrifying as to spur a wave of protest against pipelines, thereby making a real if ever so small mark on CO_2 levels, but its narrative constructs can never in and of themselves produce anything climatic. The status of the freely imagined future mega-desert covering most of California in Claire Vaye Watkins' *Gold Fame Citrus* is qualitatively different from that of the recent Californian drought. The unicorns of cli-fi may wield influence on their readers, but as such they are still distinctly less real than the climate as it is. Or, saying things about what happens in the climate does not *in itself* in the slightest affect what happens in the climate.[42] But saying things about climate, and about what is being said about it, can be tremendously important, because future climate is now conditioned by relations between humans.

10.) In the high postmodernist era, critics of natural science liked to assert that it was oppressive, conservative, tied up and tasked with reproducing the established order.[43] Today, 'science is not the enemy; suppression of science – by Exxon for example – is the enemy', with Hamilton.[44] Surviving the warming condition requires full alignment with cutting-edge science. If some of it has served to legitimate the ruling classes, one branch has now delivered perhaps the most damning indictment ever to their rule: it is putting the material foundations for human civilisation in peril. It should therefore come as no surprise that this particular science is the object of so much denial in so many different forms, visceral and comatose, woolgathering and venomous. Emotional and psychic investments in bourgeois civilisation run deep. But they are differentiated.

Thankfully, we now possess an extensive body of research on how this works in the general category of *literal* denial – that is,

42 Cf. the ever brilliant Elder-Vass, 'Disassembling', 116.
43 The early Steven Vogel is one example: see Vogel, *Against*, e.g. 16–20.
44 Hamilton, 'Defence'.

explicit rejection of knowledge about anthropogenic climate change.[45] In a seminal paper from 2011, Aaron McCright and Riley Dunlap notice the fact that denialists in the American debate – contrarian pseudo-scientists, media pundits, think tank mouthpieces, Republicans – are almost invariably conservative white men. Is that pattern also replicated in the American public? Indeed: in a nationwide poll, 59 percent of conservative white men hold that 'there is no scientific consensus that global warming is occurring', as against 36 percent of all other adults; 65 percent of the former subscribe to the view that the media generally exaggerates the problem, compared to 30 percent of the latter. 'Liberals', women, non-whites are significantly more in tune with the science. In a reflection of the global pattern, lower positions on the economic ladder likewise predict better judgement. Why this should be so is perfectly logical. Conservative white men 'have disproportionately occupied positions of power within our economic system, controlling stocks and flows of various forms of capital'. They are 'likely to favor protection of the current industrial capitalist order which has historically served them well'.[46] Climate science throws that order into question, and so the beneficiaries of the status quo will – rationally, in a twisted sense – respond with literal denial: these scientists are denigrating my system? They are lying!

The findings of McCright and Dunlap have been broadly confirmed in other parts of the world, from Sweden and New Zealand to Brazil, with slight variations in the determining power

45   For an overview of the research, see Susan Clayton, Patrick Devine-Wright, Paul C. Stern et al., 'Psychological Research and Global Climate Change', *Nature Climate Change* 5 (2015): 640–6.

46   Aaron M. McCright and Riley E. Dunlap, 'Cool Dudes: The Denial of Climate Change Among Conservative White Males in the United States', *Global Environmental Change* 21 (2011): 1165. Cf. Aaron M. McCright, Sandra T. Marquart-Pyatt, Rachael L. Shwom et al., 'Ideology, Capitalism, and Climate: Explaining Views about Climate Change in the United States', *Energy Research and Social Science* 21 (2016): 180–9.

of ideology, gender, race and income.[47] Support for existing social hierarchies strongly predisposes people to denial. So does approval of capitalism.[48] 'We find', one team of researchers describe the base logic, 'that the more individuals are invested in the status quo, and the more motivated they are to justify and uphold extant systems, the less willing they are to admit and confront' the reality of a warming world.[49] If knowledge of that world is a threat to their positions, and if the perception of that threat fuels their denial, it follows that vocal denialism is not an atavism or a fading force, as many were lulled into thinking in the years of Barack Obama. Rather, one is led to the prediction that the higher the temperatures, the more conclusive the science, the more radical the required measures of mitigation, *the more confident and belligerent the denialism of the winners will be.* The oft-reported trend for the US public to lose belief in climate change in the twenty-first century is not, then, so freakish after all. (The conviction spread dramatically in Latin America and sub-Saharan Africa in the same years.)[50] For

47   E.g. Rachel E. Goldsmith, Irina Feygina and John T. Jost, 'The Gender Gap in Environmental Attitudes: A System Justification Perspective', in Margaret Alston and Kerri Whittenbury (eds), *Research, Action and Policy: Addressing the Gendered Impacts of Climate Change* (Dordrecht: Springer, 2013), 159–71; Taciano L. Milfont, Petar Milojev, Lara M. Greaves and Chris G. Sibley, 'Socio-Structural and Psychological Foundations of Climate Change Beliefs', *New Zealand Journal of Psychology* 44 (2015): 17–30; Kirsti M. Jylhä and Nazar Akrami, 'Social Dominance Orientation and Climate Change Denial: The Role of Dominance and System Justification', *Personality and Individual Differences* 86 (2015): 108–11; Kirsti Jylhä, Clara Cantal, Nazar Akrami and Taciano L. Milfont, 'Denial of Anthropogenic Climate Change: Social Dominance Orientation Helps Explain the Conservative Male Effect in Brazil and Sweden', *Personality and Individual Differences* 98 (2016): 184–7.

48   Yuko Heath and Robert Gifford, 'Free-Market Ideology and Environmental Degradation: The Case of Belief in Climate Change', *Environment and Behavior* 38 (2006): 48–71; McCright et al., 'Ideology'.

49   Goldsmith et al., 'Gender', 168.

50   Stuart Capstick, Lorraine Whitmarsh, Wouter Poortinga et al., 'International Trends in Public Perceptions of Climate Change Over the Past Quarter Century', *WIREs Climate Change* 6 (2015): 35–61.

there is no greater and more powerful concentration of winners – conservative, white, male, rich – than in that particular nation: a caste that has, in the age of Trump, also ascended to untrammelled state power.

If recent trends are anything to go by, then, the rise and rise of the political right can be expected to usher in more brazen indifference towards the problem of climate change, no matter what the science says or the heavens bring (at least up to some point). One meta-analysis of studies from fifty-six countries found that identification with the right is by far the strongest predictor of scepticism towards climate science: people affiliated with conservative parties, loyal to the free market and 'inclined to value elites and the status quo' exhibit the deepest reluctance to take in the knowledge of what is going on.[51] This divide, with recognition of the science ranged on the left and superstitious belief in the excellence of business as usual on the right, cuts the world in halves; it has been corroborated in study after study after study, with no sign of the reverse pattern appearing to date.[52] There is even evidence that, at least for the United States, personal experiences of climate change impacts have virtually zero effect on the conservative deniers, so strong are the ideological blinders, so forcefully does the loyalty to power trump everything else – and there has not exactly been a shortage of climate disasters in the US of late.[53] So what else can the surge of the right bring in its wake?

---

51   Matthew J. Hornsey, Emily A. Harris, Paul G. Bain and Kelly S. Fielding, 'Meta-Analysis of the Determinants and Outcomes of Belief in Climate Change', *Nature Climate Change* 6 (2016): 623.

52   E.g. Bruce Tranter and Kate Booth, 'Scepticism in a Changing Climate: A Cross-National Study', *Global Environmental Change* 33 (2015): 154–64; McCright et al. 'Ideology'; Aaron M. McCright, Riley E. Dunlap and Sandra T. Marquart-Pyatt, 'Political Ideology and Views about Climate Change in the European Union', *Environmental Politics* 25 (2016): 338–58.

53   Sandra Marquart-Pyatt, Aaron M. McCright, Thomas Dietz and Riley E. Dunlap, 'Politics Eclipses Climate Extremes for Climate Change Perceptions', *Global Environmental Change* 29 (2014): 246–57.

Now this presents an embarrassment for Latour. He thinks that climate denialism is driven by excessive criticism of existing networks, an ornery attitude to the order of things. As another Latourian scholar, Rita Felski, sums up the posture: 'instead of criticizing institutions, can we also learn to trust them?'[54] But not only does it seem bad advice to trust the institutions of a society that is rushing headlong into calamity, *it is precisely an excess of such trust that generates denial*, the refusal to acknowledge the science a conspiratorial corollary of a deep-seated allegiance to the status quo. The demographic segments least invested in the prevailing order and therefore most prone to mistrust it – inhabitants of the global South, women, people of colour, the left – are also most appreciative of climate science: the correlation is crystal clear. Felski thinks it is time we give up on 'the rhetoric of revolution and vanguard' and learn to play our role 'in conserving and taking care of the past'. But exactly that approach is amply documented as the carrier of a serious malady. Indeed, literal denial is a poisonous pre-emptive strike against the revolutionary implications of climate science, launched by those who seek to defend a capitalist system in which white men consistently come out on top (which also happens to disprove the idea that environmentalism is a pastime of the privileged). As we shall see in the next section, Latour is unwilling to admit even the existence of that structure, while the science of the reception of climate science suggests that a confrontation with it is unavoidable. Such is the consequence of climate realism. The subalterns of the world are the bearers of truth: such is the springboard for scientific socialism.

Then there is, in the taxonomy used by Kari-Mari Norgaard in her still unsurpassed *Living in Denial: Climate Change, Emotions, and Everyday Life*, the second general category of *implicatory* denial, which is not so much a set of beliefs as a way of living. It is the art of professing awareness of climate change while going about one's daily business as though nothing in particular was

---

54   Rita Felski, 'Introduction', *New Literary History* 47 (2016): 218.

happening. Insidious and ubiquitous, subalterns and the left are certainly guilty of this form of denial. It is sustained as much by a sense of helplessness in the face of overwhelming power structures as by fidelity to them.[55] So far, this leaves us with a fringe of more or less deviant personality types ready to *act* on climate realism – a woefully inadequate demography that must, if there is to be any hope, combine with a mass of people whose material interests are so threatened that they one day, in the not too distant future, burst out of the torpor and lend the science their muscles.

WHAT WE DROWN IN

At the moment of this writing, the wind is blowing in the other direction at considerable speed. The far right is in the ascendancy, and it knows where to point its guns. Donald Trump, with all his feeling for spectacle, has performed a public merger of white supremacy with primitive fossil capital, but the convergence of xenophobia – Islamophobia in particular – with climate denialism has been underway for some time; it deserves more than the parenthesis we will offer here.

In the early years of the twenty-first century, the spike in Islamophobic ideology production in advanced capitalist countries spelled out a choice of threat: global warming is a hoax; the Muslim invasion is drowning us. In his bestseller from 2006, *America Alone: The End of the World as We Know It*, praised by Christopher Hitchens and Martin Amis and recommended by George W. Bush to his staff, Mark Steyn combines all the central tropes of contemporary Islamophobia: the Muslims are having too many babies; they are imposing sharia on Europe; they might appear assimilated on the surface but are always hatching plans for a hostile takeover; they have exploited feminism and social democracy to weaken our

---

55   See Kari Marie Norgaard, *Living in Denial: Climate Change, Emotions, and Everyday Life* (Cambridge, MA: MIT Press, 2011), e.g. 84, 192–3.

defences; their religion is a manual in theft and rape. This is 'the dawn of the new Dark Ages'.

> And, unlike the ecochondriacs' obsession with rising sea levels, this isn't something that might possibly conceivably hypothetically threaten the Maldive Islands circa the year 2500; the process is already well advanced as we speak . . . Long before the Maldive Islands are submerged by 'rising sea levels' every Spaniard and Italian will be six feet under. But sure, go ahead and worry about 'climate change.'[56]

Two pages later, Steyn offers his central policy recommendation: 'if you can't outbreed the enemy' – the Muslims – 'cull 'em'.[57] He is one of the contributors to *Climate Change: The Facts*, an anthology featuring Richard Lindzen and other heroes of denialism, published in 2015 by the Australian think tank Institute of Public Affairs, among whose donors one finds Shell and ExxonMobil.[58]

At the height of the War on Terror, Melanie Phillips added her piece to the groundwork by disdaining the Muslim minority in the UK in one *Daily Mail* column and deriding climate science in the next; in Sweden, the leading conservative magazines – *Neo* and *Axess* – alternated between sounding alarms about Muslims and attacking climate alarmism. Organised Islamophobia began to dispatch forces to this second front. In 2008, Siv Jensen, leader of the Norwegian Fremskrittspartiet – 'the Party of Progress' – coupled the suggestion that borders should be closed to anyone from Muslim countries such as Somalia, Afghanistan and Pakistan with

---

56 Mark Steyn, *America Alone: The End of the World as We Know It* (Washington D.C.: Regnery, 2006), xiii, 3.

57 Ibid, 5.

58 The donors: Brad Norrington, 'Think Tank Secrets', *The Sydney Morning Herald*, 12 August 2003; 'The global warming sceptics', *The Age*, 27 November 2004. As of this writing, *Climate Change: The Facts* is the top result when searching for 'climate change' on amazon.com.

denunciation of 'the climate hoax'.[59] In 2013, Nigel Farage of the UK Independence Party opined that 'we may have made one of the biggest stupidest collective mistakes in history by getting so worried about global warming'.[60] In 2014, the French Front National launched a 'New Ecology' movement to oppose international climate negotiations, the environmental spokesperson for the Front branding the UN Framework Convention on Climate Change a 'communist project' and declaring that 'there are pros and cons to the scientific evidence'.[61] Since they took off their Nazi boots around the turn of the millennium, Sverigedemokraterna – now the second-largest party in Sweden, with its eyes set on government power – has denied climate change with roughly the same frequency as it has lashed out against Jews, although hatred against Muslims is its main vocation. In early 2017, the party copied Donald Trump's promise to terminate all climate research at NASA by proposing that the Swedish meteorological institute should have its budget slashed.[62]

These are the parties that, at the moment of writing, win election after election after election in the advanced capitalist countries (and beyond). A fresh paper provides robust statistical evidence of the link between 'right-wing authoritarianism' and climate change denial.[63] With the recent temperature records, the planet is moving into uncharted terrain, and the most successful political forces of the conjuncture are doing all they can to speed up the process.

59   Frode Hansen, 'Siv skal ta klima-bløfferne', *Verdens Gang*, 28 March 2008; Kristoffer Rønneberg, 'Frp vil stenge grensen', *Aftenposten*, 7 April 2008.

60   Brendan Moore, 'Climate Change Skepticism in the UK Independence Party', *Environmental Europe*, http://environmentaleurope.ideasoneurope.eu, 2 March 2015.

61   Arthur Neslen, 'French National Front Launches Nationalist Environmental Movement', *Guardian*, 18 December 2014.

62   Tidningarnas Telegrambyrå, 'SD-politiker: SMHI bedriver propaganda', *Aftonbladet*, 10 January 2017.

63   Samantha K. Stanley, Marc S. Wilson and Taciano L. Milfont, 'Exploring Short-Term Longitudinal Effects of Right-Wing Authoritarianism and Social Dominance Orientation on Environmentalism', *Personality and Individual Differences* 108 (2017): 174–7.

What can be said about it? For now, only this: climate realism can make headway solely at the expense of fascism. It somehow has to learn to be militantly and efficiently anti-fascist.

FOR SOCIALIST CLIMATE REALISM

Another question for theory: is social power the root of technology? When baboons hang out, they chatter, bite, pull, copulate, negotiate, charge, retreat, laugh, huddle together and groom one another and immerse themselves in other social activities all the time. Humans do not need to behave like that. We have found a way to avoid constant testing of ranks and relations by *stabilising them in material objects*. Baboons are nothing more than their naked bodies and thus have to communicate incessantly, but humans can make face-to-face interaction superfluous by mobilising a whole gamut of extra-somatic resources that render their arrangements more cohesive, durable and, as it were, indirect. This analysis of the peculiar nature of human vis-à-vis primate society helped catapult Latour into the pantheon of theory in the 1980s and 1990s, while he adroitly elaborated it with several now famous examples.[64] Instead of reminding his guests to drop their keys on the way out, a hotel manager can attach so heavy and unwieldy metal objects to them that even the most absent-minded customer will eagerly go to the front desk to return his property. The social interaction – the manager demanding that the guests drop the keys – has been transposed onto an intermediary object.[65] Or, the administration of a university wants drivers to slow down their cars when they

---

64   Michel Callon and Bruno Latour, 'Unscrewing the Big Leviathan: How Actors Macro-Structure Reality and How Sociologists Help Them to Do So', in K. Knorr-Cetina and A. V. Cicourel (eds), *Advances in Social Theory and Methodology: Toward an Integration of Micro- and Macro-sociologies* (Boston: Routledge and Kegan Paul, 1981), 277, 283–5; S. S. Strum and Bruno Latour, 'Redefining the Social Link: From Baboons to Humans', *Social Science Information* 26 (187): 783–802.

65   Bruno Latour, 'Technology is Society Made Durable', *The Sociological Review* 38 (1990): 104.

enter the campus, but not by *telling* them every minute: instead concrete speed bumps are installed.[66] Similar examples can be multiplied on end.

This is surely the rational kernel of actor-network theory and Latour's thinking more broadly: the insistence on seeing human relations as mediated through matter and, more particularly, technology. Given the need to countervail idealism, this is a facet of society that cannot be stressed enough. But there is also a sense in which Latour has reinvented a wheel. The first volume of *Capital*, and indeed the entire oeuvre of Marx and Engels, can be read as one long analysis of how relations between humans become embodied in things: in sheep pasture, yarn, coats, corn, self-acting mules, steam-engines, slave-ships, ports, soil, money. The theory of the shift from formal to real subsumption of labour offers the insight Latour later pulled out of primatology: relations of rank are unstable as long as they are not fixed in (extra-human) matter; to become something more than an alpha male of a baboon troop, the capitalist must incarnate his dominance in the machine. Latour rebukes Hobbes for having neglected how power is materialised, how the sovereign becomes formidable by virtue of 'the palace from which he speaks, the well-equipped armies that surround him, the scribes and the recording equipment that serve him', but the charge could hardly stick to Marx.[67] Now Latour's deep animus towards historical materialism has never been in any doubt.[68] Yet he can still admit in passing that 'it is also true that a look at many Marxist schools would provide a wealth of the same linkages that have been established [by Latour himself] between material and social

---

66 Latour, 'On Technical', 38.

67 Callon and Latour, 'Unscrewing', 284.

68 The claim that Marxism is Latour's 'real target' certainly carries force. Noys, *Persistence*, 81. One does not need to be a Marxist to observe the animosity: see e.g. Oscar Kenshur, 'The Allure of the Hybrid: Bruno Latour and the Search for a New Grand Theory', *Annals of the New York Academy of Sciences* 775 (1995): 291.

conditions.'[69] If this is so, what is there to recommend *his* take on such linkages?

By now, the answer should not come as a surprise. Historical materialism teaches that if an exploiter attaches himself to some thing, that thing increases his power. Such an account is anathema to Latour, for it draws the picture of 'an all-powerful human agent imposing his will on shapeless matter, while nonhumans also act, displace goals, and contribute to their redefinition'.[70] A historical materialist would say – as the historical record does – that the steamboats of the Royal Navy calling at Labuan soon after the discovery were entrusted with the task of opening up the peripheries and subordinating them to Britain, the goals of the metropole engraved in their boilers and hulls.[71] But Latour recoils at the suggestion that objects can '"express" power relations, "symbolize" social hierarchies, "reinforce" social inequalities', since they cannot then 'be at the origin of social activity'. Incidentally, he mentions steam-power technology as a case. It should not be regarded as a '"mere reflection" of "English capitalism"'; Latour sides with those of a 'technical determinist' inclination, who would rather emphasise the '"weight of material constraints"'.[72] The historical record for this case (as isolated to capitalism in Britain) has been examined elsewhere.[73] Leaving it aside, do Latour's interpretations fit his own high-profile examples?

Let us start with the baboons. As a foil to the human mobilisation of instruments, they serve their role well: elucidating a threshold between our close primate relatives and our distant hunter-gather ancestors.[74] Contrary to the wishes of posthumanism, Latour and his co-author Shirley Strum add another brick to

---

69   Latour, 'Politics', 73. It says 'Marxist many schools' in the sentence, but this typo has been corrected.

70   Latour, 'On Technical', 38.

71   For just a small taste of the historical record, see Malm, 'Who'.

72   Latour, *Reassembling*, 72, 84.

73   Malm, *Fossil*.

74   'Threshold' is the word used by Harman, *Bruno*, 21.

the wall. Our 'efforts', they write, 'do not erase the significant differences between ants, baboons and, for instance, the technocrats of the Pentagon. Rather they highlight the source of those differences in a new way: the resources used and the practical work required in mobilizing them.'[75] So the detour through the world of the baboons led Strum and Latour back to the Pentagon, with the insight that it bases its power on material resources. Did their study also prop up the idea that objects are 'at the origin of social activity'? If so, one has to ask why all objects decided to throng to hominins and humans in particular. Why did not at least some of them decide that their 'goals' and 'aims' might be served by associating with some other species? If the tools were at least as active in creating the tool-human alliance, how is it that they *exclusively* partnered up with humans? The argument for human monopoly on using extra-somatic resources as buttresses for their relations seems difficult to square with the notion of these resources as the originators of social activity. Or are we asked to believe that the material world congregated one night in some parliament of things and agreed to select our species as its sole carrier for adventures?

The whole thrust of the baboon study appears to be another: humans have a unique propensity to *actively order matter so that it solidifies their social relations*. Some formulations of Latour lend further credence to this interpretation. 'Nonhumans are at once pliable and durable; they can be shaped very quickly but, once shaped, last far longer than the interactions that fabricated them. Social interactions are extremely labile and transitory.'[76] The social element, in other words, *is the moving element* – volatile, transitory, historical – while the matter provides *the inertia* it needs for reproduction. But that brings us right back towards historical materialism. So do, at a closer look, the hotel key and the speed bump anecdotes. Latour provides no indications that a metal weight could take the first step towards a hotel manager or indeed any step at all;

---

75   Strum and Latour, 'Redefining', 797.
76   Latour, 'On Technical', 61.

cement seems to be an eminent case of 'shapeless matter' before it has been moulded into a bump. Latour wants us to see the actants as 'imposing their aims' and 'shifting from one opinion to another' and 'fomenting their own plots' and 'betraying our expectations': they 'use us to prosper': each of them acts 'on its own behalf'.[77] He strives to establish absolute *symmetry* – a key word – so that all properties are swapped and shared between the actants, and so that there can be no residual impression of a human 'initiative' (if anything, the initiative lies with the objects).[78] But his words tell other stories. They support the view that things such as the bulky key and the bulging bump possess *'derivative intentionality'*, with Jacquette: a task delegated from a proprietor with a goal. Rather than a one-to-one symmetry, something like a ten-to-zero asymmetry structures the configuration. For 'who would want to claim that a telegram saying "Sell the farm!" is itself intelligent just because it expresses an author's thoughts and is causally connected in a chain of events that may help to accomplish the author's purposes?'[79] Yes, who?

Alf Hornborg, in *Global Magic: Technologies of Appropriation from Ancient Rome to Wall Street*, supplies two other examples that cap the primacy of the social. Consider a key and a coin. Both manufactured out of metal, rather similar in shape and form, they are used to unlock two very different doors: one to a specific house, the other to any object in the marketplace. Why do they have such disparate functions? The explanation must be that humans have fashioned keys for houses on the one hand, and established and upheld the convention that money shall accord its owner access to

77   Latour, *Pasteurization*, 35, 197; Bruno Latour, 'How to Write *The Prince* for Machines as well as for Machinations', in Brian Elliott (ed.), *Technology and Social Change* (Edinburgh: Edinburgh University Press, 1988), 9.

78   Latour, 'On Technical', 53. See further e.g. 34–5, 54; Latour, *Pasteurization*, 35–7; Latour, 'Technology', 108–10; Jim Johnson (pseudonym for Bruno Latour), 'Mixing Humans and Nonhumans Together: The Sociology of a Door-Closer', *Social Problems* 35 (1988): 303.

79   Jacquette, *Philosophy*, 80, 69. Emphasis in original.

freely selected commodities on the other – or, that we humans 'externalise our relations' – or, that 'social relations of power in different ways are delegated to material artifacts.' From the most primitive key to the most vaporous financial instrument, across the terrain of extra-somatic resources pocketed by humans, 'the driving forces and the glue that reproduce them are irreducibly *social* in the sense that they hinge on the incentives, intentions, and agency of interacting subjects.'[80]

We may just as well accept the new materialist slur and call this view 'socialism', or 'socialist realism'. It is implied by every hotel and every car. A hotel with a manager who worries about the return of keys presupposes private property and the interest in running it with a profit; a speed regulation is prompted by a contradiction between private ownership of cars and the safety of pedestrians guarded by some institution.[81] Or take the razor wires rolled out along European borders in 2015 and 2016 to keep refugees out. They derived from nation-states, citizenships, bureaucracies, perceptions of some humans as aliens without a right to protection – relations that, during some months in 2015, were indeed challenged by 'extremely labile and transitory' movements of people. To endure, they had to be anchored in some pliable and durable material that can cut up a human body. The fences have derivative intentionality. Socialist realism holds.

If socialist realism posits relations as the moving element in the development of new technology, it also suspects, in the spirit of critique, power as a central vector. To drive back this bugbear, Latour proposes that power can never be '*possessed*. We either have it "in potentia", but then we do not *have* it; or we have it "in actu", but then our allies are the ones that go into action.' Either a British imperialist is naked and has no power; or he gets equipped with a steamboat and some coal mines, and then it is those allies that go into action, and he still possesses no power. Fundamentally, humans

---

80   Hornborg, *Global*, 104, 162, 35. Emphasis in original.
81   Cf. Newton, *Nature*, 32.

146

are no more than hapless, vulnerable adolescents. 'Either no one helps you out and so no power is granted to you; or they do help you out but then they pursue their own goal, *not yours*.'[82] If there is power in the world, it is a property of the network as such – not of one human agent over and against another.[83] The configuration hereby excluded is that of some people exercising their power over others by means of objects such as steamboats or razor wires. The refusal to conceive of objects as passive in the hands of human subjects makes *power projected through the medium of a thing* inconceivable.[84]

One might think that before the British imperialists disembarked on Labuan, they must have already possessed some edge over the natives and the people in the region at large, even if only a narrow one, and that their appropriation of the material resources in question served to *widen the differential*, so that they returned towards the metropole more powerful than before. Something similar should apply to the relation between European nation-states and propertyless people from the Middle East and sub-Saharan Africa looking for a home. Latour, however, is unambiguous on this count: 'Domination is an effect not a cause.'[85] But to understand why there is so much domination in the world, one needs to see it as *a cause that has an effect that loops back to further strengthen that cause*, and so on and so forth – the kind of dialectic Latour loathes, and the key to understanding why certain relations of inequality seem to be etched in stone. An idea of power as the outcome of the things themselves is impossible to make sense of. It marks, as Hornborg points out, another crucial difference from Marxian approaches: by attributing agency and power to the objects rather than to the relations and people behind them, *it mirrors*

82 Latour, *Pasteurization*, 174–5, 12. Emphasis in original.
83 See e.g. Latour, 'Technology', 110, 123. Cf. Joyce and Bennett, 'Material', 1–2; Otter, 'Locating', 46.
84 See further Hornborg, 'Technology'.
85 Latour, 'Technology', 130.

exactly the sort of fetishism Marx set out to unmask.[86] Latourianism is mysticism and unabashed fetishism.

By logical extension, if not yet by any comprehensive empirical demonstration, the fossil economy must have been built up through this kind of dialectical processes, solidifying into a structure that, at the moment of this writing, is getting more stable than the climate by the day.[87] We have touched upon one such recursive loop: the segment of the capitalist class prosecuting primitive accumulation of fossil capital, starting with money invested in the extraction of fossil fuels and ending up with more money when they are sold – with more power, that is, to command the resources of others and resume the circuit. Some 200 years old and still expanding, the fossil economy has been radiating from its Western centre over its *longue durée* and sustained into this day by the exceptional concentration of power invested in business as usual. That is why victories such as that over the Keystone XL pipeline remain such fragile exceptions.

But if the analytical targets we have already picked up were not enough, Latour is also famously averse to the category of structure – there is nothing but motley actants bumping into each other, agglomerating for a moment and splitting off, never permitting any central source of power to form a vertical structure around itself. Latour wants to 'keep the social flat'.[88] He does not say anything

---

86   Hornborg 2016, *Global*, e.g. 15. For excellent clarifications of these and related points, see further Hornborg, 'Technology'; Hornborg, 'Political Economy'; Hornborg, 'Political Ecology'; Scott Kirsch and Don Mitchell, 'The Nature of Things: Dead Labor, Nonhuman Actors, and the Persistence of Marxism', *Antipode* 36 (2004): 687–705; Hylton White, 'Materiality, Form, and Context: Marx contra Latour', *Victorian Studies* 55 (2013): 667–82.

87   See further Malm, *Fossil*, e.g. 12–13.

88   Latour, *Reassembling*, 165. Cf. Harman, *Bruno*, 110. This strand of Latour's theory is subject to remorselessly effective critique in Elder-Vass, 'Searching'. See also e.g. Noys, *Persistence*, 93; Benjamin Noys, 'The Discreet Charm of Bruno Latour', in Jernej Habjan and Jessica Whyte (eds), *(Mis)readings of Marx in Continental Philosophy* (Basingstoke: Palgrave Macmillan, 2014), 197; Keir Martin, 'Knot-work not Networks, or Anti-anti-antifetishism and the ANTipolitics

about what this would mean for the fossil economy, but he often does so for the entity that has spawned and become one with it: capitalism. 'Like God, capitalism does not exist.' In the world Latour has seen, including in the United States itself, 'capitalism is still marginal even today. Soon people will realize that it is universal only in the imagination of its enemies and advocates.'[89] Or, as clear as he can be: 'don't focus on capitalism.'[90]

It is about time we take leave of Bruno Latour, and while we do so, we can just as well revive another of his detested categories: totality. He wants to turn our attention away from the global scale and towards the strictly local, but in the warming condition, every local site is a plaything in the hands of the earth system.[91] A superstorm does not strike a shoreline because of something that has happened there. Behind it is the totality of the fossil economy, and so we can briefly sum up three tenets of a socialist climate realism: 1.) social relations have real causal primacy in the

---

Machine', *HAU: Journal of Ethnographic Theory* 4 (2014): 99–115; Rebecca Lave, 'Reassembling the Structural: Political Ecology and Actor-Network Theory', in Perreault et al., *Handbook*, 213–23; White et al., *Environments*, 133–5, 201; cf. Mark Edward, 'From Actor Network Theory to Modes of Existence: Latour's Ontologies', *Global Discourse* 6 (2016): 1–7.

89   Latour, *Pasteurization*, 173.

90   Latour, *Reassembling*, 179. The advice is repeated in Latour *Reset*, 53. But possibly the crisis of global warming has pushed Latour to reconsider some of his earlier hostility to the concept of capitalism. If so, it has produced another round of confusion: 'I will take *capitalism* to mean not a thing in the world, but a certain way of *being affected* when trying to think through this strange mixture of *miseries and luxuries* we encounter when trying to come to terms with the dizzying interplays of "goods" and "bads".' Latour, 'On Some', 2. Emphases in original. The gibberish prize again.

91   As pointed out by Hamilton, 'Defence'. For a desperate attempt to hold the category of totality at bay even while endorsing Gaia theory, see Latour, 'Why Gaia'. For a critique of Latour's anti-totality line, see Kai Jonas Koddenbrock, 'Strategies of Critique in International Relations: From Foucault and Latour towards Marx', *European Journal of International Relations* 21 (2015): 243–66. For Latour's programme of 'relocalizing the global', see Latour, *Reset*, e.g. 52, 91, 112, 168.

development of fossil energy and technologies based on it; 2.) by recursive loops of reinforcement, these relations have been cemented in the obdurate structure of the fossil economy; 3.) that totality has in its turn fired up the totality of the earth system, so that (some) humans have real reasons to be afraid. This gives us nothing more than clues to further investigations. But the point we have tried to make here is that Latour, and much associated theory, can provide only poor guidance to studying the social dynamics of a warming world and, a fortiori, to intervening in it. With that, we can move on to the political implications of all this quarrel over theory.

A PATH TO MILITANCY

Contemporary hybridism comes in two main forms: constructionism and new materialism. If the former collapses nature into society, the latter does the reverse. As we have seen in the figure of Latour, the two are closer than it might first appear; indeed, they sometimes seem to be ensnarled branches growing out of the same ideological trunk (to whose identity we shall return). We have argued that this thicket is of sparse analytical value for orientation in a warming world. What of the politics?

The policy recommendations of idealist constructionism are not hard to come by. One scholar who sometimes falls under its spell, Mike Hulme, is on record as saying that 'there is no such thing as a "good" climate or a "bad" climate, only "good" or "bad" ways of imagining and living with climate.' Imagine 4°C in a good way and it might turn out fine. Hence 'it really is *not* about stopping climate chaos' – it is about telling stories, and the story of approaching climate chaos is a distraction, a diversion, a myth that has blinded us to

our contemporary crisis. Why, for example, do we not see the same political energy and diplomatic capital being invested in the achievement of the Millennium Development Goals (MDGs) as we see daily being invested in the drive to establish an international climate regime with its sights half a century hence?[92]

One must hesitate to impute such a far-out opinion to anyone, but the logic of this argument is that too much is being done for long-term stabilisation of the climate. If it is a matter of imagining the good climate, any summit – or climate camp, or divestment campaign, or initiative for a just transition – must indeed be a waste of time. And verily, Hulme has consistently toned down the need for urgent mitigation and berated even the Kyoto Protocol for being too hierarchical and top-down.[93]

Constructionists of this breed tend to fault others for over-simplifying the problem, overblowing the risks, overlooking the complexities and spreading undue alarmism. They are very interested in the vagaries of knowledge and much less so in structures of economy.[94] Not infrequently do they fail to maintain a proper distance from the denialist discourse: thus Noel Castree, while posing as the spokesperson for the humanities and social sciences in the climate research community, is on record as alleging that 'epistemic uncertainty looms large', that the IPCC reports are guilty of 'over-confidence' in creating 'the impression that scientists are now relatively [sic] sure that anthropogenic warming is occurring', and that media should continue to give denialists airtime.[95] These statements are worse than inaccurate.

---

92   Mike Hulme, 'Four Meanings of Climate Change', in Stefan Skrimshire (ed.), *Future Ethics: Climate Change and the Apocalyptic Imagination* (London: Continuum, 2010), 42, 53–4. Emphasis in original. This is an extrapolation of the argument developed in Mike Hulme, *Why We Disagree About Climate Change: Understanding Controversy, Inaction and Opportunity* (Cambridge: Cambridge University Press, 2009), see e.g. 361–2.

93   Hulme, *Why*, 297, 311–12; see further Antonio and Clark, 'Climate', 341–3.

94   See the excellent overview in Antonio and Clark, 'The Climate'.

95   Castree, *Making*, 257–8, 242.

Literalist constructionism, on the other hand, tends towards the position that we can do more or less whatever we want with nature, for there is no external nature, only the one we ourselves build. To Neil Smith, the idea of an external nature is so unpleasant because 'it renders non-human objects and processes intractable barriers to which humans must at some point submit', whereas in his theory, apparently, those barriers are removed and humans never have to submit to anything.[96] The one political demand constructionists of this disposition like to raise is that of *democratisation*: we can do whatever we want, but we should take the decisions about what to do together, more democratically than at present.[97] Paul Wapner brushes aside the 350.org movement as the purveyor of an impossible goal – we cannot return to 350 ppm: 'climate stability is unreachable' – and instead advocates democratic deliberation: 'The atmosphere has no preferred level of carbon concentrations. There is no natural ideal toward which humans must tack. Rather, we need to agree upon our own targets and directions for policy.'[98] Yes, but *on what grounds* should we choose between the available options if there are no imperatives, no signals, no boundaries to be crossed or respected in the biophysical world?

Similarly, Jedediah Purdy wants to replace the current 'neoliberal Anthropocene' with a 'democratic Anthropocene', in which the

96 Smith's argument summed up in Noel Castree and Bruce Braun, 'The Construction of Nature and the Nature of Construction: Analytical and Political Tools for Building Survivable Futures', in Braun and Castree, *Remaking*, 7.

97 See e.g. Smith, 'Production', 50; Smith, 'Nature as Accumulation Strategy', in Leo Panitch and Colin Leys (eds), *Socialist Register 2007: Coming to Terms with Nature* (London: Merlin Press, 2006), 34. For a splendid critique of this constructionist idea of democratisation, see John Bellamy Foster and Brett Clark, 'Marx's Universal Metabolism of Nature and the Frankfurt School: Dialectical Contradictions and Critical Syntheses', in James S. Ormrod (ed.), *Changing Our Environment, Changing Ourselves: Nature, Labour, Knowledge and Alienation* (London: Palgrave Macmillan, 2016): e.g. 130.

98 Wapner, *Living*, 174; Paul Wapner, 'The Changing Nature of Nature: Environmental Politics in the Anthropocene', *Global Environmental Politics* 14 (2014): 47.

making of that thing called nature is 'everyone's authorship politically'. Citing Amartya Sen – 'no democracy has ever suffered a famine' – he suggests that disasters can be avoided in such an Anthropocene.[99] But that seems to miss an important aspect of climate change. By force of temperatures, there will be more famines in a considerably hotter world *whether or not institutions are democratic*. Egalitarian adaptation might ameliorate the worst effects, but even if the world were a perfect democracy, it would still at some point become very hungry insofar as it allowed CO_2 emissions to continue. The first precondition for minimising that risk is the destruction of business as usual – a matter of political content, which might very well require a certain democratic form but *cannot be reduced to it*.

Steven Vogel is of another mind: he thinks that any talk of non-human power is sabotage of the democratic process. 'To believe that there is a "nature" beyond us and above us' is to 'escape the need for us to figure out what to do'.[100] But it is, of course, precisely the other way around. If there is nothing but us, then there is nothing to figure out – at least not in the department of ecological politics. Here literalist constructionism sounds a bit like an exhortation to film critics to stop watching any actual movies, look only at each other and then pin down their criticism of contemporary cinema. A democratic assembly can make a prudent decision only if it stands in relation to something outside its windows; if the assembly were all that is, its democracy would ring hollow. Any line on global warming that is not denialist must take cognizance of forces and causal powers oblivious to human predilections: one cannot abolish thermal expansion of the oceans by democratic decree. That is why one must have a line on global warming in the first place. That is also

---

99 Purdy, *After*, 48–9; cf. e.g. 271. And Sen could be inverted: no democracy has ever flourished on a seabed or a parched planet.

100 Vogel, *Thinking*, 93. For Vogel's democratisation programme, see also Vogel, *Against*.

why it is a bad idea to dig up all fossil fuels and set fire to them – without practical application of the category of nature, it would be impossible to make that argument. In no way does this imply that nature is a source of normative value or moral arbiter in itself. Following Soper again, nature might determine the effects of human actions, 'but it does not endorse any particular way of living or being'.[101] It does not tell us whether it is righteous or heinous to burn all known fossil fuels reserves: it is up to humans to mull over that question, but on the basis of the *descriptive* information gleaned from nature. Having internalised the natural into the social, the constructionist programme for ecological democracy runs on empty.

If literalist constructionism tends towards the view that we can do anything, new materialism veers, as we have seen, towards the ditch where nothing can be done.[102] Here the 'limitation of humans' agentic efficacy' is extolled – or, as Jessica Schmidt begins her essay: 'Today's complex, interconnected and globalised world seems to tell us mainly one thing: this world that we are bound to live in is no longer ours. Although humans are still held to be its chief "drivers", their formative capacities seem to have been substantially curtailed.'[103] That is the powerlessness she and her peers drape in ontology. Learn to enjoy the chastening.

As for Latour himself, things get a little more complex. In a wonderful critique of his 'political ecology', Rebecca Lave concludes that it is more likely to inspire the self-organisation of fax machines than workers: '"fax machines unite, you have nothing to lose but

---

101   Soper, 'Disposing', 8.
102   For splendid critiques of the politics of new materialism and actor-network theory, see Martin, 'Knot-work'; Lave, 'Reassembling'; Washick and Wingrove, 'Politics'; cf. White et al., *Environments*, xix, 142. A feeble attempt to distil emancipatory potentials out of new materialism is Erika Cudworth and Stephen Hobden, 'Liberation for Straw Dogs? Old Materialism, New Materialism, and the Challenge of an Emancipatory Posthumanism', *Globalizations*, 12 (2015): 134–48.
103   Coole and Frost, 'Introducing', 14; Schmidt, 'Empirical', 174.

your electrical cords"?'[104] Latour and his acolytes, however, make a great deal out of the presumption that the extension of agency to all objects under the heavens will contribute to a process of *politicisation* – at last, things will be allowed entry into the sphere of the political. But the effect is rather the opposite. How do the European border fences become better recognised as political entities if we say that they cut immigrant bodies on their own behalf? All the technomass permeated by fossil fuels and weighing down this planet with the heaviest burden would be *emptied* of its political substance by such a programme. Similarly, Latour fancies that he is opening up venues for engagement by denying that structure stands in the way – but as Benjamin Noys has noted in another biting critique, 'this inflation of "local" agency is bought at the cost of an inability to change or challenge any of the terms of the game.'[105] Agency banned from taking down structures is circumscribed, not empowered.

'Having known Latour personally for fifteen years', Graham Harman informs us as he takes on the mission of systematising and popularising his politics, 'I can safely describe him (*qua* voter, citizen, and reader of the news) as a politically benevolent French centrist with progressive tendencies', or as 'a liberally minded Hobbesian who adds inanimate entities to the political sphere'.[106] How the warming world is crying out for more benevolent French centrists, particularly of the Hobbesian slant. Latour has spent his career supplying ideological nourishment to the Western centre; indeed, his lifework can be read as one of the subtlest anti-Marxist constructions of the last half-century, albeit never fully suppressing tics of fear at the prospect of renewed revolutionary ferment.[107] Latour will not cease combatting the 'infatuation with emancipation politics' and impressing on the reader that the most we can

---

104 Lave, 'Reassembling', 218. The example and slogan are borrowed from Elaine Hartwick.

105 Noys, 'Discreet', 203. Cf. Noys, *Persistence*, 85–6.

106 Harman, *Bruno*, 5.

107 Noys, 'Discreet'; Noys, *Persistence*.

ever achieve are 'small extensions of practices'.[108] But what we need now are very great changes in practices.

There is, however, a more sinister side to Latour's politics that Harman does nothing to conceal: his Hobbesianism-plus-things. The moral of the baboon story is that the Leviathan of entrenched technologies saves us from chaos. Without it, humans would plunge into apelike anarchy, and so we must learn to appreciate the techno-Leviathan, treasure it, care for it as one would for a unifying father figure. Industrial technology is an index of progress towards stability.[109] 'It follows that our *primary* attitude towards institutions should be to build and extend them rather than critique or destroy them', and – given what Latour adds to Hobbes – this attitude should *primarily be directed at their material infrastructure*. Criticism of the networks 'misses the point', namely that 'any transcendence would threaten peace'.[110] In his account of Latour's affirmation of victorious technologies, Harman reuses another old case: the failure of a French public utility to convert the country's car fleet to electricity in the 1970s; the resounding triumph of Renault in beating back the challenge and reconfirming the supremacy of petroleum.[111] So that is an example of the successful technology serving as the glue that holds human communities together and deserving respect as a guarantor of peace. Little surprise that Latour ends up in the company of the Breakthrough Institute, the extreme fringe of technological optimism in the spectrum of green politics, which, among other fixes, touts natural gas as a path to sustainability.[112] Smashing the fossil infrastructure would presumably not be to his taste.

---

108   Latour, *Reassembling*, 52; Latour, *We*, 48.

109   See Strum and Latour, 'Redefining', 792–3; Latour, 'Technical', 47.

110   Harman, *Bruno*, 31, 17, 19. Emphasis in original.

111   Ibid., 27. For the original example and its use in the development of Hobbesianism-plus-things, see Callon and Latour, 'Unscrewing', particularly 287–93.

112   See Bruno Latour, 'Love Your Monsters: Why We Must Care for Our Technologies As We Do Our Children', *Breakthrough Institute*, thebreakthrough. org, Winter 2012.

Nature is real; nature and society form a unity of opposites; society is constructed; agency cannot be found in inanimate matter but may still appear among human collectives, which can potentially target the incumbent technology that embodies social power – these are some of the necessary premises for an activist theory. Rejecting hybridism and its two branches, then, is not a matter of staking out some bland third way or middle course. It is about recovering the theoretical basis for ecological militancy.

5

On the Perils of Property: Sketches for Tracking the Storm

HISTORICAL MATERIALISM AS ALTERNATIVE

Like the best of bibles, the tradition of historical materialism is rich enough to inspire a vast array of incompatible interpretations. If new materialism aims to unseat the 'old', constructionist thinkers such as Castree, Smith and Vogel profess varying degrees of fidelity to the Marxist project and buttress their argument with select quotations (the parts on Feuerbach, the cherry-tree, the coral islands). It is eminently possible to be Marxist and mistaken. Exegesis of the founding fathers is an unreliable fountain of theory: external evidence must adjudicate. Indeed, the incoherence in Marx's corpus as a whole is such that he turned from a clear-cut constructionism about nature in the Paris manuscripts to a full-fledged realism in the mature works – or so Andrew Feenberg argues in *The Philosophy of Praxis: Marx, Lukács and the Frankfurt School*. If the young Hegelian wished to see nature as the product of human labour and historical practice, he soon knew better.[1] The break occurred in *The German Ideology*, where ambivalences are still on view, while a fresh vantage point for historical materialism is being worked out:

---

1 Andrew Feenberg, *The Philosophy of Praxis: Marx, Lukács and the Frankfurt School* (London: Verso, 2014), e.g. 43–9, 121.

The first premise of all human history is, of course, the existence of living human individuals. Thus the first fact to be established is the physical organisation of these individuals and their consequent relation to the rest of nature. Of course, we cannot here go either into the actual physical nature of man, or into the natural conditions in which man finds himself – geological, oro-hydrographical, climatic and so on. All historical writing must set out from these natural bases and their modification in the course of history through the action of men.[2]

Humans find themselves within climatic conditions, which they subsequently modify through the course of history: a most promising schema for our purposes. Yet whatever happens, 'the priority of external nature remains unassailed'.[3]

Come the *Grundrisse* and there is not much ambiguity left. When the working subject encounters nature, 'this condition is not his product but something he finds to hand – presupposed to him as a natural being apart from him'.[4] This is the view historical materialism must commit to, because, as Feenberg accepts, it is the only defensible one.[5] The encounter is repeated anew in every generation. Any toddler casting an eye towards her closest adults must grapple with the friction, the gravity, the light and the darkness and the physicality of the objects surrounding her, and however perfectly she and her contemporaries subsequently learn to navigate, manipulate, refashion and seemingly subdue these and other

2 Karl Marx and Friedrich Engels, *The German Ideology* (New York: Prometheus, 1998), 37.

3 Ibid., 46.

4 Marx, *Grundrisse*, 488. Cf. e.g.: 'the chief objective condition of labour does not itself appear as a *product* of labour, but is already there as *nature*'. Ibid., 485. Emphases in original.

5 Feenberg, *Philosophy*, e.g. 123, 129, 136. Strangely, given this argument and the explicit rejection of Vogel's interpretation in *The Philosophy of Praxis*, Feenberg endorses *Thinking like a Mall* as 'the environmental philosophy for our time'. Vogel, *Thinking*, back cover.

aspects of nature, they cannot extricate themselves from the exterior materiality in which they once learned to walk and work. Some circumstances will never be of their making.

The first historical fact is the act of staying alive in those circumstances. A short list of primary needs – a minimum of caloric intake, bodily warmth, rest – must be satisfied, and unless the nourishment, the clothing and the sheltering are renewed on a daily basis, the body will disintegrate.[6] Hunger, thirst, shivering, fatigue are functions of material structures and processes independent of human will, but residing within the bodies of all members of the species: it is nature that formulates the most basic corporeal needs. The general form for meeting them and staying alive is, of course, labour. Labour is the praxis by which the physical organisations of humans remain intact. Labour regulates the *Stoffwechsel*, or metabolism, between body and external matter, which means that however inventive it becomes, whatever intelligence it applies to the building of drones or the implantation of chips, it can only work out laws and draw out latent processes from nature: 'If we subtract the total amount of useful labour', Marx says in a formulation of utmost importance,

a material substratum is always left. *This substratum is furnished by nature without human intervention.* When man engages in production, he can only proceed as nature does herself, i.e. he can only change the form of the materials. Furthermore, even in this work of modification he is constantly helped by natural forces. Labour is therefore not the only source of material wealth, i.e. of the use-value it produces. As William Petty says, labour is the father of material wealth, the earth is its mother.[7]

6   This draws on John Bellamy Foster and Paul Burkett, 'The Dialectic of Organic/ Inorganic Relations', *Organization and Environment* 13 (2000): 403–25; Joseph Fracchia, 'Beyond the Human-Nature Debate: Human Corporeal Organisation as the "First Fact" of Historical Materialism', *Historical Materialism* 13 (2005): 33–62.

7   Marx, *Capital I*, 133. Emphasis added. See further John Bellamy Foster, *Marx's Ecology: Materialism and Nature* (New York: Monthly Review Press, 2000);

Here the pieces fall into place: a realist, anti-purist definition of nature; a distinction between labour and earth; a bond that is unbreakable.

Now this focus on labour might indeed seem old-fashioned. New materialists would have us reorient our sensibilities to the materiality of *life as such* in all its aspects, none more central than any other.[8] But in a warming world, there is good reason to privilege labour as the pivot of material flows. The rise and rise of large-scale fossil fuel combustion has not occurred in the sphere of play, sex, sleep, leisure, philosophical contemplation or aesthetic appreciation but precisely, and evidently, in that of labour. But how is that possible, if labour is some sort of eternal mode of human existence, as fixed in place as the sun and the moon? It is so because labour is the site of the permanent *and* the dynamic, the given *and* the transient, in a dialectic outlined in what could be called the fragment on human ecology in the *Grundrisse*.[9]

All labour, Marx specifies, 'all production is appropriation of nature on the part of an individual within and through a specific form of society.' A human body cannot regulate her *Stoffwechsel* in solitude, any more than she could speak in a private tongue: she must do it as a communal being. Her relation to the rest of nature is therefore mediated through her relations to other humans. All labour is, in a basic and tautological sense, realised through property – some piece of nature is appropriated by the subject – but what *form* that property takes is nowhere carved in stone:

Paul Burkett, *Marx and Nature: A Red and Green Perspective* (London: Macmillan, 1999); John Bellamy Foster and Paul Burkett, *Marx and the Earth: An Anti-Critique* (Leiden: Brill, 2016); Alfred Schmidt, *The Concept of Nature in Marx* (London: Verso, 2009); Feenberg, *Philosophy*, 149; Ted Benton, 'Ecology, Socialism and the Mastery of Nature: A Reply to Reiner Grundmann', *New Left Review* I: 194 (1992): 55–74; Implantation of chips: Rory Cellan-Jones, 'Office puts chips under staff's skin', *BBC News*, 29 January 2015.

8   For a very pertinent critique of this inclination, see White et al., *Environments*, 140–1.

9   The core of this fragment spans Marx, *Grundrisse*, 485–98.

originally, humans hunted and fished and tilled the earth as members of families, clans or tribes, whose properties were collective in essence. Then irrupted the moment of history.

> It is not the *unity* of living and active humanity with the natural, inorganic conditions of their metabolic exchange with nature, and hence their appropriation of nature, which requires explanation or is the result of a historic process, but rather the *separation* between these inorganic conditions of human existence and this active existence, a separation which is completely posited only in the relation of wage labour and capital.[10]

Again and again, in *Grundrisse* as in *Capital*, Marx insists on a sharp line between nature and society: the creation of private property, the divorce between the direct producers and the means of production, the accumulation of capital are *not* acts or mechanisms of nature. 'All relations as posited by society, not as determined by nature.' Dependent on that binary for contrastive effect and concrete analysis, the Marxian theory of capital would unravel the instant it became blurred. So would any theory of how capital causes environmental degradation. 'Nature builds no machines, no locomotives, railways, electric telegraphs, self-acting mules', all those things that are 'no longer productive but destructive forces' – a particular form of society does.[11] Or, 'it is just as impossible to make the transition directly from labour to capital as it is to go from the different human races directly to the banker, *or from nature to the steam engine*.'[12]

Once history has taken off from the ground, it really is the relations that determine the trajectory of the metabolic exchange. What relations? Those of property, first and foremost, because they structure how humans labour, for what purposes, with what

---

10   Ibid., 87, 489.
11   Ibid., 276, 706; Marx and Engels, *German*, 60.
12   Marx, *Grundrisse*, 259. Emphasis added.

instruments and raw materials: social property relations form the central axis along which humans relate to the rest of nature *through* relations to one another.[13] Like any other species in the material world, this one is forever tied to nature, but the nature of the ties is never natural. If the body must be clothed, there is no end to the variety of tools, skills, fashions, family units, supply chains, management structures, other arrangements by which that need can be satisfied; condemned to live in and with and through nature, humans can do it in an almost infinite number of different ways.[14] That dialectic of utter inextricability and utter variability is the source of the current curse, as well as of any hypothetical future blessing.

In the English language, 'property' is one of those words ('power' and 'right' being other instances) where two distinct aspects have fused: property as possession and as quality. (The fusion has not happened in Swedish, which separates *egendom* from *egenskap*; even less so in Farsi, with its *maalekiat* and *vijegi*.) Hence we have to say that *property relations are emergent properties of societies.* The organisation of the *Stoffwechsel* through the systematic division of members of the species into direct producers and exploiters that must relate to each other is a property at the level of the whole, impossible to locate in any of the component bodies, imposing certain rules for their reproduction, compelling them to behave differently than they otherwise would. It cannot be understood in the language of physics or chemistry or biology, nor can it be deduced from simple aggregation of the modules. *It does not exist in nature.* Nothing in nature dictates whether a particular group of people have feudal or capitalist property relations, or slave-based or post-capitalist or any other conceivable variety – but these relations

---

13   This interpretation aligns itself, of course, with political Marxism and other currents emphasising the primacy of property relations over productive forces. On property as the central axis of human ecology, cf. Hailwood, *Alienation*, 155, 158, 172.

14   Cf. Ted Benton, 'Biology and Social Theory in the Environmental Debate', in Ted Benton and Michael Redclift (eds), *Social Theory and the Environment* (London: Routledge, 1994), 43–4; Soper, 'Disposing', 8.

do dictate how people under their dominion relate to extra-human nature. They exert causal powers in their own right. They set off downward causation.

Capitalist property relations, for instance, compel people to sell their wares on a market and maintain at least average productivity when manufacturing them, on the penalty of being outcompeted. They also institute a pattern of increase in material throughput.[15] When that happens, the causation reaches all the way down, deep into the layers of evolution from which the human species itself once emerged: Marx and Engels take the example of freshwater. Essential to fish, it

> is no longer a suitable medium of existence as soon as the river is made to serve industry, as soon as it is polluted by dyes and other waste products and navigated by steamboats, or as soon as its water is diverted into canals where simple drainage can deprive the fish of its medium of existence.[16]

Water itself – and there is no more basic thing – is no longer fit for fish, because industry, which sits at the top of the historical chain, has transformed it. The arrow of causation runs downwards. In accordance with a similar logic, but one that Marx and Engels could not have predicted, the biosphere itself might one day cease to be a suitable medium of existence, because its fossil substrata have been made to serve industry – from, as it happens, the time of the steamboats. That critical phrase 'made to serve industry' marks a historical event, a turning point in the annals of labour, when the everlasting condition of metabolism is pressed into a form that pushes all the wrong buttons: and there is nothing natural about *that*.

Nature did not suddenly alter itself in the nineteenth century, and so it must have been society that did, sending forth plumes of CO_2 through its antecedent. Nature is not reducible to humans,

---

15   This draws on the reading of political Marxism in Malm, *Fossil*, 279–92.
16   Marx and Engels, *German*, 66.

who are part of it; humans are not reducible to nature, which is part of them; it is precisely in the interstices of that unity-in-difference that something like global warming can develop. Any counter-measures will occupy the same precarious place of inception.

HOW HUMANS COULD HATCH CAPITAL

As inexact as it is to blame humankind rather than capital for the warming condition, it would be fantastical to think of any other species than *Homo sapiens sapiens* hatching a capitalist mode of production. Baboons could not do it, nor badgers or bats. So what exactly separates us from nonhuman animals? Posthumanists seize on the refutation of some old answers – notably the idea that we use tools while they do not – as a reason for throwing the question overboard, but that is premature. Given the ecological ramifications of capitalism in general and large-scale fossil fuel combustion in particular, it would presumably be of some interest to understand how our species but no other could do this to the earth (a question obviously not to be conflated with the view that humans are *much better* than animals). Now this is not the place for an exhaustive inquiry into the age-old puzzle, but we may at least surmise that it has something to do with the capacity for abstraction.

Animals possess intentionality in the rudimentary sense of having thoughts about things – Jacquette refers to his aquarium fish expecting to be fed in the morning; Marx observes that 'a horse has a head of its own' – and should therefore count as being endowed with minds, and hence also with an elemental form of agency (perhaps somewhere on Anderson's first level).[17] But humans appear to have a special ability to think about their own thoughts and, crucially, about the thoughts of others. They can distinguish between the propositions 'I believe that it is raining'

---

17 Jacquette, *Philosophy*, 158–60, 182–6 (cf. Frankfurt, 'Problem', 31); Marx, *Capital I*, 497. See further e.g. Hans-Johann Glock, 'Animal Agency', in O'Connor

and 'it is raining' and the equivalent thoughts of their conspecifics, adopt collective beliefs that may or may not be true, share symbols for taking perspectives on things, engage in 'meta-representation' and complex forms of collective intention and reach orders of abstraction dogs and dolphins only rarely, if ever, attain (no post-dolphinists among dolphins, etc.).[18] At least on Anderson's second and third levels, agency is only for them.

Some animals use tools. Most species do not, but the phenomenon is fairly widely distributed across taxa, from insects to primates. In September 2016, scientists added to the list the Hawaiian crow, adept at utilising sticks when extracting food from crevices in logs.[19] Fewer animals manufacture tools, but some do. None manufacture tools out of a range of different materials, such as when humans choose between wood and stone and hair and bone and metal and other substrata. None build composite tools, with several components functionally integrated – a knife with a handle, a blade, a binding material – and, perhaps most importantly, none produce tools *for the production of other tools*, such as when humans fashion a flake for carving a sling out of skin. These distinctions are based on the most recent research and so remain falsifiable, as one should expect from a scientific theory.[20]

Nor – so it seems – do animals transport their creations across vast distances and store them for later use, or manufacture tools out of stone. The choice to attack such a solid and recalcitrant material

and Sandis, *Companion*, 384–92. The radicalism of the views of Marx and Engels on the topic is brought out in Foster and Burkett, *Marx*, 44.

18   Michael Tomasello and Hannes Rakoczy, 'What Makes Human Cognition Unique? From Individual to Shared to Collective Intentionality', *Mind and Language* 18 (2003): 121–47; Derek C. Penn, Keith J. Holyoak and Daniel J. Povinelli, 'Darwin's Mistake: Explaining the Discontinuity between Human and Nonhuman Minds', *Behavioral and Brain Sciences* 31 (2008): 109–78.

19   Christian Rutz, Barbara C. Klump, Lisa Komarczyk et al., 'Discovery of Species-wide Tool Use in the Hawaiian Crow', *Nature* 537 (2016): 403–7.

20   Richard W. Byrne, 'The Manual Skills and Cognition that Lie Behind Hominid Tool Use', in Anne E. Russon and David R. Begun, *The Evolution of Thought: Evolutionary Origins of Great Ape Intelligence* (Cambridge: Cambridge

as stone manifests the ability to project a series of abstract images on matter – the characteristic intentions of an architect. Indeed, specialists in the field have offered the hypothesis that apes and humans relate to tools in rather different ways: the former tend to focus on their perceptually obvious physical affordances – this pole can be used to fish those termites – while the latter take their cues from *the goals for which the tools were designed* as displayed to them by other humans.[21] Our species has a 'tendency to naturally track social over physical information' when watching tools in the making or in use, asking for what they were intended and learning to imitate the process: 'achieving a specific behavioral goal, which is driven by social conformity'. Or, 'social relations promoting intense cooperation may be the integral aspect' of human tool-making, not compelling but *allowing* members of the species to visualise novel solutions, let their imagination run riot over the earth, attack even the most unyielding materials and transmit the innovations across generations.[22] If this hypothesis were to be confirmed, primatology – the field where Latour once sought to anchor actor-network theory – would lend itself to a very fundamental socialist realism.

University Press, 2004): 31–44; Kathleen R. Gibson, 'Tool Use, Language and Social Behavior in Relationship to Information Processing Capacities', in Kathleen R. Gibson and Tim Ingold (eds), *Tools, Language and Cognition in Human Evolution* (Cambridge: Cambridge University Press, 2008): 251–69; Peter C. Reynolds, 'The Complementation Theory of Language and Tool Use', in ibid., 407–28; Robert Aunger, 'What's Special About Human Technology?', *Cambridge Journal of Economics* 34 (2010): 115–23; Christophe Boesch, 'Ecology and Cognition of Tool Use in Chimpanzees', in Crickette M. Sanz, Josep Call and Christophe Boesch (eds), *Tool Use in Animals: Cognition and Ecology* (Cambridge: Cambridge University Press, 2013): 21–47; Gavin R. Hunt, Russell D. Gray and Alex H. Taylor, 'Why Is Tool Use Rare in Animals?', in ibid., 89–118.

21   April M. Ruiz and Laurie R. Santos, 'Understanding Difference in the Way Human and Non-Human Primates Represent Tools: The Role of Teleological-Intentional Information', in Sanz et al., *Tool*, 119–33; Matthew V. Caruana, Francesco d'Errico and Lucinda Backwell, 'Early Hominin Social Learning Strategies Underlying the Use and Production of Bone and Stone Tools', in ibid., 242–85.

22   Ruiz and Santons, 'Understanding', 130; Caruana et al., 'Early', 270.

Some animals, finally, approximate certain features of language. But only humans routinely utilise complicated linguistic codes; however hard scientists have tried, they have not managed to induce apes to master the abstract grammatical structures and the tens of thousands of words we command as a matter of course. Moreover, 'unlike the best animal examples of putatively referential signals, most of the words of human language are not associated with specific functions (e.g., warning cries, food announcements) but can be linked to *virtually any concept* that humans can entertain' – hence the open-ended character of human language, by which meaningful units can be conjoined in an infinity of different expressions.[23]

If we combine those levels of abstraction, we can begin to see how humans could develop the two prerequisites for capitalist property relations: means of production that can be monopolised by some; a universal equivalent that can be exchanged for anything.[24] Tools assembled out of diverse parts, distributed and stocked, produced for the production of other tools, amenable to rapid development; an empty symbol – money – that can stand in for any material object and be opposed to none – these are the two basic ingredients of the witches' brew we know as capital. Without the apparently unique human capacity for material and symbolic abstraction, that brew could not possibly have been set to boil.

Needless to say, capital does not thereby become the biologically inevitable destiny of *Homo sapiens sapiens*.[25] Rather, it should be seen as a process historically promoted by – in the last instance – group agents, who have exploited certain potentialities inherent in the species for their own contingent ends (think of landlords ramming through the commodification of land). What we have crudely outlined here are just some hints at an answer to the

---

23   Marc D. Hauser, Noam Chomsky and W. Tecumseh Fitch, 'The Faculty of Language: What Is It, Who Has It, and How Did It Evolve?', *Science* 298 (2002): 1576 (emphasis added). Cf. e.g. Penn et al., 'Darwin's', 121–2; Newton, *Nature*, 73.

24   On money, see Hornborg, *Global*, e.g. 39, 72.

25   Cf. ibid., 162; Hornborg, 'Artifacts', 11.

question of how humans could *possibly* generate something as formidable as capital, which no other animals can (thankfully – what would it look like?). Graced with unparalleled 'technolinguistic plasticity', radically '*under*-determined by nature', humans can arrange their metabolism with the rest of nature in almost any way they like, or at least with a historical richness and variety no other species comes close to – it is only that one type of relations has seized hold of them rather firmly (for which they perhaps, at some metaphysical level, have to carry responsibility).[26] But the very same potentialities that made capital possible are the only conceivable sources for its transcendence. Given the abstractness of their minds, humans can evidently come to believe that this is not the way to go about it.

ON THE PROLIFERATION OF COMBINATIONS

Every productive force, nay every human artefact can be seen as a combination of the social and the natural. Talk of 'hybrids' should be skipped, since the term has acquired the connotation of erasure of the hybridised categories; 'combination', in Marxist parlance, is rich with allusions to unevenness, movement, dynamic non-equilibrium, internal contradiction. It suggests that the combined elements persist and may well continue reacting upon one another.

Consider an Egyptian pyramid. Here slave labour, an ancient polytheistic belief system, the institution of the state have been combined with the durability of the stone material, gravity, friction, lower temperatures below ground and other facets of nature. Or, a vertical water-wheel combines the seigneurial privileges of feudal lords with the properties of water flowing down an incline. Even if the social component has long gone out of business, the extant artefact can be subject to such dissection in the interest of understanding it better; it can be performed all the way back to the earliest hunting tools and domesticated animals. Indeed, human

---

26 Newton, *Nature*, 80; Soper, 'Humanism', 366. Emphasis in original.

bodies themselves, emaciated by hard work or adorned with tattoos, are susceptible to the analysis: the possibility of torture and medicine and intoxication and all the rest is constituted by the nature of the body, on which the social can work in any number of different ways. The branded body of a slave might be the ultimate example of how property relations and corporeal nature can be combined.

In bringing forth a combination, human agents use some natural relations – or 'material substrata' – for their purposes. They must proceed from the knowledge of causal powers independent of their will, adapt to, ride on, mobilise them in their labour. A smartphone surfs on the nature of silicon, which it does nothing to constitute or alter; even the wildest Promethean schemes like terraforming distant planets could only be successful by relying on things unproduced.[27] This is an ineluctable axiom of human existence. But when the combinations materialise, some feature of the earth is changed: a field cleared, a fabric woven, a stream diverted, a rock blasted, a current of electricity dispatched. If the combinations proliferate, they leave marks – scars of the social, so to speak – that may well be indelible. In that sense, they effect a historicisation or *socialisation* of the biosphere, but that process does not cut one way only. It advances by integrating material substrata deeper into society, as a bed on which it now comes to rest, and in that sense, the proliferation of combinations affects a *naturalisation* of social life – in short, an escalating interpenetration of the poles.

Now, capitalist property relations usher in a development of productive forces of a magnitude and intensity unlike anything seen before, in a break as abrupt as the primordial oxygenation of the earth's atmosphere. Bruno Latour claims that 'whenever we discover a stable social relation, it is the introduction of some non-humans that accounts for this relative durability.'[28] But the

---

27 This draws on Ted Benton, 'Marxism and Natural Limits: An Ecological Critique and Reconstruction', *New Left Review* I: 178 (1989): 70–3; Benton, 'Ecology', 61–2, 66; Newton, *Nature*, 41–2; Soper, 'Disposing', 7–11; Hailwood, *Alienation*, 137–8.

28 Latour, 'Technology', 111.

Catholic Church or the nuclear family has not lasted for so long because they have invented such a profusion of novel artefacts to stand on. Not all relations are restlessly productive in mobilising non-human matter; because of the *perpetuum mobile* of the pursuit of profit, capitalist property relations exceed all others in this regard, and it is this that makes them both stable *and* more destabilising than any other known relations. Under their reign, an extreme socialisation of nature advances in tandem with a no less pervasive absorption of material substrata into the fabric of social life. This is no reason to feel calm or confident. It introduces all manner of fresh hazards. 'Naturalisation' here refers to a process more unsettling than solidifying: everything being connected to everything else, the natural substrata are plugged into a whole planet of social relations, and so their usage might kick off cascades of unintended consequences where least expected. As much as the combinations extend the sway of the social over the natural, it places the natural *under* and *inside* the social, smuggling in some spontaneously generated explosive devices.

In the case of the fossil economy, humans had laboured for thousands of years with the currents of the water and the wind, adjusting to their comings and goings, making the most of their distributions and fluctuations. Fossil energy changed all that, most dramatically when mobilised to propel machines and vehicles.[29] A qualitatively novel set of combinations arose, and its functionality rested on a range of natural relations that had to be taken as given: the geographic positions of the deposits underground, their fixed supply (being the legacy of past photosynthesis), the presence of oxygen in the atmosphere, the power of combustion to release potential energy, and so on. That was when the storm was set brewing. For as long as they had existed, humans had lived as though the climate of the earth was utterly beyond their reach, the realm of gods or, later in history, anonymous forces and causal powers too

29 See Malm, *Fossil*. Of course, pre-fossil energy sources also included e.g. wood and animals.

vast in scope, too inert and gradual to be disturbed by the doings of humans. But the productive forces of the fossil economy turned out to be able to hot-wire the climate.

Constructionists with an urban bias sometimes ask a rhetorical question: if you look out of your window and take in the world around you, where can you find nature?[30] But not only is Simon Hailwood correct in responding that 'there is no place in which nonhuman nature has been eliminated entirely'; the moments of shock and surprise global warming brings into the hearts of affluence – say, Californian suburbanites fleeing a firestorm – are reminders, if only ever so temporary, of how even the most artificial enclaves sit on top of it.[31] Their fortunes have been built through capitalist property relations that have internalised *more* of nature, more thoroughly, more destructively than any prior variants. Not only does the realm not end with the combinations: it streams into the cracks of society, ticking with its own laws and pulses – and climate change as such might not be the end of this part of the story.

Until very recently, it could be taken for granted that 'the incidence of radiant energy from the sun is absolutely non-manipulable.'[32] Who would have thought that humans could govern the amount of incoming sunlight? And yet it is now clear that late capitalism possesses a set of productive forces that can, at the push of some buttons, initiate 'solar radiation management', the form of geoengineering that seems to be mostly in the cards. At a first glance, that looks like the final socialisation of the natural, the ultimate subsumption of the biosphere, the absolute end of nature – but all indications are that it would rather push the contradictions towards some new bursting point. Switching to reliance on other substrata – most obviously, particles with the ability to block rays of sunlight – it would also link up with a host of other natural relations, extending

30   E.g. Wapner, *Living*, 110.
31   Hailwood, *Alienation*, 184.
32   Benton, 'Marxism', 68.

the surface of the social across even greater unknown fields (current research has identified quite a few risks: collapsing monsoons, generally declining precipitation, dislocated weather systems, spiking ozone depletion, lethal air pollution, disruptions to photosynthesis, the frying of the planet if particle injections cease, and more).[33] Solar radiation management would in no way eliminate nature, only raise the stakes in a society that seeks to overmaster it. And onwards the history of capital goes, from one combination to the next, the perils mounting along the curve and, with Benjamin, the debris growing 'towards the sky. What we call progress is *this* storm.'[34]

Similar sequences of combinations could conceivably be tracked for a number of other ecological pressure points; various aspects of the food crisis and bioengineering spring to mind. Related paradoxes would then be expected there. In his 1962 classic *The Concept of Nature in Marx*, Alfred Schmidt repeatedly stresses the inescapability of nature: anything but a 'vanishing appearance' that dissolves in social fluid, it 'retains its genetic priority over men and their consciousness'.[35] No matter what productive forces are conjured up, even at the end of capitalist history nature will not disappear. Rather, it 'triumphs over all human intervention'; the more deeply

---

33 For one prudent analysis, focusing on the dislocation of weather systems, see Mike Hulme, *Can Science Fix Climate Change? A Case Against Climate Engineering* (Cambridge: Polity, 2014). Most remarkably, Ted Benton anticipated the current discussion on geoengineering in the second of his seminal *New Left Review* articles, when he argued that incidence of solar radiation might be manipulable after all – but due to the 'immense complexity of the interacting forces', such attempts at mastery would likely turn into its opposite. Benton, 'Ecology', 65.

34 Walter Benjamin, *Selected Writings, Volume 4, 1938–1940* (Cambridge, MA: Harvard University Press, 2006), 392.

35 Alfred Schmidt, *The Concept of Nature in Marx* (London: Verso, 2009), 29. See further e.g. 26–7, 63–4, 69, 95–8, 137–140. Schmidt's work, however, reproduces the inconsistencies of constructionism *and* realism in Marx's corpus to a higher level. For instances of the former, see e.g. 35, 46, 50, 55, 60, 71, 86, 119, 154–8. For a close and illuminating reading of Schmidt and his ambiguities, see Foster and Clark, 'Marx's'.

the forces cut into it, the more nature asserts itself at ever higher stages and 'congeals into an abstract in-itself external to men': the paradox of historicised nature anticipated.[36]

This would be a *dialectical* analysis of combinations. It can extend beyond productive forces, other artefacts and human bodies to historical conjunctures, phases of capitalist growth, biophysical processes unleashed by them and almost any other entity or development, on a macro or a micro scale, that mixes the two elements. Most importantly, when applied to the process of climate change, such an analysis can articulate the real tensions, be sensitive to deadly embraces and downward spirals, maintain that the natural and the social are locked in 'a dialectic whose boundaries are to be determined, and which does not suspend the real difference'.[37] Why determine the boundaries? To identify the points for strategic intervention: in our present conjuncture, this is what we can change, in relation to what must be taken as given.

MAKING HISTORY WITH NATURE AS BODY

Some anthropologists point to cultures where no boundaries are drawn between the social and the natural, where the sun and the mountains are attributed full intentionality and stones have souls; and, granted, such animist ontologies have been prevalent in human history. But that fact in itself hardly ratifies them. Given the fabulous diversity of all the cultures that are not one's own, a willingness to embrace their beliefs leads down the slope where everything and nothing is true and false at the same time. Moreover, it just might be the case that the modern distinction between society and nature registers a real disjuncture and imbalance, introduced by capital and now a fact of life wherever its power extends – across

---

36   Schmidt, *Concept*, 89, 82. Cf. Raymond Williams, *Culture and Materialism* (London: Verso, 2005), 106–13.

37   Marx, *Grundrisse*, 109. Marx is here talking about the dialectic of the productive forces and the relations of production.

all cultures. The warming condition is as universal as any can be, no matter how parochial its origins. Under the heavy skies, it is, in principle, reasonable and imperative for *everyone* (perhaps for committed animists more than most) to reflect on how the two poles have become so dysfunctionally integrated. This climate calls for concrete analysis of the concrete conjuncture, where 'the concrete is concrete because it is the concentration of many determinations, hence unity of the diverse'.[38]

The purpose of such analysis, then, should be to feed into resistance or, preferably, revolutionary ecological practice. Here one can do neither without the subject or the object. Humans and humans alone might still make ecological history, but they cannot do so as they please; not under self-selected circumstances, but under circumstances already existing, given and transmitted from the past. The limits imposed by the natural relations form the parameters for action, and revolutionary ecological practice then aims to take control over the social relations, break them down and replace them with others so as to remove the dangers of destabilisation. Marx can be read as recommending as much: for the Communist 'man' of *Grundrisse*, the goal is 'the grasping of his own history as a *process*, and the recognition of nature (equally present as the practical power over nature) as his body'.[39] Something similar is perhaps afoot in the climate movement.

Consider, for instance, 350.org. With a brand name referring to the atmospheric concentration of CO_2 identified by James Hansen and other climate scientists as a safe level for humanity, and under the spiritual leadership of Bill McKibben, this organisation has been instrumental to the recent upswing in climate activism as visible in the divestment campaigns, the People's Climate March, the (apparently short-lived) victory over the Keystone XL pipeline, the global 'Break Free' weeks of direct action against fossil fuels in

---

38 Ibid., 101. Cf. Collier, *Critical*, 117, 255–7.
39 Marx, *Grundrisse*, 542. Emphasis in original.

2016, and onwards. Recognising nature as the body, determined to grasp history as a process, 350.org resolutely locates the political in society and, more particularly, through its targeting of the fossil fuel industry, in the economy. It appears to have been a fairly effective recipe for de-naturalising and politicising climate change. Even the circuits of financial capital, so far removed from the remit of politics in our time, have been called into question: why do some people profit from the extraction of fossil fuels? How can these profits be allowed to continue soaring? Should not more money be blocked from flowing under the ground – and towards the end of that road: should not all investment in energy be placed under public control, so that fossil fuels are ejected from the economy *in toto*?

It is the pretension of the dialectical theory we have sketched here that it is more in line with the assumptions implicit in the actual praxis of the climate movement – whether it tears apart fences or petitions municipalities – than the alternatives reviewed above. That movement can obviously grow without theory. But, at the very least, it should be somewhat revealing that even in the Western capitalist heartlands, climate activists have so far been indifferent to constructionism, Latourianism, new materialism, posthumanism and the rest of it, while continuing to draw inspiration from Marxism and anarchism and their various converging and diverging currents in slogans, banners, aesthetics, thinking and reading.[40] The fact that the movement is still nowhere approaching the critical mass required for taking down the fossil economy does not diminish its status as benchmark for theoretical utility. It remains weak and scattered – which may have something to do with the fact that most other social movements

---

40   For a good overview of the movement, see Matthias Dietz and Heiko Garrelts (eds), *Routledge Handbook of the Climate Change Movement* (London: Routledge, 2014). The one book that could lay claim to being the bible of the movement, Klein's *This Changes Everything*, draws extensively on ecological Marxism, berates Latour for his techno-optimism (278–9) and does not care to mention the key new materialist or constructionist thinkers.

are too, including, centrally, the organised working class – but these are but so many reasons to join and assist it in every way possible. For if anything is ever going to turn in a better direction, a lot of action will be needed.

6

On the Use of Opposites:
In Praise of Polarisation

Since the turn of the millennium, one Marxist line of inquiry into environmental problems has outshone all others in creativity and productivity: the theory of the metabolic rift. Developed by John Bellamy Foster and his colleagues Richard York and Brett Clark, with crucial contributions from Paul Burkett and Marina Fischer-Kowalski and many others, it can be summed up in the following, highly condensed sequence. Nature consists of biophysical processes and cycles. So does society: human bodies must engage in metabolic exchanges with nonhuman nature. That need not be particularly harmful to any of the parties. Over the course of history, however, the relations through which humans have organized their *Stoffwechsel* might be fractured and forcibly rearranged, so that they not only harm the people disadvantaged by this change, but also, at the very same time, disturb the processes and cycles of nature. A *metabolic rift* has opened up.

Distilled through Foster's pioneering exegesis, the theory makes inventive use of Marx's comments in the third volume of *Capital* on how capitalist property relations 'provoke an irreparable rift in the interdependent process of social metabolism, a metabolism prescribed by the natural laws of life itself'; operationalised in a variety of ways, it has elucidated everything from the imbalances in the global nitrogen cycle to climate change.[1] It is a method for tracking disruptive combinations of the natural and the social. In a recent tour de force of metabolic rift analysis, *The Tragedy of the Commodity: Oceans, Fisheries, and Aquaculture*, Stefano B. Longo, Rebecca Clausen and Brett Clark start from the self-evident yet so often lost premise that 'ecological concerns are not problems derived internally, originating from ecosystems themselves, but are produced externally, by social drivers. For example, the oceans are not polluting themselves; humans are doing it.' That tragedy is possible, however, only because 'human society exists *within* the earthly metabolism'.[2] In the case of fishing – a primordial form of *Stoffwechsel* – a dramatic shift occurred in the middle of the nineteenth century, when companies armed with steamboats could catch hauls at new orders of magnitude; since then, but particularly since the post-war period, global fish stocks have come under lethal pressure. Rifts in the reproductive cycles of fish have opened up everywhere, from the bluefin tuna of the Mediterranean to the salmon of the Pacific Northwest – a result of how the elements of company and commodity mix with water. If this sounds like a

---

1 Karl Marx, *Capital: Volume III* (London: Penguin, 1991), 949. The two key works in which the theory is formulated and applied are Foster, *Marx's*; John Bellamy Foster, Brett Clark and Richard York, *The Ecological Rift: Capitalism's War on the Earth* (New York: Monthly Review Press, 2010). Some of the most noteworthy articles on climate change and fossil energy emerging from the metabolic rift school are Brett Clark and Richard York, 'Carbon Metabolism: Global Capitalism, Climate Change, and the Biospheric Rift', *Theory and Society* 34 (2005): 391–428; Richard York, 'Do Alternative Energy Sources Displace Fossil Fuels?', *Nature Climate Change* 2 (2012): 441–3; Richard York, 'Asymmetric Effects of Economic Growth and Decline on CO_2 Emissions', *Nature Climate Change* 2 (2012): 762–4; Brett Clark, Andrew K. Jorgenson and Daniel Auerbach, 'Up in Smoke: The Human Ecology and Political Economy of Coal Consumption', *Organization and Environment* 25 (2012): 452–69; Kelly Austin and Brett Clark, 'Tearing Down Mountains: Using Spatial and Metabolic Analysis to Investigate the Socio-Ecological Contradictions of Coal Extraction in Appalachia', *Critical Sociology* 38 (2012): 437–57.

2 Stefano B. Longo, Rebecca Clausen and Brett Clark, *The Tragedy of the Commodity: Oceans, Fisheries, and Aquaculture* (New Brunswick: Rutgers University Press, 2015), x, 23. Emphasis added.

theory and a method that abide by all the precepts suggested above, it is because any twenty-first-century ecological Marxism necessarily stands on their shoulders.

Of late, however, the metabolic rift school has come under sustained fire from Jason W. Moore. In a series of essays culminating in *Capitalism and the Web of Life*, he seeks to demonstrate that Foster and colleagues repeat the original sin of Cartesian dualism. The proof of their guilt lies, first of all, in their choice of conjunctions: they speak of nature *and* society, of interaction *between* the spheres, of capital as *having* an ecological regime. Moore wants the 'and' replaced with an 'in'. It should be labour-*in*-nature, capital-*in*-nature, and so on – never *and*, the false bridge that betrays a worldview of nature/society as two hemispheres divided by a chasm. Likewise, one must not talk of metabolism *between* any two things, but always have to say *through* – and most essential of all: capitalism does not *have* an ecological regime, it *is* an ecological regime. By developing these series of conjunction swaps, in effusions of supposedly non-Cartesian language games of hyphenation and formulae, Moore proposes his 'world-ecology' as a superior dialectical framework, to great acclaim from parts of the academic radical ecology community.[3]

What the analytical advantages consist of, beyond a new terminology, is initially unclear. So, for instance, Moore faults Foster and colleagues for using the word 'interaction' to describe the relation between nature and society, since this wrongly presupposes that the two can be separated to begin with – for two things to interact, they must first be apart – and proposes that we should instead ask how

---

3   See particularly Jason W. Moore, 'Transcending the Metabolic Rift: A Theory of Crisis in the Capitalist World-Ecology', *The Journal of Peasant Studies* 38 (2011): 1–46; 'Toward a Singular Metabolism: Epistemic Rifts and Environment-Making in the Capitalist World-Ecology', *New Geographies* 6 (2014): 10–19; *Capitalism in the Web of Life* (London: Verso, 2015). The most systematic picking apart of Moore so far is Kamran Nayeri, '"Capitalism in the Web of Life" – A Critique', *Climate and Capitalism*, climateandcapitalism.com, 19 July 2016.

the two '*fit together*'.[4] But exactly the same critique can of course be levelled against that choice of words. For two pieces to fit together, they must first be two different pieces. Moore himself seems forced to employ the foul conjunction in phrases such as 'human *and* extra-human nature', 'the soil *and* the worker', perhaps because a language of permanent *in*-hyphenation would be unreadable.[5] It certainly would not solve any real conceptual problems.

Why all this phraseology? It seems, at a closer look, that Moore has fundamentally misunderstood the requirements for transcending the Cartesian legacy. In a sentence of the kind repeated ad nauseam in *Capitalism*, he declares: 'In place of a Cartesian optic – the "exploitation of labor *and* nature" [words from Foster et al.] – I would begin with two forms of labor-*in*-nature.'[6] But there is nothing Cartesian about saying 'labour and nature'. Foster et al. would be Cartesian if they thought that labour and nature consisted of different substances or inhabited separate spheres, so that the one could be analysed without reference to the other – a very common perception in the history of capitalist modernity *but precisely the opposite of what the metabolic rift school teaches*. As Foster himself retorts, 'there is no contradiction in seeing society as both separate from and irreducible to the Earth system as a whole, and simultaneously as a fundamental part of it. To call that approach "dualist"' – in the Cartesian sense – 'is comparable to denying that your heart is both an integral part of your body and a distinct organ with unique features and functions.'[7] What Moore does here is simply to succumb to the temptation of substance and property monism.

---

4   Moore, *Capitalism*, 47. Emphasis in original.

5   Ibid., e.g. 228, 291, 293.

6   Ibid., 230.

7   John Bellamy Foster and Ian Angus, 'In Defense of Ecological Marxism: John Bellamy Foster Responds to a Critic', *Climate and Capitalism*, climateandcapitalism.com, 6 June 2016. See further John Bellamy Foster, 'Marxism in the Anthropocene: Dialectical Rifts on the Left', *International Critical Thought* 6 (2016): 393–421.

Beneath the arid semantic quibble, then, there is substantial disagreement on whether nature and society should at all be distinguished from one another. It is here that one finds the core of Moore's theoretical project: an unbridled hybridism in Marxist garb. He has taken on the task of importing 'the philosophical victory' of such thinkers as Neil Smith and Bruno Latour into the theory of capitalist development, setting out from a postulate that should by now be familiar: 'The old language – Nature/Society – has become obsolete. Reality has overwhelmed the binary's capacity to help us track the real changes unfolding, accelerating, amplifying before our eyes.'[8] The aim of 'world-ecology' is to act as a solvent on all related distinctions. 'Put in these terms, the apparent solidity of town and country, bourgeois and proletarian, and above all Society and Nature, begins to melt.'[9] Moore has found a way to abolish even the opposition between the classes – in language.

Several versions of hybridism are here banded together: much influenced by the production of nature theory, Moore opposes references to 'a nature that operates independently of humanity', and to external limits, and to biophysical flows as having 'ontological priority' over social relations, leading him right back into the blind alley: 'We can dispense with the notion that something like climate change can be analyzed in its quasi-independent social and natural dimensions.' If so, we can dispense with the notion of analysing it at all. Skidding in the other direction, Moore adopts the terminology of the material turn, defines agency as a *relational property* of specific bundles of human and extra-human nature', dresses up water and oil as 'real historical actors', attributes agency to climate as such, says that capitalism is 'co-produced by manifold species' and, logically, contends that coal formations were *'subjects* of historical change' in England. They were not, of course, in any

---

8 Moore, 'Toward', 14; Moore, *Capitalism*, 5. White et al. share Moore's ambition of developing a hybridist eco-Marxism and present a very similar critique of Foster et al. See White et al., *Environments*, e.g. 104, 152.

9 Moore, 'Toward', 15.

meaningful sense of the word, subjects in what happened in England or anywhere else, and the picture does not become a speck clearer by labelling coal an 'actant' possessing 'agency'. The singular achievement of Moore turns out to be a double collapse, such as in the following précis of his view: 'Capitalism makes nature. Nature makes capitalism.'[10] Neither of those propositions is true. Capitalism emphatically does not make nature; nature most definitely does not make capitalism. It is the utter disharmony between the two that needs to be accounted for, and it is that which the theory of the metabolic rift has so consistently foregrounded.

The double collapse partly flows from a view of dialectics as a method not so much for articulating antagonism as for achieving *holism*. It would be edifying here to keep in mind the admonition of Levins and Lewontin: 'There is a one-sidedness in the holism that stresses the connectedness of the world but ignores the relative autonomy of parts.'[11] Among the effects of that one-sidedness is that the parts disappear from view. Moore casts doubt on the belief 'that such a thing as "society" exists' and suggests that 'entropy is reversible and cyclical', when entropy is defined by the second law of thermodynamics precisely as never being that.[12] With no laws of society and no laws of nature – what is there left to study?

On the other hand, there *are*, symptomatically, passages where Moore seems to accept the need for a binary of the social and the natural. When it comes down to saying something concrete about what capitalism actually does to (or in) the web of life, the explanatory model of historical materialism slips through cracks in the jargon. Now Moore argues that certain societies in the long sixteenth century developed the law of value as a new set of relations between people, which induced a complete shift in how these people related to non-human nature: for the first time in human

---

10 Moore, *Capitalism*, 6, 180, 85, 36–8, 4, 179, 196, 8. Emphases in original.

11 Richard Lewontin and Richard Levins, *Biology under the Influence: Dialectical Essays on Ecology, Agriculture and Health* (New York: Monthly Review Press, 2007), 107.

12 Moore, 'Transcending', 8; Moore, *Capitalism*, 97 (cf. 84).

history, 'the law gives priority to labor productivity, and mobilizes uncapitalized natures without regard for their reproduction.' Further, 'a civilization premised on money and labor-time called forth a very different kind of time', based on which capital sought to remake material reality 'in its own image, and according to its own rhythms': again, an impulse at changing nature emanating from property relations. Moore is then able to identify a clash 'between the finite character of the biosphere and the infinite character of capital's demands'. Or: 'Nature is finite. Capital is premised on the infinite' – hence ecological crisis.[13] And there we have the whole package again: a duality, a separation and conjunction, an attribution of inherent and antithetical properties, an intelligible argument about why capital must go berserk in nature.

Hybridism resists any juxtaposition between relations and laws of motion internal to *capitalist* society, on the one hand, and relations and laws of motion internal to *nature* on the other. But when Marxists write about the environment, they are pulled to the magnetic opposition between those poles. Take for instance the greatest classic of Marxist ecological feminism, *The Death of Nature: Women, Ecology and the Scientific Revolution* (which, contrary to appearances, contains no end-of-nature thesis). In this groundbreaking study from 1980, Carolyn Merchant traces the historical shift from a conception of nature as a mother to be revered and respected, an organic living being, sometimes benevolent and sometimes wrathful, to one of nature as a dead, inert object to be manipulated and controlled with maximum efficiency. The shift pivoted on a transition in social property relations in Europe, England in particular: starting in the fourteenth century, the English ruling class moved towards capitalist arrangements in agriculture, drained the fens, enclosed the fields, cut down the forests, removed the taboos on mining and pitted the peasant as worker against the landlord as capitalist.[14] Some priceless things were broken in the process.

---

13   Moore, *Capitalism*, 60, 234–5, 112, 87.
14   Carolyn Merchant, *The Death of Nature: Women, Ecology and the Scientific*

The Death of Nature departs from the postulate that 'natural and cultural subsystems' develop 'in dynamic interaction.' Moore would presumably disapprove of this wording, but it allows Merchant to identify a contradiction appearing at a specific moment in time: 'Particularly important is the question of how environmental quality was affected by the transition from peasant control of natural resources for the purpose of subsistence to capitalist control for the purpose of profit.' The latter type of property relations fathered a force that conflicted with environmental quality. 'Built into the emerging capitalist market economy was *an inexorably accelerating force of expansion and accumulation*, achieved, over the long term, *at the expense of the environment*' – in the fens, for instance, the hitherto abundant wildlife collapsed as the pumps and windmills took over. It was this epochal transition that called forth the abandonment of the old conception of nature, which suited the novel relations and their inbuilt expansionary force poorly; instead, more and more people came to regard nature as a depot of resources to be owned and mastered. Since nature remained widely associated with women, this – the most well-known aspect of Merchant's argument – translated into more aggressive subordination of the female body under the brute mechanisms of male power. At the end of her book, she turns to the environmental woes of the present and offers a strategic suggestion that has since become the stock of the trade of ecological Marxism: we need 'a revolution in economic priorities.'[15]

Or, to take but one other example: in an excellent, long overdue Marxist intervention into the debate over the biodiversity crisis, *Extinction: A Radical History*, Ashley Dawson observes that 'capital must expand at an ever-increasing rate or go into crisis'. As it does so, 'it commodifies more and more of the planet, stripping the world of its diversity and fecundity', puncturing holes in the web

---

Revolution (San Francisco: HarperCollins, 1980), 43–68. Her superb account owes much to Robert Brenner.

15 Ibid., 43, 51, 295. Emphasis added.

of life with incalculable consequences: 'biologists are only just beginning to understand the cascading, ecosystem-wide impact of the destruction of the megafauna.'[16] One emergent property comes into conflict with a whole planet of other emergent properties. This is the necessary and fundamental *form* of a Marxist account of ecological crisis, which does not exclude other drivers but centres on a feature unique for capitalist relations: the compulsion for perpetually expanding absorption of biophysical resources. Such a property cannot be found in nature. Any creature that had it would be fantastically maladaptive and quickly go extinct; capital has been able to maintain it into the twenty-first century only by establishing complete dominion over tellurian nature. But it cannot go on forever.

The ongoing sixth mass extinction looks particularly amenable to the sort of analysis outlined here. Thus we have strong evidence that the long postponement of the crackdown on the bustling London ivory market promised by the Tories has provided continuous incentive to criminal syndicates to slaughter African elephants and smuggle their tusks into Britain, but we have no signs of the elephants jumping off cliffs or otherwise committing mass suicide.[17] The biodiversity being torn apart is neither a human creation nor a source of agency in this disaster. On that environmental issue as well as on any other, it is possible to say something of ecological Marxist import only by practising property dualism.

THE VALUE OF BINARIES

For one genus of scholars, however, there can still be no higher pitch of ecstasy than the dissolution of binaries. The greatest pleasure and joy come the moment they can say: 'those two categories

---

16   Ashley Dawson, *Extinction: A Radical History* (New York: O/R Books, 2016), 12–13, 16, 24. See further e.g. 42–3, 53.

17   Jamie Doward, 'Tories' Failure to Halt Ivory Trade "Risks Extinction of Elephants"', *Guardian*, 27 August 2016.

you *thought* were two are one – I hereby proclaim them united!' This is the intellectual concupiscence firing up Jason W. Moore and many of the other theorists we have come across here – Latour perhaps most of all, Haraway as well, while Braidotti goes after the final binary: events like Hurricane Katrina and Australian bushfires 'simply blur the distinction between life and death'.[18] They do no such thing, of course. Here we find renewed calls to 'elude the politics of polarity' and self-declared 'antipathy towards oppositional ways of thinking'.[19] Hybridism, then, can also be seen as a strident current of *dissolutionism.*

This has consequences for the analytical equipment. 'Analysis', the Merriam-Webster dictionary informs us, is 'a careful study of something to learn about its parts, what they do, and how they are related to each other'; it means 'separation of a whole into its component parts', 'the identification or separation of ingredients of a substance', and so on.[20] Analysis demands razor blades. But the effect of the dissolutionist crusade is that the blades are blunted and scrapped one after the other. Consider some of the binaries listed by Haraway as ripe for dissolution: self/other, mirror/eye, mind/body, reality/appearance, right/wrong, truth/illusion, base/superstructure, slave/master, rich/poor.[21] With all of them and more gone, what rigorous analysis can still be performed? Because they work in the department of writing about things, however, the dissolutionists have no choice but to erect *other* binaries – such as, in Moore's case, that of 'Cartesian dualism' versus 'world-ecology', or 'the Moderns' versus everyone else in Latour's – in which all evil is ranged on one side no less sweepingly (often rather more) than in the models they choose to attack.[22] Hybridist dissolutionism, then, is another

---

18   Braidotti, *Posthuman*, 112. See further e.g. 115, 134.

19   Desblache (quoting Homi Bhabha), 'Hybridity', 246; Coole and Frost, 'Introducing', 8.

20   Merriam-Webster, merriam-webster.com, consulted 25 September 2016.

21   Haraway, *Manifestly*, 11, 36, 57, 59, 96. One wonders if any other guild has engaged in so much vandalism against its own tools as academics.

22   This draws on Terry Eagleton, *The Illusions of Postmodernism* (Oxford:

performative contradiction, one that seeks to ruin as much analytical equipment as possible while charging with lowered lances.

This also has consequences for the prose. As Terry Eagleton reminds us, 'any term which tried to cover everything would end up meaning nothing in particular, since signs work by virtue of their differences.'[23] As they wage war on distinctions, the dissolutionists not infrequently end up with a prose evacuated of meaning, a sludge dumped on the poor reader, who has to be on permanent watch for something to hold onto. Latour is the master of the genre.[24] A book like *The Politics of Nature* is an orgy in the mud. The average new materialist essay runs on sentences like this:

> Choratic reading, by contrast, begins from the assertion that acts of literature – very much including scholarly readings – are performed in material composition with the affordances of their media, the sensorium of their audiences, and the deformations of dissemination as they transduce across and are deformed by the irruptions of the choratic plane.[25]

It is not that such chunks of text are difficult; rather, they seem devoid of propositional content almost on purpose, leading the non-initiated to ask whether these scholars really want to say something or are simply fooling around. In a refreshing outburst, anthropologist Ellen Hertz finds it

> hard to avoid the conclusion that there is an awful lot of fluff floating around in the anthropological 'conversation' today, accompanied by preposterous amounts of posturing. Furthermore, it is impossible not to acknowledge the emperor's-new-clothes syndrome that so effortlessly fuels this obscurantism: who wants to admit in public that she just doesn't understand?

Blackwell, 1996), 25–6. A recent iteration of Bruno Latour has decided to cut up the world into 15 distinct 'modes of existence': see Latour, *Inquiry*.

23   Eagleton, *Illusions*, 103.

24   For two examples, see notes 20 on p. 124 and 90 on p. 148.

25   Sheldon, 'Form', 216.

The same goes for much political ecology and contemporary theory in general.[26] The fluff rarely resonates with either masses or vanguard. The case against academic obscurantism has had to be made frequently over the past three or four decades, and unfortunately the need has not passed away; we can venture the prediction that the more nature and society are smudged into one grey stain, it will grow.

Finally, dissolutionism has political consequences. It tends, for a start, to locate the roots of social and environmental ills in the sphere of conceptions. Haraway believes that the breakdown of distinctions 'cracks the matrices of domination', Plumwood that anti-dualist theory can 'shake the conceptual structures of oppression to their foundations'.[27] Moore has the same inclination. He thinks that the binary of nature/society is at the root of all ills, in itself 'fundamental to the rise of capitalism'.[28] But power does not stem from notional dichotomies; it is of a far more earthly nature, the tracing and dislodging of which might require both hammers and sickles. Scholars hypnotised by the rigidities of language and the prospects of fluidifying them are, as Eagleton observes, involved in 'a fantastic displacement of a genuine political deadlock'; the current desire to dissolve nature and society is a splendid illustration of his point.[29] Equally sublimating is the belief that there is something violent and oppressive about the very practice of distinguishing between things.[30] Our sordid realities point in a rather different direction.

---

26   Ellen Hertz, 'Pimp My Fluff: *A Thousand Plateaus* and Other Theoretical Extravaganzas', *Anthropological Theory* 16 (2016): 147.

27   Haraway, *Manifestly*, 53; Plumwood, *Feminism*, 1. Cf. the critique of such beliefs in Newton, *Nature*, 35–7; Pellizzoni, 'Catching', 4.

28   Jason W. Moore, 'The Rise of Cheap Nature', in Jason W. Moore, *Anthropocene or Capitalocene? Nature, History, and the Crisis of Capitalism* (Oakland: PM Press, 2016), 87.

29   Eagleton, *Illusions*, 6.

30   Some formulations of Moore seem to indicate that any type of distinction is bourgeois: 'It is often difficult to discern the analytical difference between the use-/exchange-value binary of metabolic rift analysis and the utility/exchange binary

When eight individuals – as of 2017; the number seems to shrink as fast as CO_2 concentrations rise – possess as much wealth as half of humanity, one cannot afford *not* to draw lines of separation.[31]

Just how thoroughly the phenomenon of CO_2 emissions is bound up with such polarity was highlighted by two reports released for COP 21. One tenth of the human species accounts for half of all present emissions from consumption, half of the species for one tenth. The richest 1 percent have a carbon footprint some 175 times that of the poorest 10 percent; the emissions of the richest 1 percent of Americans, Luxembourgians and Saudis are two thousand times larger than those of the poorest Hondurans, Mozambicans or Rwandans. Shares of the CO_2 accumulated since 1820 are similarly skewed.[32] In a world like this, where the contradictions between the apex of wealth and the conditions supporting human existence are reaching catastrophic intensity, the instinct of critical scholars should not be to dissolve binaries, but to strive towards *more radical polarisation* so as to clarify the stakes and gather the forces. If the politics of polarity and oppositional ways of thinking are avoided, there will be peace on our way into the abyss. Political warfare against an ever more pestiferous ruling class demands manuals brimful with binaries.

In the latest instalment of Dipesh Chakrabarty's campaign for disconnecting climate change from issues of justice – this one dedicated to Bruno Latour – we are treated to a different argument. Because global warming has such ruinous consequences for other species than our own, we can no longer give struggles for human justice pride of place. Let us put intra-species polarisation to the

---

of neoclassical reasoning.' Moore, 'Toward', 14. The former binary runs, of course, through the entirety of Marx's theory of capital.

31 Larry Elliott, 'World's Eight Richest People Have Same Wealth as Poorest 50%', *Guardian*, 16 January 2017.

32 Lucas Chancel and Thomas Piketty, *Carbon and Inequality: From Kyoto to Paris*, Paris School of Economics, 3 November 2015; Oxfam, 'Extreme Carbon Inequality', Oxfam Media Briefing, 2 December 2015.

side for the sake of the animals.[33] But if the richest eight members or 1 percent of *Homo sapiens sapiens* were to vanish tomorrow, among the luckiest would surely be the rodents, bears, birds and butterflies of this planet – only they have no capacity to make that happen. The grotesque concentration of resources for burning at the top of the human pyramid is a scourge for all living beings; an effective climate policy would be the total expropriation of the top one to ten percent. That could eliminate up to half of all emissions in one fell blow and finance a global transition several times over. Some humans would have to induce such a measure, but they would scarcely gain more from it than the animals, whose objective interest – as subjectively mute as it might be – aligns neatly with that of the human enemies of the 1 percent. Other species, too, await our liberation.

THE LIGHTS OF GOLDMAN SACHS

Much ado about nothing, then, it would seem, in the fight over the metabolic rift. But there is also a second point of disunity, beyond the contortionist sideshows, regarding which aspects of environmental degradation are of critical interest. If Foster and colleagues are often regarded as the nucleus of a second generation of ecological Marxism, Moore harks back to the key thinker of the first, James O'Connor, who put his emphasis on how ecological problems throw spanners in the works of *capital*. If capital has a tendency to overproduce commodities ('the first contradiction'), it is no less prone to *underproduce* – deplete, overtax, destroy – the ecological conditions for high rates of profit ('the second contradiction').[34] Against this model, the theory of the metabolic rift adduces two observations: 1.) the

---

33 Dipesh Chakrabarty, 'Humanities in the Anthropocene: The Crisis of an Enduring Kantian Fable', *New Literary History* 47 (2016): 377–97.

34 See James O'Connor, *Natural Causes: Essays in Ecological Marxism* (New York: Guilford Press, 1998). Moore acknowledges his debt to O'Connor in Moore, 'Transcending', 12–15, but for some reason omits to mention it in *Capitalism*.

most serious consequences of environmental degradation afflict people and other species *outside of the capitalist class and its circuits of accumulation*, and 2.) the balance of evidence suggests that capital can *thrive by ravaging the earth* – not forever, of course, but under the crucial time span when crises such as climate change can still potentially be mitigated.[35] But, for Moore, that argument smacks, of course, of Cartesianism. In his zeal to eliminate any trace of a division between nature and society, he resurrects O'Connor and refines his second contradiction into a general theory of capitalism and the environment that is perhaps best labelled a species of *internalism*.[36]

The theory says, in short, this. For profit rates to be high, nature – here understood as consisting of food, labour-power, energy and raw materials – must be cheap. Through environmental degradation, one or more of these 'four cheaps' becomes expensive, which puts a downward pressure on rates of profit. A veritable *capitalist* crisis then ensues. Now this leads Moore to stress the *price* of material substrata as the main vector of socio-ecological – well, shall we say 'fitting' – so that, for instance, the transition to steam-power is said to have been caused by the cheapness of coal relative to alternative fuels.[37] Here is an empirically testable hypothesis, and it turns out that it fails to correspond with extant data from the crucial frontlines of that transition: in the mills, water was cheaper than steam until long after the shift had been completed in both the UK and the US; on the seas and rivers, wind was cheaper than steam throughout the period when the British Empire filled them

---

35   See the brilliant critique of O'Connor's theory in John Bellamy Foster, *The Ecological Revolution: Making Peace with the Planet* (New York: Monthly Review Press, 2009), 201–12.

36   Ecological limits are said to be not external, but internal to capital: 'We are speaking of *internal* as methodological premise.' Moore, *Capitalism*, 101. Emphasis in original. This is clearly a crucial choice of words.

37   Ibid., 92, 104; Jason W. Moore, 'Cheap Food and Bad Climate: From Surplus Value to Negative Value in the Capitalist World-Ecology', *Critical Historical Studies* 2 (2015): 36–7.

with its steamboats.[38] Entirely different factors were at work. A history of the fossil economy must juggle many more factors than price levels.[39]

Far more pernicious, however, is the narrowing of the eco-Marxist optic that Moore, in his revival of O'Connor, effects. He is not interested in ecological crisis 'in a Cartesian sense', by which he means aspects unrelated to the rates of profit, suffered by others than capitalists, outside the process of accumulation, which would indicate some sort of division of reality into different compartments. In his polemics against Foster and colleagues, he sneers at the attention paid to environmental destruction as such – that is, as unrelated to the fortunes of capital: 'Capitalism wages war on the earth and all that. I wish to suggest, however, that the more interesting – and practically relevant – problem is how nature gets *maxed out*' so that profits begin to fall.[40] Hence the one aspect of climate change that interests Jason W. Moore is the arrow running from agricultural crises to rising food prices to growing wage bills to declining rates of exploitation to falling rates of profit. The food of workers will get dearer in a warming world; capital will have to pay them better; profits will shrink. On the basis of this one causal loop, Moore states: 'Global warming poses a fundamental threat not only to humanity, but also, *more immediately and more directly*, to capitalism itself.'[41]

A quick survey of the landscape of climate change should suffice to disprove that statement. The immediate, direct, fundamental threat does not concern capitalists: the storm is sweeping

---

38   For the former frontline, see Malm, *Fossil*; the second will be dealt with in detail in a sequel entitled *Fossil Empire*.

39   And preoccupation with that factor can clearly lead to incorrect predictions: in 2014, Moore proclaimed the end of 'cheap oil in the Middle East'. Moore, 'Toward', 17.

40   Moore, *Capitalism*, 125, 113. Emphasis in original. Cf. e.g. 5, 15, 27–9, 77, 100–1, 180, 292–5; Moore, 'The Rise', 113.

41   Moore, 'Cheap', 42. Emphasis added. Moore's analysis of that loop is developed in this article, overlapping with chapter 10 in Moore, *Capitalism*.

into the lives of others. Moore's arrow rests on a deduction from the historical importance of cheap food for capitalist development, but its existence in the warming present remains to be demonstrated. Prima facie, this old Ricardian law – food scarcity → high wages →low profits → crisis for capital – appears rather distant from the killing fields of extreme weather. Consider the floods in Pakistan in 2010, one of the worst climate-induced agricultural disasters in recent years, during which 2,000 people were killed and some 10 million displaced, more than 70 percent of the country's farmers lost more than half of their expected income, fields and stocks were wiped out, rice imports surged and prices soared.[42] Did this in any way translate into a downward pressure on the rate of profit? Or were the victims primarily people so poor and peripheral to the central circuits of capital as to not even have a wage, their misfortune worse than that of a productive worker? And if they did have a wage, was it raised to compensate for their squeezed household budgets? And if some capitalists as a result did lose money, and if that did indeed contribute to a profit crisis, *would that be the point at which ecological Marxists should awaken to an event of theoretical and political interest?* (And we have not then mentioned the losses sustained by other species.)

If rising food prices might, at some point in the future, cause profits to plunge, they will do so long after famines have killed off millions with no presence in processes of accumulation. Indications are that the capitalist class will be the *last* to suffer from global warming, and that it can profit from quite a few facets of it in the meantime: GMO technologies for adapting crops to heat stress, water desalination equipment, the sudden accessibility of Arctic oil, disaster insurances and carbon trading and other fresh financial markets, military hardware, *expensive* water – naturally, the potentials for profit increase when previously abundant

---

42 FAO (Food and Agriculture Organization of the United Nations), *The Impact of Disasters on Agriculture and Food Security* (2015).

resources become scarce – not to mention the final frontier of geoengineering.[43] Anna Plowman has demonstrated the operation of a causal loop opposite to Moore's: climate change accelerates migration from rural areas such as the Ganges-Brahmaputra delta into industrial cities such as Dhaka, where the replenishment of the reserve army further undermines the bargaining position of labour, leading to *rising* rates of exploitation and profit.[44]

If climate change will ultimately choke the accumulation of capital – long after it has killed those at the greatest distance from the bourgeoisie – there are certainly countervailing tendencies along that road. There is little evidence that profitability is under any atmospheric sword of Damocles, but plenty of proof that people with no advanced means of production occupy such a position.[45] The prototypical scene of the warming condition is that famous moment captured by Ben Lerner's protagonist as he walks through a New York City where the storm has shut down almost all lights:

> We saw a bright glow to the east among the dark towers of the Financial District, like the eye-shine of some animal. Later we would learn it was Goldman Sachs, see photographs in which one of the few illuminated buildings in the skyline was the investment banking firm . . . Its generators must have been immense; or did they have special access to a secret grid?[46]

---

43   See the magnificent McKenzie Funk, *Windfall: The Booming Business of Global Warming* (New York: Penguin, 2014).

44   Anna Plowman, *Could the Effects of Climate Change be Profitable? A Case Study of Climate Induced Migration into the Bangladeshi Readymade Garments Industry*, master's thesis in human ecology, Lund University, 2015; 'Bangladesh's Disaster Capitalism', *Jacobin*, 22 January.

45   For the little evidence, see e.g. Simon Dietz, Alex Brown, Charlie Dixon and Philip Gradwell, '"Climate Value at Risk" of Global Financial Assets', *Nature Climate Change* 6 (2016): 676–9.

46   Lerner, *10:04*, 236–7.

Or, in the words of Naomi Klein: 'This is happening because the wealthiest people in the wealthiest countries in the world think they are going to be OK, that someone else is going to eat the biggest risks, that even when climate change turns up on their doorstep, they will be taken care of.'[47] Let them eat chaos.

Inverting that scene, Moore's internalist theory of capitalism as world-ecology is beyond anthropocentric: it is *capitalocentric*. Its political implication seems to be that we should eagerly anticipate the imminent climate-induced collapse of the capitalist mode of production. Moore wants us to be less 'catastrophist' and 'apocalyptic' and more cheerful. Global warming and its attendant crises are making him 'skeptical (about capitalism's survival), which means I am optimistic (about ours)'; he draws a parallel to the fall of Rome, which ushered in a golden age for the vast majority.[48] But there is a flaw in that analogy. Rome did not have property relations that demanded self-sustaining growth on the basis of fossil fuels. If capital is allowed to continue doing what it is doing to the earth, it will leave it utterly scorched to anyone who comes after. As long as there are only few signs of it being toppled on a global scale, there is reason to be pessimistic – and correspondingly intransigent in militancy and negativity.[49]

Were it to gain traction, Moore's capitalocentric internalism might do damage to radical ecology and the climate movement, not the least by blunting their crucial normative edge directed against the capitalist class: *you did this to enrich yourselves, and now we are paying with our lives.* A well-grounded perception, it is also the foundation for ecological class hatred, perhaps the emotion most dearly needed in a warming world. Surely the capitalist class deserves a pinch of hatred for turning forces of nature into mass killers of poor people – and then, among many other feats,

47   Naomi Klein, 'Let them Drown: The Violence of Othering in a Warming World', *London Review of Books*, 2 June 2016, 14.

48   Moore, 'Cheap', 36; Moore, 'Toward', 17.

49   See Terry Eagleton, *Hope Without Optimism* (New Haven: Yale University Press, 2015), and the perspective developed in the journal *Salvage*.

spreading denial of that fact and sabotaging attempts to defuse the scattered bombs.

Far from any Hegelian sublation of purportedly Cartesian eco-Marxism, then, Moore has accomplished a big step backwards. That does not necessarily mean that the school of the metabolic rift provides the final word in the search for a unified red-green theory. The proceedings of historical materialism are rich enough to contain other resources, beyond what Marx himself wrote. Taking a cue from his words on labour and the earth as the two parents of every valuable thing, we may experiment with some ideas developed by Marxists exclusively preoccupied with labour and, *mutatis mutandis*, apply them to the earth. It is to that task we now turn.

7

On Unruly Nature:
An Experiment in Ecological Autonomism

THE AUTONOMY OF LABOUR AND NATURE

Labour and nature possess an ineradicable *autonomy* from capital. Both are ontologically prior to it, antedate its appearance on earth, have a history as long as human history in the former case and geological history in the latter of operating according to their own laws, and however hard various ruling classes have subsequently sought to control them – and none has had more power at its disposal than the bourgeoisie – that autonomy persists below the surface, even when the volcanoes seem dormant. The autonomy of labour has, of course, been theorised for more than half a century by autonomist Marxism. Labour, claims Antonio Negri in *Marx Beyond Marx: Lessons on the Grundrisse*, is its own self-generating power or force or, in Italian, *potenza*, because it is indistinguishable from the lives of people. Capital has not produced that *potenza*. It is not an artefact, not a manufactured commodity; it appears with human bodies themselves, much like the mind or the voice, as a result of their reproductive cycles and thus, one could say, as a function of their belonging to nature. Therefore labour eludes capital. Its existence, the life it leads cannot fully pass into the hands of the capitalist, who always runs into residuals of subjectivity that can refuse his authority. Negri posits 'the radical estrangement, *the autonomy of the working class from the development of capital*'.[1]

---

1 Antonio Negri, *Marx Beyond Marx: Lessons on the Grundrisse* (New York:

In more senses than one, as a corollary of the realist definition, *nature has an analogous autonomy*. Some environmental philosophers and historians have lately commenced the work of pinning it down. Keekok Lee defines the autonomy of nature as that which 'has come into existence, continues to exist, and finally, disintegrates/decays, thereby going out of existence, in principle, entirely independent of human volition or intentionality, of human control, manipulation or intervention'.[2] More simply, nature is autonomous because it has a capacity for regulating its own behaviour. That is the literal meaning of 'autonomy', made up of *autos*, self, and *nomos*, rule or law: setting oneself one's own laws.[3] Instances include rocks falling, stars orbiting, animals reproducing, predators preying, plants growing, trees decomposing, cliffs eroding, lightning striking, mountain ranges forming on their own. All of that and very much more happened, came and went and came again before any humans were around because it was, and is, intrinsically independent of them.[4] Since capital is a human creation, it follows that nature is *intrinsically independent of capital*, its production and management and domination – which can, from a capitalist standpoint, be highly unnerving.

But the autonomy of nature is far from identical to that of labour. Among several dissimilarities, it has, in the words of Lee, 'nothing to do with consciousness at all, never mind with reason and freedom'.[5] She thereby draws a sharp distinction between human and natural autonomy, and between the latter and the concept as usually associated with Kant, for whom autonomy

---

Autonomedia, 1991), 101. Emphasis in original. Cf. e.g. Antonio Negri, *Factory of Strategy: 33 Lessons on Lenin* (New York: Columbia University Press, 2014), 10, 282.

2 Lee, 'Is Nature', 59. The sentence is emphasised in original.

3 Thomas Heyd, 'Introduction: Recognizing the Autonomy of Nature: Theory and Practice', in Heyd, *Recognizing*, 5; William Throop and Beth Vickers, 'Autonomy and Agriculture', in ibid., 102; R. Jordan III, 'Conclusion: Autonomy, Restoration and the Law of Nature', in ibid., 190–1.

4 Lee, 'Is Nature', 59–60; Woods, 'Ecological', 177.

5 Lee, 'Is Nature', 59.

referred to the individual will rationally legislating for itself. While acknowledging that higher animals have consciousness, Lee considers human consciousness unique, the only one for which the Kantian notion might be appropriate. Given the weight of brainless matter in nature as a whole, she defines its autonomy – the one that interests her most – as primarily non-conscious. Nature can very much propel itself towards states of affairs and generate its own patterns, but without a mind it does not think about things and act on one of the alternatives it has surveyed: the volcano erupts with no intention.[6] Hence the appropriate formula in this case would be *autonomy without agency*.

From the capitalist standpoint, however, the most disconcerting aspect might be the moment of uncontrollability as such, whether founded in a will or not. Calm or strike can shut down the circuit alike. Here, autonomy denotes not a moral capacity, but an ontological fact that capital has to wrestle with throughout its history. It is that fact that binds labour and nature together from the perspective of capital: as something that came before it, could go on perfectly well without it, does not need it for existence and might one day refuse to cooperate, whether as a crop failure or a mass resignation. Even without Kant, from the point of view of capital the two might be more alike than different.

In *Autonomous Nature: Problems of Prediction and Control from Ancient Times to the Scientific Revolution*, whose cover portrays the eruption of Vesuvius, Carolyn Merchant traces perceptions of nature as an 'unpredictable, unruly, and recalcitrant' force, the unproduced *potenza* par excellence, 'self-acting' and 'self-creating'.[7] Just as in the case of labour, nature does not lose this autonomy because it comes to enter a relationship with others: both can be stamped with brands all over their bodies and retain autonomy in their core. Indeed,

---

6   Cf. Ned Hettinger, 'Respecting Nature's Autonomy in Relationship with Humanity', in Heyd, *Recognizing*, 90; Throop and Vickers, 'Autonomy', 102; Woods, 'Ecological', 177.

7   Carolyn Merchant, *Autonomous Nature: Problems of Prediction and Control from Ancient Times to the Scientific Revolution* (New York: Routledge, 2016), 1, 161.

autonomy is manifested precisely in the feedback, in the influence exerted *in return*, unexpected and uncalled-for. Being autonomous does not mean being isolated or alone; to the contrary, the autonomy comes to the fore precisely when bonded to another party.[8] Merchant emphasises that 'the way in which nature as an autonomous system behaves *depends on how humans behave in relationship to it*', and the same can, of course, be said about labour in relation to capital.[9] Here is a source of paradoxes and loops.

Autonomy in this sense, then, points towards a particular dynamic in time. For Negri and his associates, the autonomy of labour is the external engine of capitalist development. Capital cannot do without the stranger of the worker, so it chases her and seeks to subordinate her, integrate her into a disciplinary regime and make her most subjective impulses redundant to the process of production, always on the move towards the mirage of total control: capital is 'a rule imposed on a separation'.[10] This, the autonomists contend, is the inducement to technological innovation. Automatic machinery is introduced in the hope of annihilating 'every residue of working-class autonomy', of incorporating the movements of the worker into the physical organisation of capital itself, so that it can produce commodities with a minimum – preferably but impossibly zero – contribution from living labour. [11] Or, the 'history of capital is *the history of the successive attempts of the capitalist class to emancipate itself from the working class*' – or, all productive forces are 'weapons of capital. Any time capital plans a new organization of useful labour, or the introduction of a new technology, such plans should be analysed in terms of their role in decomposing the present level of working-class power.'[12]

---

8   Heyd, 'Introduction', 5; Hettinger, 'Respecting', 89, 92; Throop and Vickers, 'Autonomy', 101.

9   Merchant, *Autonomous*, 150. Emphasis added.

10   Negri, *Marx*, 133.

11   Raniero Panzieri, 'Surplus Value and Planning: Notes on the Reading of "Capital"', in *The Labour Process and Class Strategies* (London: Conference of Socialist Economists, 1976), 9.

12   Alberto Toscano, 'Chronicles of Insurrection: Tronti, Negri and the Subject

In nearly all of these propositions, 'labour' could be exchanged for 'nature' and we would have some useful signposts towards the history of the fossil economy. Capital cannot do without the stranger of nature, so it chases it and seeks to subordinate it, integrate it into a disciplinary regime and make its most erratic impulses redundant: here too, capital is a rule imposed on a separation. Automatic machinery is introduced in the hope of annihilating every residue of natural autonomy, of activating the potentialities of material substrata in such a way as to provide capital with a fitting corporeal shape that allows it to produce the maximum amount of commodities, without having to adapt to the swings and convulsions of external nature. The history of capital is thus also the history of successive attempts of the capitalist class to emancipate itself from nature – but, as the autonomists teach us, it is precisely for this reason *a self-contradictory, self-undermining enterprise*, because the only weapons capital can use for bringing down labour and nature are, of course, labour and nature. When it introduces a new technology for subsuming them, that force is predicated on the work of *other* workers and on the functionality of *other* substrata than those it serves to control, displace, absorb or process faster. Capital, say the autonomists, seeks to emancipate itself from workers only to be drawn back into their inescapable net.[13]

The machine is the fulcrum of this impossible quest. We can try the exercise of swapping 'nature' for 'labour' in a passage from autonomist Raniero Panzieri:

> The capitalist objectivity of the productive mechanism with respect to nature finds its optimal basis in the technical principle of the machine: the technically given speed, the coordination of the various

of Antagonism', *Cosmos and History* 5 (2009): 81; Harry Cleaver, *Reading* Capital *Politically* (Edinburgh: AK Press, 2000), 132. Emphasis in original. Cf. e.g. Negri, *Factory*, 17–19, 82.

13   The unparalleled analysis of this logic is Beverly Silver, *Forces of Labor: Workers' Movements and Globalization since 1870* (Cambridge: Cambridge University Press, 2003).

phases and the uninterrupted flow of production are imposed on nature as a 'scientific' necessity, and they correspond perfectly to the capitalist's determination to suck out the maximum amount of material substrata.[14]

The machine, then, is the favoured capitalist platform or swivel in its war against labour *and* nature, promising victory in the form of a productive mechanism free from dependence on their turbulent *potenza*: just push the button or touch the screen, and capital's artefacts will do the job in perfect submission. The machine holds some material substrata (say, iron) captive so as to better suck out others (say, cotton). As a combination, it fuses certain relations with certain objects. It is built so as to extinguish all traces of autonomy inside it, the matter remoulded until the thing has become the extended arm of its owner: Marx says that 'the material quality of the means of labour' is 'transformed into an existence adequate to fixed capital and to capital as such'. While the matter might be recalcitrant, it has no agency, and so capital really can dress itself in it, dwell in the passive flesh, assume the machine as its own 'coarsely sensuous form' – project power through the medium of a thing.[15]

The immediate object of that objectified power may be, as classical autonomism would have it, labour. The machine imposes its discipline on workers, squeezes out more of their time, ratchets up the rate of exploitation – but that process is at one with accelerating the material throughput, reducing nature to standardised form, dissipating ordered matter, usurping, processing, degrading the earth; the rise in productivity takes its toll on both. Hardly a coincidence, it is the chapter on 'Machinery and Large-Scale Industry', where Marx lays out his elaborate analysis of the machine in *Capital*, that ends with the celebrated declaration that capitalist production only develops 'by simultaneously undermining the original sources

---

14   Panzieri, 'Surplus', 9. First 'nature' exchanged for 'the workers' in the original, second for 'the will of the worker', 'material substrata' for 'labour-power'.

15   Marx, *Grundrisse*, 692, 704.

of all wealth – the soil and the worker.'[16] The machine is a combination for speeding up the appropriation and solidifying the control over labour *and* nature. If it breaks down, it is because either autonomous labour or autonomous nature has re-emerged inside it and fiddled with some cogwheel or other. Then capital tries anew. This is the process of real subsumption of the two strangers, in which they star as both guns and targets.

Now, one substratum no machine can do without is energy. The machine may have 'a soul of its own in the mechanical laws acting through it', but it 'consumes coal, oil etc. (*matières instrumentales*), just as the worker consumes food, to keep up its perpetual motion'.[17] On the terrain of energy – so foundational for all production – capital first encountered fuels used since time immemorial, notably water in mills and wind on oceans and rivers. They flowed along given trails in the landscape and ceased when the weather so decided. Dry weeks, doldrums and downstream currents could bring the manufacturing and transportation of commodities to a halt. Interrupting circuits from within the most fundamental base, such energy evinced an overbearing autonomy and made capital a hostage to nature – but there was an alternative, seemingly lacking even a vestige of autonomy: fossil energy. Its realisation required massive amounts of capital in whose absence it would never emerge above ground, giving the impression that the resulting mechanical power was a pure product of engineering and investment. Hence – to make long and complicated stories extremely short – the transition, on factories as well as on boats.[18] *Fossil energy appeared to be a power intrinsic to capital itself.* Capital could not find any kinetic energy within its own abstract circuit but had to locate it outside itself in nature and channel it into its mechanical implements: but the flow of energy, or what we would

---

16   Marx, *Capital I*, 638.

17   Marx, *Grundrisse*, 693.

18   For the factories, see Malm, *Fossil*. 'The weather exemplified nature's most unruly aspect', notes Merchant, *Autonomous*, 93.

today call renewables, constantly erupted in unruly oscillations. Fossil capital is a rule imposed on a separation.

The mechanised vehicles known as steamboats followed the same logic: when the British Empire sent them up rivers and along ocean highways from the second quarter of the nineteenth century onwards, these marvellous combinations promised to outclass the old sailing ships at sucking in raw materials – cotton, flax, silk, palm-oil, tea, sugar, timber, rubber, ivory, beeswax . . . – subjugating the required foreign labour and, of course, trashing any military force so foolish as to block the way. But the boats had to consume coal to keep up their perpetual motion. As it injected steam into its machines and vehicles, capital projected a reinforced power over autonomous labour – not the least on distant fields and plantations – and autonomous nature as manifest in, for instance, the locality and seasonality of the desired raw materials. That laid down a very persistent pattern. Over the past two centuries, fossil energy has been a kind of meta-weapon in the successive attempts of the capitalist class to emancipate itself from labour and nature, constructing a world of productive mechanisms entirely under its dominion. Or, as Klein puts it:

> The promise of liberation from nature that Watt was selling in those early days continues to be the great power of fossil fuels. That power is what allows today's multinationals to scour the globe for the cheapest, most exploitable workforce, with natural features and events that once appeared as obstacles – vast oceans, treacherous landscapes, seasonal fluctuations – no longer even registering as minor annoyances. *Or so it seemed for a time.*[19]

It is a doctrine of autonomist Marxism that, sooner or later, the *potenza* strikes back. When capital believes it has finally extricated itself from the dependence on labour, something blows up in one backyard or another. And here we have climate change – the

---

19   Klein, *This*, 173–4. Emphasis added.

ultimate blowback; the return, as Merchant notices, of utter unpre-
dictability: 'Climate change is the twenty-first century's *marquee*
exemplar of autonomous nature responding to humanly produced
greenhouse gases.'[20] Or, in the words of renowned climate scientist
Wallace Broecker: 'the Earth's climate system has proven itself to be
an angry beast. When nudged, it is capable of a violent response.'[21]
Solar radiation management is then exactly what autonomism
would predict the capitalist response to be: a fresh technology for
calming things down. It would be an attempt to treat the entire
climate system *as though it were a machine.* In *The Planet Remade:
How Geoengineering Could Change the World,* currently the most
influential gospel in the field – and preaches it does, passionately –
The Economist editor Oliver Morton consistently speaks of the
earth as a mechanical structure: 'finding a powerful lever is the key
to moving the earthsystem', which must be guided 'with precision'.
Dreaming of aeroplanes spewing soot into the sky, Morton cannot
wait to see this 'unabashed utopia' and 'technological sublime' rise
before his eyes; the prospect of 'holding back great sheets of ice and
re-routing planet-spanning currents of air thrills' him.[22] Thus
speaks the proprietor of the machine.

The rationale of that geomachine would obviously be to decom-
pose the present level of natural autonomy, but even Morton, who
shrugs off concerns about cataclysmic side effects, concedes that
this is a futile endeavour. 'The climate system works in such a way
that if you perturb one bit of it you would expect to see responses
in other bits a long way away.' For the moment, this is probably the
greatest, most elusive, least subsumable autonomous system
humans can possibly tinker with. Even in a geoengineered world,
the social and the natural are not, with Morton, 'inseparably
conjoined, nor indistinguishable; *they still have their separations,*

20   Merchant, *Autonomous*, 149. Cf. Lee, 'Is Nature', 60.

21   W. S. Broecker, 'Does the Trigger for Abrupt Climate Change Reside in the
Ocean or in the Atmosphere?', *Science* 300 (2003): 1522.

22   Oliver Morton, *The Planet Remade: How Geoengineering Could Change the
World* (London: Granta, 2015), 51, 81, 345, 347, 372.

and there is always room for the unintended' – another rule imposed on a separation, then, and one that might turn out to be unprecedentedly dangerous.[23] The current state of research and debate on solar radiation management provides strong proof of the autonomy of nature. We do not need to see it corroborated in practice.

YOUR WARS, OUR DEAD

None of this is to say that autonomist Marxism should be swallowed lock stock and barrel. Leaving aside questions of political strategy, its more recent iterations have slithered towards ultra-monism, hybridism, posthumanism and a host of other theoretical dead-ends. There is, as Noys observes, a correlation between the flat networks of Latour and those of *Empire*, whose authors are just as loath to recognise any central power.[24] In its classical forms, on the other hand, autonomism has its share of other blind spots and hyperboles, such as a naturalisation of working-class insurrection or, in the words of Perry Anderson, a 'romanticization of proletarian revolt as a more or less continuous flow of lava from the factory floor'.[25] The volcanoes do not always erupt; as the current state of the world indicates, smouldering is the rather more common condition. The Italian industry of the 1960s and 1970s was the site of exceptionally ferocious combat ill-suited for generalisation, but the autonomists theorising that experience have often fallen into the trap of '*ontologisation* of the class struggle'.[26] Capitalist property relations are here rendered as a permanent, if epic, drama, without significant lulls or leaps, lasting seasons and breaks.[27]

---

23 Ibid., 293, 372.

24 Noys, *Persistence*, 124. For posthumanism and hybridism, see e.g. Michael Hardt and Antonio Negri, *Empire* (Harvard: Harvard University Press, 2000), 215–16.

25 Perry Anderson, *The New Old World* (London: Verso, 2009), 331.

26 Axel Kicillof and Guido Starosta, 'Value Form and Class Struggle: A Critique of the Autonomist Theory of Value', *Capital and Class* 31 (2007): 22. Emphasis in original.

27 Andreas Bieler, Ian Bruff and Adam David Norton, 'Acorns and Fruit: From Totalization to Periodization in the Critique of Capitalism', *Capital and Class*

Incidentally, something similar could be said about nature: it does not flaunt its autonomy every minute. The matter of carbon seemed perfectly under control for nearly two centuries. One can imagine a period when solar radiation management works smoothly and the repercussions are minor. Major blowbacks happen *in specific historical conjunctures*, when the displaced and condensed contradictions come to the fore in explosive unity, for labour as for nature – but these two, needless to say, follow their own rhythms, with no tendency to synchronicity. If the conjuncture of the 1960s and 1970s was characterised by the flare-up of labour, we seem to be heading deeper into one determined by the turbulence of nature. (One might speculate about how the struggle against climate change would develop were the eruptions to coincide.)

Ecological autonomism, if such a thing could exist, would then primarily be a theory of acute crisis. But it is precisely the *ontological* status of the autonomy of nature, like that of labour, which makes such crisis a possibility. Here is the taproot of the unintended consequences, the counterforce driving the paradox of historicised nature. Moreover, because of the way capital deals with nature – and here might be a second difference to labour – the trend seems to be a secular rise in volcanicity. This is nothing to salute: and here is a third, crucial difference. One does not cheer on a superstorm as one does a strike combined with a sit-in.

The other of labour is capital; the other of nature is society and therefore humanity as a whole. Nature can never, even hypothetically, be a subject of revolution; its blowbacks are non-subjective and random. The capitalist class and its allied strata have accumulated sufficient access to biophysical resources to withstand the blows and have, in this sense, succeeded in emancipating themselves from nature, at least for the time of greatest political interest. They can turn on their immense generators when the lights have gone out for those who live directly off biophysical resources,

---

34 (2010): 27, 30–4. Another major problem with autonomism is, of course, its monocausal explanation of technological change.

without money to concentrate – a farmer in Burkina Faso, a family of fishers in the Philippines – and people with no property at all (factory workers in Alexandria, the homeless in New York). *Pace* Jason W. Moore, the capitalist war on the earth takes the form of *vos guerres, nos morts* – 'your wars, our dead'. As Klein has pointed out, this goes for solar radiation management as well: the worst impacts are likely to befall people in South Sudan, not in South Dakota, which is probably why some rich white men can be so sanguine about it.[28] Objectively speaking, it follows, the liberation of nature is a global class demand.

FOR THE LIBERATION OF NATURE

If constructionism wants to liberate humanity from the shackles of nature, the idea that the shackles on nature should be lifted along with those on humanity has a venerable Marxist pedigree. Friedrich Engels famously intuited one part of the logic:

> Let us not, however, flatter ourselves overmuch on account of our human conquest over nature. For each such conquest takes its revenge on us. Each of them, it is true, has in the first place the consequences on which we counted, but in the second and third places it has quite different, unforeseen effects which only too often cancel out the first

– springing from what we have here posited as the autonomy of nature. He proceeded with some ancient examples of the dangers of trying to subjugate nature: farmers around the Mediterranean clearing up land and inadvertently desiccating the region; merchants introducing potato to Europe and unknowingly spreading the disease of scrofula. 'Hence at every step we are reminded that we by no means rule over nature like a conqueror over a foreign people', and if we do try to rule this way, the argument implies, sure as

---

28   Klein, *This*, 275–6.

shooting the reminders will come.[29] Engels' examples suggest that attempts to subdue nature and their infelicitous combinations precede the capitalist mode of production.[30] So do money and markets and egoism. 'What distinguishes capitalism from other historical forms of life', to borrow from Eagleton again, is that it 'plugs directly into' the most destabilising drives: 'Constant transgression is of its essence.'[31] No longer an option, the real subsumption of nature – as of labour – is an imperative of the system itself, which piles up resources for pressing on with it. 'For the first time', Marx writes of the arrival of bourgeois society,

> nature becomes purely an object for humankind, purely a matter of utility; ceases to be recognized as a power for itself; and the theoretical discovery of its autonomous laws appears merely as a ruse so as to subjugate it under human needs, whether as an object of consumption or as a means of production.[32]

The spiritual father of this *Weltanschauung* is not so much Descartes as Francis Bacon. If radical political ecology needs a bête noire, he is, as Hailwood proposes, the better candidate; unlike the French philosopher, he was directly linked to the emerging fossil economy and made domination of nature the centrepiece of his thought. Bacon conceived of miners as his shock troops. Any scruples about 'penetrating into these holes and corners' had to be discarded, for 'there are still laid up in the womb of nature many secrets of excellent use having no affinity or parallelism with anything that is now known'. Through the concerted efforts of miners, mill-owners, smiths and other practical men, nature could finally be 'bound into service' and made a 'slave'; this, as Merchant argues at length in *The*

---

29 Friedrich Engels, *Dialectics of Nature* (New York: International Publishers, 1940), 291–2. Foster and Burkett have dug up plenty of quotations from Marx himself with a similar thrust, see e.g. Foster and Burkett, *Marx*, 42.

30 As likewise documented in Merchant, *Autonomous*.

31 Terry Eagleton, *On Evil* (New Haven: Yale University Press, 2010), 31.

32 Marx, *Grundrisse*, 410.

Death of Nature, was the worldview most appropriate for the rising class of mine-owners, manufacturers and merchants.[33] The original ideological sin of the bourgeoisie is not so much dualism as subsumptionism.

After Engels and Marx, two luminaries of mid-twentieth-century Marxism developed this perspective further: Ernst Bloch and Herbert Marcuse. Whereas Theodor Adorno and Max Horkheimer tended towards the view that destructive technology inhered in human nature, Bloch, in his chapter on technological utopias in *The Principle of Hope*, considered the appearance of capital the true watershed. Until some point well into the eighteenth century, innovation most often took the form of dilettante experimentation or alchemical fantasy schemes, moored in magic and organic cosmologies. Advances in mining were discouraged by beliefs in water-spirits and blood-sucking demons under the ground – but then again 'there is no inner urge as such to invent something. A mandate is always necessary', more specifically a 'social mandate', without which the machines of the industrial revolution wouldn't have 'flashed into the mind of any inventor, out of inner vocation for instance'.[34] No matter how 'remarkable Roman plumbing, Chinese paper and gunpowder (only used for fireworks), and Egyptian cranes are: only with the mandate under capitalism did larger technological projects also get under way'. 'Look', Bloch says, 'what became of Papin's old steam digester' – one of the many abortive precursors to Watt's engine – 'once capital was interested in making steam do some work.'[35] When Bacon preco-ciously fantasised about steam-engines and other mechanical marvels, he articulated the confidence of the newborn bourgeoisie and smoothed its way by deleting from consciousness the category of catastrophe. This pertained particularly to the previously feared activity of burrowing deep in the ground.[36]

---

33 Bacon quoted in Merchant, *Death*, 168–9. Cf. 177, 185

34 Ernst Bloch, *The Principle of Hope: Volume 2* (Cambridge, MA: MIT Press, 1995), 658.

35 Ibid., 646, 659.

36 Ibid., 655–7.

Here is the break: in the epoch of capital, nature comes to be perceived as a repository of exchange-value. It is plundered and pillaged for the material substrata of profit and handled with anti-septic, hyper-abstract gloves: 'Bourgeois thinking as a whole has distanced itself from the materials with which it deals. It is based on an economy which, as Brecht says, is not interested in rice at all but only in its price.' The symbolic straitjacket of the universal equivalent is pressed onto nature, in a double move of 'exploitation' and 'abstractness' that manages everything as substitutable for everything else. Although it has pushed deeper into nature than anyone before it, capital 'stands in a pure commodity-relation, one alienated from the start, to the natural forces with which it operates *from outside*'. So while the whole of life is now 'surrounded by a belt of artificial creations which have never existed before', this is – paradoxically but logically – due to a form of technology that disparages the material world, effaces its qualitative properties, refuses to establish lasting relationships with it, rides roughshod over it, not at all 'interested *in being indigenous to it*'.[37] The proper analogy is colonial occupation.

> The capitalist concept of technology as a whole . . . exhibits more domination than friendship, more of the slave-driver and the East India Company than the bosom of a friend . . . Thus it becomes evident again and again that our technology up to now stands in nature like an army of occupation in enemy territory, and it knows nothing of the interior of the country.[38]

The curse of capital is that it can emancipate itself from nature in all its sparkling autonomy only by colonising it, lining it up in rows and marching it off to the chimneys of accumulation: and over its long history, the instances when it has operated in that way by *treating humans in the same manner* have been legion. Herbert

---

37   Ibid., 666, 667, 627, 671. Emphases added.
38   Ibid., 670, 696.

Marcuse tied the two threads together in the rallying cry 'nature, too, awaits the revolution!' Under the gathering clouds of the warming condition, his essay in *Counterrevolution and Revolt* reads, together with Bloch's chapter, as some of the most penetrating words on ecology in the Marxist canon. Capitalism approaches nature 'in an aggressively scientific way: it is there for the sake of domination; it is value-free matter, material. This notion of nature is a *historical* a priori, pertaining to a specific form of society.'[39] Capital fastens itself on nature and labour and sucks them dry; both need to shake it off; both have a capacity for ruling themselves, and the safest way to achieve not so much a future of freedom as *any* future is to institute their full self-government – a definition, if one so wishes, of sustainability.

But the liberation of nature cannot be the work of nature itself (at least not if it is to accord with that of humanity). Any ecological politics must, we remember, be anthropocentric, in an elemental, methodological and as such fairly harmless way. Marcuse makes as much clear:

> The idea of the liberation of nature stipulates no such plan or inten-
> tion in the universe: liberation is the possible plan and intention of
> human beings, *brought to bear upon nature*. However, it does stipulate
> that nature is susceptible to such an undertaking, and that there are
> forces in nature which have been distorted and suppressed – forces
> which could support and enhance the liberation of man. This capac-
> ity of nature may be called 'chance', or 'blind freedom',

or autonomy without agency.[40] It blows with every wind and falls with every ray of sunlight. Free humans pin their future on such forces.

39   Herbert Marcuse, *Counterrevolution and Revolt* (Boston: Beacon, 1972), 74, 61. Emphasis in original.

40   Ibid., 66. Emphasis added.

AUTONOMY IN *VICTORY*

The British coal colony at Labuan ended in commercial failure. After the annexation of the island in 1846, the Empire set up an Eastern Archipelago Company to run mining operations and feed the nearby steamers, but it soon encountered a stubborn obstacle: labour. The natives proved utterly averse to working in the mines, absconding as soon as they had sat foot underground. Indentured workers from China and India had to be imported. They, however, turned out to be scarcely more reliable; in report after report to the Company, managers complained of their juvenile and feckless demeanour. Because of the troubles in manning the enterprise to even half of the required extent, Labuan became an embarrassment, and in the late 1870s, the mines were closed.[41]

This debacle forms the background to *Victory*, Joseph Conrad's most underappreciated novel.[42] It opens with a précis of the ideology of the fossil economy:

> There is, as every schoolboy knows in this scientific age, a very close chemical relation between coal and diamonds. It is the reason, I believe, why some people allude to coal as 'black diamonds'. Both these commodities represent wealth; but coal is a much less portable form of property. There is, from that point of view, a deplorable lack of concentration in coal. Now, if a coal-mine could be put into one's waistcoat pocket – but it can't! At the same time, there is a fascination in coal, *the supreme commodity of the age in which we are camped like bewildered travellers in a garish, unrestful hotel.*

The supreme commodity, one can add, that has built this garish hotel right over an abyss; in a warming world, words like these take

---

41 For details, see Malm, 'Who'.

42 Andrew Francis makes a convincing case for Labuan as the model for the novel's island of 'Samburan' in *Culture*, 165–7.

on another layer of meaning.[43] They set the tone of transience and imminent ending that pervades *Victory*. The protagonist of the novel is Heyst, identified as a Swede, who, we learn in the first pages, personally discovered most of the coal outcrops in the tropical islands. Rushing over the archipelago, jumping in and out of packets, restlessly preparing for his business, 'he was heard by more than a hundred persons in the islands talking of "a great stride forward for these regions."'[44] A manager of the specially formed Tropical Belt Coal Company, he was stationed at Samburan, the island modelled on Labuan and setting for most of the action.

When the novel takes off, the Company has been dissolved. No coal leaves the ground. Heyst leads the life of a hermit on the island, desolate and pitiful, accompanied only by Wang, a Chinese indentured worker who has stayed on after the closure of the mines. The hierarchy between the former 'Number One' and his worker is vaguely unsettled. Wang cooks food for Heyst, but he has an uncanny ability to vanish and appear on a whim. Having married a woman from the indigenous population, 'the Alfuros', Wang lives with her in a hut and cultivates a plot of land away from the central settlement. A line divides the island in two zones: forests on the one side, the relics of the Company on the other – some bungalows, the shafts, a clearing 'in which the black stumps of trees stood charred', derelict storerooms, a jetty in 'Black Diamond Bay'.[45] On the opposite side, in the dense woods, live the Alfuros. To mark their resistance to the Company, they have built a barricade of trees on the boundary of their realm.

Heyst finds a new purpose in life by cajoling a woman, Lena, to come and live with him on the island; most of the novel is concerned with the intrigues between the couple and some other Westerners,

---

43 Joseph Conrad, *Victory* (London: The Book Society, 1952), 9. Emphasis added. See further Andreas Malm, '"This Is the Hell That I Have Heard Of": Some Dialectical Images in Fossil Fuel Fiction', *Forum for Modern Language Studies* 53 (2017): 121–41.

44 Conrad, *Victory*, 11. 'Heyst' is anything but a Swedish-sounding name.

45 Ibid., 172.

with Wang and the Alfuros in the background (typically for a Conrad novel, no Alfuro ever says a word). But Heyst has the appearance of a bourgeois zombie. He has lost his Company, his energy, his belief in the great stride forward; on a walk on their side of the island, Lena tells him that 'it seems as if everything that there is had gone under'. Heyst is then reminded 'of the story of the deluge . . . The vision of a world destroyed.'[46]

As the plot thickens, the two henchmen of his European rival creep up on Heyst. In his greatest moment of danger, Wang sneaks into the bungalow and makes off with his only revolver: the old worker has decided to abandon the master once and for all and relocate to the Alfuros on the other side of the rampart. Of those people, Heyst knows that 'they are peaceable, kindly folk and would have seen me shot with extreme satisfaction'.[47] Desperate for physical safety, he takes Lena with him on a march up to the barricade to try to persuade Wang to hand the gun back. They approach the mass of foliage and discover several spear-blades protruding:

> 'This', Heyst explained in his urbane tone, 'is a barrier against the march of civilisation. The poor folk over there did not like it, as it appeared to them in the shape of my company – a great step forward, as some people used to call it with mistaken confidence. The advanced foot has been drawn back, but the barricade remains.'[48]

Laughing, standing on higher ground, Wang declares that he would rather shoot Heyst than return the revolver. The unarmed couple head back to their fate. In the final pages, they and the two henchmen all die.

When Penguin Classics reissued *Victory* in 2015, readers again asked the question that has puzzled many a critic: who is the victor

---

46 Ibid., 151.
47 Ibid., 270.
48 Ibid., 267.

in this novel?[49] Given that the four main characters on the Western side of the story perish, there seems to be no win in sight. But that is, of course, to forget their foil: *Victory* belongs to Wang and the Alfuros, who inherit the island without any coal company and Westerners around. What strategic asset seals their triumph? Only a patch of the island has been cleared. Beyond the barricade is nature in autonomous bloom, enhancing and supporting the autonomy of the islanders. Spared the tools of the Company, that nature is at liberty to develop on its own: hence so are the people who live by working inside it – free to withdraw, shake off the intruders and pluck the fruits of the island in peace. Conrad's is a tale of double autonomy, victorious in the end when the coal is left unperturbed, no black diamonds exported, no steamers call, 'Number One' is gone, the trees in the clearing beginning to regrow.

As a fantasy about the denouement of the fossil economy, *Victory* is, naturally, too good to be true. In reality, it is rather Heyst and his descendants who have inherited the earth, filled it with jetties and railroads, cleared the surrounding vegetation and driven Wang underground. But if only negatively, Conrad here dramatizes the conditions for liberation (or even survival). An island for the Alfuros and Wang, all to themselves, with no one there to drive them into mines and cut the trees down. That is what victory would look like.

---

49   Sam Jordison, 'Who Is Joseph Conrad's Winner in Victory', *Guardian*, 20 October 2015.

8

Conclusion:
One step back, two steps forwards

FROM THE DAY BEFORE TOMORROW

A genealogy of the main ideas we have here scrutinised and discarded would take us back to the old rhizome of post-structuralism and other postmodernist thinking. More generally, these ideas are outpourings or reflections of the postmodern condition, insofar as they cannot come to terms with nature and history and their imbrications. In the warming condition, they are ideas from the yesterday that refuses to let go.

More specifically, the theoretical obliteration of nature mimics the practical attempts by capital to subsume it under the law of value – indeed, as many anti-constructionists have argued, it is the latter that makes the former seem plausible.[1] Only in a society that strives to turn every bit of nature into profit can the idea that nature has no independent existence take root. For Steven Vogel, merely to suggest that there is some realm called nature that humans cannot shape is to preach 'a religious idea'.[2] But only under a ruling class that believes itself so godlike that it can substitute its

---

1 See e.g. Kidner, 'Fabricating'; Eileen Crist, 'Against the Social Construction of Nature and Wilderness', *Environmental Ethics* 26 (2004): 5–24; Plumwood, 'Towards'; Plumwood, 'Concept'; Newton, *Nature*, 41–2; Hailwood, *Alienation*, 57, 61, 64, 85.

2 Vogel, *Thinking*, 238.

power for all others can the notion of nature as such appear offensively religious. Constructionism swims with the current when what is needed is an affirmation of nature as something *other* than the commodity.

New materialism, for its part, continues the postmodernist tradition of making a virtue out of the crisis of political agency.[3] Together with its siblings, it had to be the child of the enduring conjuncture of defeat and not, say, of the 1920s or the 1960s. If constructionism mirrors the forces that run roughshod over nature, new materialism reflects the lack of control over them and the apparent implausibility of any scheme for reining them in: when capital seems more solid and rocklike than the earth itself, the sensation of overwhelming thing-power might creep up easily. Jane Bennett justifies the material/nonhuman turn with 'the voluminous mountains of "things" that today surround those of us living in corporate-capitalist, neoliberal, shopping-as-religion cultures.' These mountains demand that we give the alluring objects themselves – the commodities – 'pride of place in our thinking'.[4] Certainly, new materialism has scored a more profound ontological success in this regard than most of its predecessors, by crowning the things the heirs apparent of agency. The wealth of societies in which the capitalist mode of production prevails appears as an immense collection of thing-kings.

Hybridism takes joy in transgression. Capitalism, Eagleton reminds us, is a system for 'restlessly transgressing boundaries and dismantling oppositions'.[5] And as Plumwood herself has pointed out, some boundaries we would be better off respecting: opening a rainforest for oil exploration muddies the lines between the natural and the social, and there is nothing to celebrate about that.[6] Hybridism is the theoretical mirror image of the homogenising

---

3   On this tradition, cf. Eagleton, *Illusions*, 13–17.
4   Bennett, 'Systems', 224.
5   Eagleton, *Illusions*, 133.
6   Plumwood, 'Towards', 46.

bulldozer of capital.[7] It is encountered some circles down in environmental hell.

TRAVEL BACK IN TIME

If modernity was the epoch when time moved forwards and postmodernity that when it stood still, there was always the possibility of it starting to move backwards.

> Trying to escape the punishing sun, Osama Sayed and his seven-year-old son, Ahmed, take shelter beneath a bush. 'It's like we've travelled back in time, having to wait with jars for the water carrier', says Sayed. Severe water cuts have repeatedly forced him and the 5,000 other farmers living in this small Nile Delta village to wait hours, sometimes even days, for drinking water, amid a severe heatwave in the Middle East,

the *Guardian* reported in August 2015.[8] Expect more gifts of history to be withdrawn, one after the other, primarily from those who never received very many of them in the first place. Historicised nature is pushing back.

UTOPIA, SIMULACRA, DYSTOPIA

It is tempting to draw up a neat dialectical scheme of three emblematic aesthetic modes: utopia for the modern, simulacra and pastiche and related forms for the postmodern, followed by dystopia for the warming condition, representing the interlinked historical moments of progress-defeat-disaster. Referring to mostly American films and novels, E. Ann Kaplan observes that 'utopian discourses have given way to dystopian imaginaries on a scale rarely seen in

---

7   Cf. Crary, *24/7*, 12–13.
8   Mohamed Ezz and Nada Arafat, ' "We Woke Up in a Desert": The Water Crisis Taking Hold across Egypt', *Guardian*, 4 August 2015.

earlier aesthetic periods.' Whereas the undercurrent of modern dystopias – Lang's *Metropolis*, Orwell's *1984*, Huxley's *Brave New World* – expressed anxieties over Fordism and totalitarianism, and while alien invasion films stretched the imagination to the utmost, Kaplan sees the 'pretrauma' form extending collapse to all ordered social life and relocating it to a place and time near the consumer, with some connection to extreme scenarios in science. Here 'future time is a major theme', but the trauma flows from the feeling of 'not having a future at all'.[9]

But there are at least four reasons to consider the possibility that such dystopia might be only a regional mode for the warming condition. First, it is stoked up by the *expectation* of disaster, just around the corner or on very early visitation. But if climate catastrophe were to become a generalised state of affairs, would that type of narrative about the future hold any traction? Second, if the climate movement and its various allies are to make any real dent in the curves, they probably – one of the key contentions of Klein – have to reinvigorate, recycle, reroute utopian impulses. Third, if fantasies of apocalypse are the order of the day in Hollywood, they seem to be somewhat rarer in Bollywood and Nollywood; a schema of utopia-simulacra-dystopia would be modelled on a particular Western sequence not necessarily corresponding to developments elsewhere. Perhaps events like Sandy really are enough to fuel some vague fantasy of losing everything among those who have it all. (And perhaps the production of credible apocalypses still requires the most advanced media technologies.)

Fourth, it is too early to count out postmodern culture: as we suggested earlier, it might not stand in any absolute contradiction to a warming world, but could rather inflame it further. The quip by Fredric Jameson that so eminently sums it up – 'it is easier to imagine the end of the world than the end of capitalism' – would then identify a crossing from the postmodern to the warming condition, on which traffic ceaselessly flows. There would be more

---

9   Kaplan, *Climate*, 8, 4, 69.

of a parallelism or dialectic between the two – both originating, of course, in a specific capitalist modernity – than a mutual exclusion. And perhaps that is also, again, one additional reason why concern is so much more rife in the poor than in the advanced parts of the capitalist world. A herder in Burkina Faso or a farmer in the Nile Delta has fewer screens to flee into. Conversely, perhaps it is wrong to say that the warming condition is one of realisation: perhaps it should rather be thought of as fundamentally fractured, rent in two, with denial and escape on the one side and realisation and suffering on the other *and the former guaranteeing the continuation of the latter.*

FORMS OF RETROGRESSION

If current trends are anything to go by, the warming condition looks set to be an era of retrogression, ecologically and politically. One of its greatest pathologies is surely the superabundance of energy thrown into the demonisation of refugees, Muslims, Mexicans, various otherwise coded others in advanced capitalist countries, while climate change receives barely a sliver of the attention. The non-threat of immigration tops the headlines and debates every day, while the super-threat of actually unfolding global warming struggles to make it there even when the most sensational records are reported. This is not a random fact about our times. As Rachel E. Goldsmith and her colleagues point out, fossil energy is a bane entirely internal to the system, but immigrants and other others can be framed as *external* enemies, so much more convenient a target of aggression.[10] Who knows what subconscious traffic there might be from the former irritant to the latter outflow. Be that as it may, the rise and rise of the far right evidently has no equivalent at the green or red-green end of the spectrum. A visitor from the future might marvel at this irrationality: but perhaps there is also some reciprocity or homology between the two trends. There

---

10   Goldsmith et al., 'Gender', 163.

are moments when the slide towards the right appears to accelerate in lockstep with the increase in temperatures. Devolution in ecosystems – say, 'the rise of slime' in the oceans: the ascent of jellyfish and toxic algae, the descent of coral reefs and apex species – has a fitting counterpart in the current state of Western politics.[11]

The far right is, of course, the first to bewail how everything is getting worse by the day and shed tears over lost splendour, translating into the universal formula 'make X great again'. Testimony to the declensionist *zeitgeist*, this current never fails to attack what actual progress has been made in recent decades – in the departments of gender, culture, welfare and, at least in certain northern European countries, the belated dissolution of white ethnic homogeneity – thereby accumulating the force of a tidal wave of reactionary slime rolling over the globe. This is the leading edge of degeneration *including in the sphere of climate*. How are the links forged? In *Climate Crisis, Psychoanalysis, and Radical Ethics*, Donna M. Orange chases the ghosts of colonial history that haunt this warming world and suggests that an unprocessed history of enslaving others primes privileged white people to callousness. 'Blindness to our ancestors' crimes, and to the ways we "whites" continue to live from these crimes, keeps the suffering of those already exposed to the devastation of climate crisis impossible for us to see or feel.'[12] And the crimes compound: against non-whites as immigrants *and* as victims of climate change. Then maybe there is some historical accumulation coming back to drive terror into the present on both planes. Consider, one last time, the picture from Labuan: does it portray the shared roots of the fossil economy and modern racism? The moment when white men with money and guns act out their belief that the jungle and its inhabitants, held conveniently invisible, are theirs to trample upon? Is colonial

11 Jeremy B. C. Jackson, 'Ecological Extinction and Evolution in the Brave New Ocean', *Proceedings of the National Academy of Sciences* 105 (2008): 11458–65.

12 Donna M. Orange, *Climate Crisis, Psychoanalysis, and Radical Ethics* (London: Routledge, 2017), 39.

aggression – Bloch's 'slave-driver and the East India Company' – more than an apt metaphor for capitalist technology based on fossil fuels? Have nature and non-whites been subjected to one and the same juggernaut, and if so, would it be so strange if the warming condition – this long fallout of subsumption – would also entail some climax of racism?

These questions aside, global warming is certainly not the sole disaster of the future in the making. Being of such magnitude, the warming would be unimaginable as a deviation from some generally wholesome trajectory. In that sense, it deserves a place, again *mutatis mutandis*, similar to that of Auschwitz in the writings of Adorno: as a catastrophe in which society as a whole discharges itself.

AGAINST AFFIRMATION

The warming condition spells the death of affirmative politics.[13] Negativity is our only chance now. Some version of Benjamin's destructive character must be rehabilitated:

> The destructive character has the consciousness of historical man, whose deepest emotion is an insuperable mistrust of the course of things and a readiness at all times to recognize that everything can go wrong . . . What exists he reduces to rubble – not for the sake of the rubble, but for that of the way leading through it . . . It is Nature that dictates his tempo, indirectly at least, for he must forestall her. Otherwise she will take over the destruction herself.[14]

---

13 A startling example of affirmative politics in this age of disaster is Braidotti, *Posthuman*. For a brilliant critique of the fashion of affirmationism – which counts Latour, new materialism and posthumanism as some of its greatest poster children – see Noys, *Persistence*.

14 Walter Benjamin, *Selected Writings, Volume 2, part 2, 1931–1934* (Cambridge, MA: Harvard University Press, 2005), 540–1.

FOR PANIC

For someone safely ensconced in a life and material position under no immediate threat from climate change, such as the average Western academic, the only way to stay conscious of the lashing urgency of the problem is to subject oneself regularly, weekly or daily, to news from the frontiers of this warming world. In July 2016 – summed up worldwide as the hottest month ever recorded – temperatures soared to the limit of liveability in the areas around the Persian Gulf. In Basra, they hit 54°C.[15] Twenty-six-year-old student Zainab Guman told the reporter of the *Washington Post* that she avoided leaving her home during the day throughout the summer, for stepping outside is like 'walking into a fire': 'It's like everything on your body – your skin, your eyes, your nose – starts to burn.'[16] In November 2016, Bolivia declared a state of emergency as the cities of La Paz and El Alto ran out of water. The glaciers feeding the cities in dry periods have shrunk or disappeared, leaving the reservoirs empty, forcing the state to impose water rationing and dig frantically for reserves. People queued for hours on end with buckets.[17] In July and September, two glaciers in Tibet

15   Michael Slezak, 'July 2016 Was World's Hottest Month since Records Began, Says Nasa', *Guardian*, 16 August 2016; Jason Samenow, 'Two Middle East Locations Hit 129 Degrees, Hottest Ever in Eastern Hemisphere, Maybe the World', *Washington Post*, 22 July 2016.

16   Hugh Naylor, 'An epic Middle East heat wave could be global warming's hellish curtain-raiser', *Washington Post*, 10 August 2016. See further Jeremy S. Pal and Elfatih A. B. Eltahir, 'Future Temperature in Southwest Asia Projected to Exceed a Threshold for Human Adaptability', *Nature Climate Change* 6 (2016): 197–200; J. Lelieveld, Y. Proestos, P. Hadjinicolaou et al., 'Strongly Increasing Heat Extremes in the Middle East and North Africa (MENA) in the 21st Century', *Climatic Change*, 137 (2016): 245–60.

17   John Rocha, 'Shrinking glaciers cause state-of-emergency drought in Bolivia', *Guardian*, 28 November 2016. See further Nick Buxton, Marisa Escobar, David Purkey and Nilo Lima, 'Water Scarcity, Climate Change and Bolivia: Planning for Climate Uncertainties', Stockholm Environment Institute, Discussion Brief, 2013, sei-international.org.

suddenly collapsed in implosions that left scientists flabbergasted, each setting off avalanches that covered some ten square kilometres of land with broken ice and strewn boulders.[18] In late 2016, the *Guardian* published a series of dispatches from villages in eastern Sudan being engulfed in sand. Swings between drought and torrential downpours spoil the soil, river levels fall, once fertile fields turn into cracked crusts and forests into drifting deserts. 'It's especially scary when the house is covered [in sand] at night and you can only wait in the dark until morning to dig your way out', said 70-year-old Hamud El-Nour Hamdallah.[19] Over in Bangladesh, villages are instead abandoned to the rising sea: '"The ocean is torturing us," said Pushpo Rani Das, 28, a mother of three who has had to move her home four times to escape storm surges. "We can't stop it. Water enters my house in every high tide, especially in the rainy season."'[20]

This war remains sorely underreported. There is still no *Planet of Slums* or *High Tide* that maps the permanent state of climate emergency settling over the global South. But the science keeps coming: one study published in *Nature Climate Change* in September 2016 used simulations and historical records to calculate how much the global wheat yield will decline per centigrade increase in temperature. On average 5.7 percent, it found, but with large variations: hot countries – those in or near the tropics, holding most of poor humanity – will suffer greater losses: 11–20 percent in Upper Egypt, compared to some 4 percent in France.[21] From Antarctica, scientists reported a batch of fresh discoveries. Ice shelves buttress inland

18   Kate Ravilious, 'Climate Change likely Cause of Freak Avalanches', *Guardian*, 4 December 2016.

19   Hannah McNeish, ' "We Have almost Been Buried": The Sudanese Villages Being Swallowed by Sand', *Guardian*, 17 November 2016; Hannah McNeish, 'Farmers in Sudan Battle Climate Change and Hunger as Desert Creeps Closer', *Guardian*, 19 December 2016.

20   Karen McVeigh, 'On the Climate Change Frontline: The Disappearing Fishing Villages of Bangladesh', *Guardian*, 20 January 2017.

21   Bing Liu, Senthold Asseng, Christoph Müller et al., 'Similar Estimates of Temperature Impacts on Global Wheat Yield by Three Independent Methods', *Nature Climate Change* 6 (2016): 1130–7.

glaciers and prevent them from sliding into the sea, but when enough water melts on their surfaces to form ponds, it might slip into cavities and work its way through the shelves until they catastrophically break up; this has happened several times in the Antarctic peninsula, but researchers on the ground have now also observed similar processes underway in the eastern part of the continent.[22] The Totten Ice Shelf holds back a volume of ice equivalent to a 3.5-metre sea level rise. Meltwater and the warm ocean are eating into it from below.[23]

And on it goes. Some on the left maintain that progressives should not stoke panic – they ought to be less 'catastrophist' and 'apocalyptic' – but if we accept the principles of climate realism and stay up to date with the science, the boot is entirely on the other foot. Donna Orange points to the classic psychoanalytical embarrassment of Sigmund Freud himself, who refused to see Nazi annexation coming and only escaped Vienna at the very last moment, leaving several family members to perish. 'The parallel with our climate emergency is clear: when we cannot panic appropriately, we cannot take fittingly radical action.'[24] Dare to feel the panic. Then choose between the two main options: commit to the most militant and unwavering opposition to this system, or sit watching as it all goes down the drain.

A BAD TIME TO CALL IT A DAY

So what, then, can still be achieved in the struggle to maximise the prospects for survival? If both the 1.5°C and 2°C guardrails turn out to have been breached, we are still far from the 8°C rise in average temperature due to burning all of the proven fossil fuel reserves. That gap covers the distance between a very dangerous and an unlivable

---

22   J. T. M. Lenaerts, S. Lhermitte, R. Drews et al., 'Meltwater Produced by Wind-Albedo Interaction Stored in an East Antarctic Ice Shelf', *Nature Climate Change* 7 (2017): 58–62.

23   Stephen Rich Rintoul, Alessandro Silvano, Beatriz Pena-Molino et al., 'Ocean Heat Drives Rapid Basal Melt of the Totten Ice Shelf', *Science Advances*, 16 December 2016.

24   Orange, *Climate*, 16.

climate. There would be no scientific support today for the position that it no longer matters whether the fossil fuels in the ground are taken up or not, or for the view that zero emissions tomorrow would make no difference. Those are the two finishing lines the resistance will have to rush towards in the decades ahead: no extraction, no emissions.[25] But it might take *many* decades to get there, and if it does, chances are that a total decarbonisation of the world-economy must be combined with negative emissions on a massive scale for the worst to be averted. Indeed, we have obviously already passed the point where such methods are required for a stabilisation of the climate – taking us back to, say, 350 ppm – and so they demand the closest consideration, if only ever *in addition to* the complete dismantling of the fossil economy. It is far beyond the scope of the present work to discuss on what scale negative emissions technologies could be feasible (empirical data might tell us it is small), but they belong to the parameters of the struggle ahead: trying and using all means to make this little planet habitable for the duration. That will not be achieved at a dinner party. Would very bad scenarios come to pass, there might even have to be a detour of fighting for a planned phase-out of solar radiation management. Perhaps a stabilisation of the climate – after which the autonomous forces of nature can rule once more without jeopardising human civilisation – should be conceived as a revolutionary project for the next few centuries or so. In the meantime, there will be plenty of struggles to wage for meaningful adaptation and just compensation; if only in the medium term, the warming condition will deepen and multiply the social fractures.[26] It is a bad time to call it a day for radical politics.

---

25 The most compelling manual for how to eliminate fossil fuel use from the world-economy in the shortest possible time is Laurence L. Delina, *Strategies for Rapid Climate Mitigation: Wartime Mobilisation as a Model for Action?* (London: Routledge, 2016).

26 For some further thoughts on this, see Andreas Malm, 'Revolution in a Warming World: Lessons from the Russian to the Syrian Revolution', in Leo Panitch and Greg Albo (eds): *Socialist Register 2017: Rethinking Revolution* (London: Merlin Press, 2016), 120–42.

EVACUATE THE OUTPOST

The fact that the autonomy of nature is ineradicable – like that of labour, including that of a person held a slave – is no reason to persist in seeking to outflank and overpower it. No one can snuff out or even reduce the ontological autonomy of nature. But it is clearly possible to try to dominate it in a way that provokes blow-backs unhealthy for humanity (not to speak of other species), and a purely anthropocentric survival instinct should then be enough to ground a policy of non-subsumption. That cannot mean a policy of non-engagement – humans *must* combine with nature – but in the critical sphere of energy, it does mean ending two centuries of capitalist rule imposed on a separation: renouncing all subsumption by means of fossil fuels. It means living with the autonomous sun and wind and waves without any more solid energy to expand on.

That makes some people jittery. 'It struck me', writes Klein, 'that this need to adapt to nature is what drives some people mad about renewables: even at a very large scale, they require a humility' that bourgeois habits of owning the earth cannot quite stomach. 'The power of the sun, wind, and waves can be harnessed, to be sure, but unlike fossil fuels, those forces can never be fully possessed', and so a turn to them would usher in 'a fundamental shift in power *relations* between humanity and the natural world on which we depend'.[27] Such relations are entirely compatible with the autonomy of nature; one does not respect someone's autonomy by withdrawing from all contact and suspending all claims to collaboration: you can ask your neighbour to cook food for you this evening without making her a slave.[28]

What matters is the ditching of the colonial attitude. 'Marxism of technology', explains the ever-utopian Bloch, 'is no philanthropy for maltreated metals, but rather the end of the naïve application of

---

27 Klein, *This*, 394. Emphasis in original. Cf. 175.
28 As argued by e.g. Hettinger, 'Respecting', 89–93; Throop and Vickers, 'Autonomy', 101–2.

the standpoint of the exploiter and animal tamer to nature.' It is an alliance with and inhabitation of the forces of nature as they come forth. 'Technology', writes Bloch – and he could have been referring specifically to energy technology – 'as an ever more advanced but also ever more lonely outpost, lacks contact with the old natural world from which capitalism pushed itself off, and also contact with an element in nature favourable to technology itself.'[29] It is that outpost that must now be evacuated.

THEODICY

In a rapidly warming world, the room for any modernist theodicy is as rapidly disappearing. Climate science has made it plain what it would mean to let business as usual run its full course. What could possibly justify such an outcome? Nothing, of course, for a worse outcome can hardly be imagined. A bourgeois civilisation that brings it about cannot get away from the guilt, and conversely, the terminus of these firmly laid down tracks shrinks the space for arguments like 'granted, capitalism has created the most abysmal inequalities ever recorded, obliterated subsistence communities and indigenous peoples, thrown billions into unemployment and exhausted billions of bodies more, but at the end of the day, it has spread the living standards of modernity – the envy of all previous history – and lifted humankind out of the ashes of poverty': into the fire. In the twilight of cataclysmic climate change, all previous disasters of the bourgeois epoch become prefigurative. Not coincidentally, Ben Lerner's *10:04* includes a reproduction of *Angelus Novus* and begins with an epigraph from Walter Benjamin: 'Everything will be as it is now, only a little different.'[30]

---

29   Bloch, *Principle*, 695, 692.
30   Lerner, *10:04*, x. See also 19, 54, 109.

PROGRESS AGAINST PROGRESS

What would real progress mean in the warming condition? Adorno: 'Progress is this resistance to regression at every stage, not acquiescence in their steady ascent.' 'For progress today really does mean simply the prevention and avoidance of total catastrophe.' In one sense, then, we might also say that 'progress occurs when it comes to an end.'[31] Making progress anew, starting to move forwards will, at the same time, in this particular condition we find ourselves in, require various forms of return: back to non-fossil energy sources, lower concentrations of CO_2, possibly a world without geoengineering. It will be a new dance of one step back and two steps forwards, in opposition to the forces of the storm.

INDUCE THE IMPLOSION

Benjamin expressed 'the experience of our generation: that capitalism will not die a natural death'.[32] Whether it would survive survival remains an open question. Climate scientists know that renewable energy technologies have to be 'scaled up exponentially' and expect that 'such a "technical explosion" will be matched by an "induced implosion" of the incumbent industrial metabolism nourished by coal, oil and gas.'[33] This includes currently operating sites for the extraction of coal, oil and natural gas, where capital is fixed and circulating in astronomical quantities – fields of accumulation which in themselves, on conservative assumptions, are enough to take the world beyond $2°C$.[34] Anyone with some understanding of

---

31 Theodor Adorno, *History and Freedom: Lectures 1964–1965* (Cambridge: Polity, 2008), 172, 143, 153.

32 Benjamin, *Arcades*, 667.

33 Hans Joachim Schellnhuber, Stefan Rahmstorf and Ricarda Winkelmann, 'Why the Right Climate Target Was Agreed in Paris', *Nature Climate Change* 6 (2016): 651.

34 Oil Change International, *The Sky's Limit: Why the Paris Climate Goals*

the workings of capital – not necessarily the field of expertise of climate scientists – can imagine what such an induced implosion might entail.[35] It would be the destructive character at work, impossible without a political movement endowed with powers not yet on the horizon. But the fact that the climate movement and its allies are still struggling to constitute themselves as a demolition crew is not a reason to give up on them. As for theory, it can only ever play a very limited part in such a project. But at least it should not be a drag on it.

35   Schellnhuber et al. themselves display a stunning naivety when trying to turn the implosion into a list of policy recommendations: to all intents and purposes, they rely on the market and trust that it will work things out. Schellnhuber et al., 'Why', 652–3.

Acknowledgements

Thanks, first of all, to Sebastian Budgen, whose energy is as generous as it is awe-inspiring; he is the wind in so many Marxist sails that we don't need no dragons. Thanks also to John Merrick, Rosie Warren and all the other comrades at Verso. This text has developed through conversations with and inspiration from three brilliant comrades: Alf Hornborg, Kate Soper and John Bellamy Foster, all of whom have read various drafts and offered invaluable comments. So have Rikard Warlenius and Harvey Shoolman. Audiences at the Historical Materialism conference in London, the political ecology research group at Lund University, the University of Essex and Goldsmiths have responded to parts of the argument and pointed out flaws. The students of the 2015–17 CPS batch engaged intensely in discussions on the issues in the spring of 2016; at the moment of this writing, they are out on internships such as supporting the olive harvest of Palestinian peasants through the agricultural branch of the PFLP, working with the one million climate jobs campaign in the UK, or participating in mobilisations against coal mining in Ecuador. I am grateful and humbled to have students like them. Last but not least, thanks to Shora Esmailian and Latifa Esmailian Malm for giving me reasons to smile and laugh every single day in these otherwise so unhappy times.

Index